WRITING
AND
LITERATURE
IN THE
SECONDARY
SCHOOL

WRITING AND LITERATURE IN THE SECONDARY SCHOOL

Edited by
Edward J. Gordon
Yale University

HOLT, RINEHART and WINSTON, Inc.

New York   Chicago   San Francisco   Toronto   London

To Pat

Copyright © 1965 by Holt, Rinehart and Winston, Inc.
All Rights Reserved

Library of Congress Catalog Card Number: 65–12795
23219–0115
Printed in the United States of America

Preface

The essays included in this book deal with the teaching of English in the secondary school. They originated as talks given at the Yale Conferences on the Teaching of English, annual meetings in New Haven for secondary school teachers. The procedure in planning the conferences is to put questions to outstanding teachers of English. In answering, the teachers illustrate their arguments with specific examples from their own experience. Since the literature on how to teach English has too long been too abtract, we are here trying to make it more concrete. The overriding question is common to every classroom: How do we teach writing and literature?

Our basic idea is that the subject matter of English is the teaching of writing and the teaching of the reading of literature. To offer some means to this end, we have organized this book. The essays are chosen from a series of conferences, 1959 through 1963.

The common thread of the various essays is that reading and writing involve hard thinking. They are more difficult to teach well than we have been willing to admit. The essays on writing emphasize that clarity of thought comes first. Writing then becomes an expression of that thought. As an aid to the teacher of literature, we have emphasized not only technique but content. How well one reads is certainly one measure of an English course; another is whether the material is worth reading.

New Haven, Conn.   E. J. G.
November 1964

Contents

Part
ONE

Writing

Introduction

Part One of this book deals with how we teach writing. The first two essays try to answer one question: Where do we begin? Philip Burnham suggests that we begin with a word, relate it to other words, and then to the paragraph. He argues that a brief paper carefully thought out and well written is more useful than a long paper which keeps repeating early errors.

A committee report, compiled by John Ragle, asks that students write about personal experiences and reactions. The subjects must be clear and limited, and the student begins with the making of good sentences. Accuracy of observation and the ability to report it in words are paramount here.

Hart Leavitt writes wittily of the Seven Deadly Sins of teen-age writing, from pretentious diction to "the Big Think," and he emphasizes that one learns to write by writing, not through analyzing "heavy baggage left over from Caesar's Gallic Wars." He argues, too, that we should end the cleavage between what students write about and what professionals write about. The student, he says, should write for an audience—his contemporaries. In his second essay he suggests that failure in writing is a failure in thinking.

Edward Irving believes that organization begins with the student's knowing what he is talking about; it is a form of "ordered thinking." He doubts a strong relation between ability to outline and ability to organize. Perhaps, he suggests, the student should write first and then outline. The teacher's job is to get attention centered on the subject, and what is to be said about it, not on the form. If one is to write well, a student must have a subject that will make him think.

Fred Godshalk, on the judging of student writing, takes us well beyond the usual methods in marking papers. He begins with a discussion of the nature of language, giving major emphasis to metaphor as a way of thinking and arguing. He touches on other possible sources of error in writing: ambiguity, redundancy, and euphemism. He reports experiments of the Educational Testing Service in trying to get judgments on the quality of student papers, and concludes with some practical suggestions that grow out of his research. After reading this essay, no one could ever again think it a simple matter to mark a paper with a 78.

Benjamin C. Nangle, who taught for many years a course at Yale in nonexpository writing, argues for more use of nonexpository or creative writing in the secondary schools. He shows the values of such writing as a form of thinking. Students might write more exactly and intelligently if their words were intended to have some correspondence with reality, something in their own experience. Should they go on writing papers on "Atomic Power" and "Dickens"?

James K. Folsom, another teacher of the same course, takes a group of papers, shows us how he reads them, and suggests that such a course is also a form of literary criticism. The student is learning firsthand the problems of the writer.

A
BEGINNING
IN
WRITING

PHILIP BURNHAM
St. Paul's School, Concord, New Hampshire

In the great juggling act which we call the teaching of English, we yearn a great deal of the time for some sort of systemized, some sort of sequential program in reading, in writing, in speaking, in listening, in whatever it may be that we think are the components of what I am sorry to find called the language arts. It would be wonderful, we are sure, could our programs be outlined in specific detail at least for the year, possibly for the term, ideally for the day-by-day classes we have to meet.

And sometimes we take out time to make some sort of organization of at least one part of the many items we have to deal with in the seventh, eighth, and ninth grades from spelling and punctuation to the writing of compositions, the reading of books, the reading of essays, the reading of poetry, and all of the other wonderfully miscellaneous activities which we welcome as a part of the English curriculum or at least the responsibility of the English class and teacher. I need not make a detailed list, for I am sure that the heterogeneous collection readily lists itself in our minds according to the responsibilities or duties which schools have placed upon us.

In the last few months—perhaps, since that well-known chariot hurries so fast, in the last few years—there have come to be quite a large number of talks and published articles dealing with the problem of the organization of the teaching of English, particularly of the teaching of writing. One such stimulating article I might remind you of: the article in *The English Journal* for November 1960, by Clarence W. Hach of Evanston Township High School, Evanston, Illinois, called "Needed: A Sequential

5

Program in Composition." And it is pleasant to report that Mr. Hach has not only stated the need but has within his own school developed a sequential course. I am anxious to note at the outset that I think that such organization into a pattern, into a sequence, into a planned and developing program, is very much our need in many schools. But in order to play my part in what I think is an honorable or at least real tradition for teachers of English, I am ready to state qualifications and conditions which I think ought to surround such a planned program. And I shall try now to make some suggestions of a kind of organization which it seems to me to be appropriate. I hope you will bear in mind that the committee which is reporting on this same topic will have other suggestions which may be fuller and better, and which may indeed run counter to what I have to say. First, then, the suggestions about certain kinds of order, with a few examples of what I think might be done. And finally, the statement of exceptions and differences with which I think we will need to cope.

My first suggestion will contain what I hope is a mild paradox: I do not think we ask our students to write enough, though we ask them to write too much. It would be far better, it seems to me, to do a great deal of what I can best describe as "fooling around" with words and sentences in the seventh grade (I choose seventh grade as an easy way of talking about this, though, depending on school organization itself, I think we can adjust ourselves to the sixth grade or the eighth grade or even the ninth grade for the kind of process that I have in mind). I would suggest that some of our writing assignments ought to consist of assignments of one word. Let each student choose his word—his own particular word—choosing it with the full knowledge that he's going to be responsible for it and have to deal with it for a long time, that he's going to have to join other words to it, that he's going to have to make sentences including that word, that he is going to have to make sentences that will add other information about the word or the idea with which he is dealing, that he will, finally, have to make a paragraph—that is to say, to express a whole unit of thought about the word and the idea with which he has begun.

We need not worry in the seventh grade (nor for that matter do I think we need to worry even in the eleventh and twelfth grades, most of the time) about the student's writing more than a paragraph. As I tried to say in a paradox a minute ago, it seems to me that we ask students to write too much at a time, but that we do not ask them to write as often as we might. Since we, like our students, become so frequently addicted to the almighty grade, we are likely to think that every paper written has to be graded—has somehow to become a part of the eternal and immortal record of the particular student who has done the writing.

A great deal can be done with that single word, both in class and out. The student needs to know as fully as he can what it means; it might even be interesting for him to know where it comes from, how it has been derived, what the meaning was, or seemed to have been, of the foreign language word from which it came. Depending upon his maturity, the student may even wish to discover—as he can in the *Oxford English Dictionary*—how the word has been used, and, perhaps stretching it a little far, who used it and where. And this I should like to insist can be classroom work in which the teacher discusses the word with the individual student while the others are themselves looking for their words, or, for that matter, are engaged in some totally un-related activity. Too often, as teachers, we become upset or worried if the whole class is not busily engaged in the very same thing at the very same time. Surely it is no crime if during our class periods the children are simply reading books or even writing letters, or, to carry this, too, a long way, are involved in some sort of activity which we can call by that cliché "a mean-ingful experience" in their lives. Stimulation and properly con-trolled enthusiasm are after all what we are looking for, and there are a good many ways other than the totally teacher-controlled whole class situation that we so often look for in our classrooms in which both stimulation and enthusiasm can be achieved.

At this point, I am sure you will agree that it is too much not to expect me to document my case with the opening words from one of the sections of an old book: "In the beginning was the Word." After the student has his word under control, or has perhaps abandoned it as not really expressing the kind of interest that he thought he originally had in it, and after he may there-fore have picked up another word, we might move on to the point where this student adds a second word to it, possibly a word that modifies it, a word that rather naturally, in the student's thinking about the first word, will go with it; or a word that expresses a contrast, or, rarely, a word that goes off at some remarkable tangent to the original word. All this, based upon the student's understanding that he's going to move this word, these words, into larger contexts.

If the word "contexts" seems too grand, then the suggestion to the student that he is going to move it into a sentence, into saying something about the word, surely ought to be clear enough even to a seventh grader. A further natural step is to take the word, or the words, and move them into a statement of some idea dealing with that word—perhaps the idea that provoked the word in the first place, perhaps an idea totally new since all the digging and worrying of the word began. Implicit in all of this is the discussion of the words with the whole class or with groups in the class, the discussion of the added word, and finally, for this point at least, the discussion of the sentences for their meaning, for their construction, for their spelling and punctuation where those items are appropriate. Some of the sentences produced will be discouragingly poor, but this is hardly a novel discovery in some of the papers in any set of compositions we have ever read. Some of the sentences will, my experience shows me, be remarkably good. And this is one of those happy circumstances of our lives.

Most of the time these sentences will turn out to be good candidates for topic sentences of a paragraph. I am not so concerned that we acquaint our seventh-graders with this fact, but I do think we ought to keep it in mind ourselves so that we can suggest in the future some kind of development of the idea with which the student is dealing. If the sentences that the students have created are reasonable topic sentences, the problem of adding one more sentence to that first sentence is a fairly simple one. One might well tell the students that several sentences are to be added, or may be added, but that for the moment just one will be enough. Though I suspect this is not likely to happen in the seventh grade, or even in the eighth or ninth, yet there may come a time when a student will see that a sentence preceding the one he has already written is going to make a better order of things than the other way around. Naturally enough, this practice is to be encouraged when appropriate.

Adding the second sentence produces not only the interest and questions and problems that the first sentence produced but also additional ones of its own, as well, indeed, as that most important aspect, the sense of transition from the first sentence to the second. Whether this transition is accomplished by one of the usual transitional words or whether it is accomplished by picking up a little bit of the old and moving on to the new or whether it is accomplished simply by the close relationship of ideas within the two sentences is a matter the teacher will have to discuss individually with the writers. Or he can, by using certain pairs of sentences as illustration for the whole class, as the concern of the whole class, raise in students' minds the question of the need for adequate linking, for adequate relationship, for adequate transition from sentence to sentence. No teacher will forget that this elementary kind of transition is a first step in moving, another year, another time, to the problem of transition from paragraph to paragraph.

Let me not fail to emphasize that what I have here, for convenience, called a topic sentence ought to be evolved from facts at the student's command, from an idea with which the student wishes to deal. And it seems to me it ought to be emphasized to students that the facts must be under control and of interest to him. In his move to his second sentence, and to the ultimate move of adding still further sentences, the question uppermost in the student's mind ought to be what facts, what relevant material, will substantiate, will prove, the general assumption of the original sentence. Clearly the prospect of adding a third or fourth sentence—possibly even more—will make itself apparent, and the teacher will have to adapt himself to the kind of original statement the student has made, to the interest of the individual, to the interest of the class, as to how far or how long he will carry out this small project.

At the moment I think I should say, somewhat to document what I mentioned earlier, that I think it would be better if a student went through this process, or a telescoped version of it, many times, possibly stopping the first time at the end of the original sentence, possibly stopping with a pair of sentences, possibly going on sometimes but not others, depending largely on the substance and seeming worth of the material with which the student is dealing. When we learn woodworking on a lathe, when we learn how to dance, we practice the individual steps a number of times, and we do it knowing full well that we are merely practicing, that we are not in our early attempts trying to turn out the finished product, the well-executed step, or the well-designed bowl or spindle.

Similarly, this process of fooling around with words and sentences appeals to me a great deal because it suggests a kind of practice that later on we can put into the full product, as on the lathe, as in the possibly gracefully executed dance. In a later year, possibly the eighth grade for our convenience in discussing it, this process can be repeated but made more mature, more complicated. Very possibly the demand can be for two words quite opposite in meaning, directly opposite in meaning if you like, or two unrelated words, two seemingly unrelated words, and then the puzzle becomes, How can some statement be made about these which makes some sense, which has some meaning? Easy to say, I realize, and hard to get even a reasonably adequate performance from a large class. But no one expects every experiment to work perfectly every time, and my contention would be that the rewards of this kind of practice, this kind of experimentation, even this kind of discovery, can be fruitful as students come in later years wanting to write, needing to write, being asked to write fuller accounts of their ideas, of their thoughts, of their experiences. What are the contrasts? What are the ways in which they may be stated? What are the ways in which they may be documented, may be detailed?

And once again it is possible at a still later stage, let us name the ninth grade to give this a sense of sequence, to ask for contrast stated as condition, to look for the "although" relationhip, or the "if" relationship, or even the "when" or the "whereas" or the "after," as the occasion and the idea may dictate. But if you allow me my phrase, I think that this kind of "fooling around" with words and sentences can be much more fruitful than the drearily repeated composition after composition, week after week, without much substance of teaching, or substance of experimentation having gone into what the student is doing. For we all know that in the two- or three-page composition the second and third pages do little but repeat the errors of the first page or produce new ones; and if they produce new ones, quantity has probably become so great that we can only overwhelm the student with the torn and bleeding quality our red pencil corrections will give it. Better, I am sure, to concentrate our attention on a small space and a small number of errors. Indeed, I have been convinced over the years that at any grade level we can treat all of the problems of writing in a one-page composition more thoroughly, more perceptively, and more understandably to the student than we can by asking for great length. As for research papers, though I may stand on a lonely eminence, I am convinced they have no use below the twelfth grade, and, indeed, very little use then. I have said before and should like to say again: I have always thought that their greatest value ended as the student wrote his first word. The grounds of my objection are somewhat the same as for large numbers of papers of two, or three, or five, or six pages, but of course there are other considerations too, though they are now not a part of our immediate concern.

Certainly there are other kinds of "fooling around" with words and phrases and sentences which can enrich and enlarge the student's skill and competence. Differences in word choices and their effect upon meaning or tone, differences in word order or the placement of phrases in the sentence and their effect upon meaning or emphasis (*The Elements of Style,* the William Strunk and E. B. White text, gives an excellent example of such differences in variants of "These are the times that try men's souls."), differences in the revisions of badly written sentences—these are a few of other ways that experimentation with sentences can lead to relative mastery and skill at any age level.

Furthermore, in the compositions we ask for, we can move into a greater sense of planning and organization if, for example, we shift the point of view in narration from grade to grade, though never losing sight of the need to return to what has been practiced in an earlier year. We could limit narration in the seventh grade to the directly personal observation, to the paper which uses the personal pronoun "I" as the center of all observation. In the eighth grade we could move to "we" or to "they"— particularly to the "they" limited to what the writer can observe. In the ninth grade we could experiment—giddy thought!—with omniscience, with the point of view of a writer who not only sees what happens but knows what goes on elsewhere, including within the minds of all the characters involved.

In description, too, we can complicate the expectation of maturity and of point of view. Similarly in exposition we can shift the point of view: how to make it, how it is made, why it is made, and what is its use represent four variants on the simplest, or at least most familiar, of expository themes.

One practice which I have found useful is to limit the call for such compositions to about every other week, for two reasons. The first is that I use the intervening weeks to call for a speech, complete with a brief set of notes, on the very topic to be used for the written paper the following week. This has two pleasant results—it gives practice in speech, at least to some in the class, and it means that there has been some thinking and organizing going on well in advance of the time when the paper itself is to be written. The second advantage of the composition every other week is that it leaves an adequate amount of time for the experimentation with words and sentences and paragraphs that I have already discussed in detail.

In being carried away, at least for myself, by the kind of approach I have been suggesting, I have not forgotten our need to teach spelling and punctuation and grammar—nor have I forgotten that the teaching of composition is certainly not the only aspect of the teaching of English with which we have to deal in the seventh grade or in any grade. But I would make the plea that we not allow our concern for spelling and punctuation to become so almighty that we fail to see the forest for the trees. Too often students come to recognize the many corrections of spelling and punctuation over the years, and thereby come to think of them as being the high points of criticism the teachers have to make. Of course they are important, and one would be foolish to deny it, but I am sure that we need to guard ourselves against the sureness of correction of these items blinding us to the virtues —or the lack of virtues—in what the student is trying to say, has had to say. We have all met teachers who have encouraged us, and alas we have met teachers who have discouraged us: one teacher who discouraged me, a man with an extraordinarily large number of years of experience, once told me that he corrected nothing in his eleventh-grade papers but spelling and punctuation. This is a sorry note, but one which emphasizes a tendency all of us may frequently have without realizing how heavily we are penalizing two extraordinarily difficult items, how little we may be allowing for reward of other important aspects of communication.

As for the teaching of grammar, the best thing I can say is that I think we ought to teach grammar, and the more, the earlier, the better. A college teacher, and a friend whom I most highly respect, once said in all seriousness that he thought boys and girls ought to be taught grammar before adolescence, for in adolescence, he said, they become interested in each other and in a deliciously expanding sense of the world, and the teaching of grammar becomes more and more remote to their interests and their understanding. I am not prepared to say that I think this is the whole word on the subject, but I think it bears remembrance and recognition. The elements of English grammar ought to be taught in the seventh grade, and I am sure that they ought to be taught again—as rapidly as previous learning will permit— in the eighth grade, with an enlarged complexity of the grammatical materials taught. I do think, however, we should always be sure that the grammar taught bears a direct relationship to the sentences the students themselves are and will be writing; that wherever possible grammatical construction will be aimed at improving the sentences which the students write. Of course not every grammatical item can so neatly be related, but those that can't ought to be taught early, or, if we are convinced that they have no relationship to the making of English sentences, they ought to be ignored until such time as individual students decide for themselves that they wish to be grammarians.

As with spelling and punctuation, so with grammar: we ought not to let the relatively mechanical details of grammar blind our eyes to what the student is trying to say. Naturally enough, the way in which anything is said is a part of what is said; but at the early levels, especially in the seventh and eighth and ninth grades, surely we can make a shrewd guess, or have a perfectly clear understanding of the idea or the fact with which the student is dealing, even though the spelling and the punctuation and the grammar may well get in our way. For the problems of good writing are not always that the reader cannot understand what the writer is trying to say because of the errors which the writer has introduced but rather that sometimes these errors impede the reader's progress more than the writer has a right to expect. There are two kinds of faulty writing: one, that containing errors so grave that the reader cannot possibly understand exactly what the writer wishes to communicate; two, that containing errors or flaws which make the reader stumble or trip, which impede his progress, which distract his attention more than the writer should allow. If you will accept such a two-part division, I think it can give quite a different view of the correction of papers, for making this distinction for ourselves and making the same distinction for our students can free us of a good many misconceptions about what the trouble may be with a given piece of writing.

However well we may plan our course in writing, however sequential we may make our program in composition, surely we will not forget that there will always be in English composition the need for going over the ground which students have been over before: sometimes at the very level at which it was approached in the past, sometimes at a slightly heightened level, but surely with another point of view, with the added complexity which the relatively increased maturity of the student can allow him to cope with. We have passed that tiresome point where we say with shock, "I wonder who taught this child last year, for surely he knows nothing!" We know well enough that what we have taught has to be learned, and that learning is not quite the sticking process that we would like to think our teaching should make it.

Within the educative process—all our lives along—two verbs must go together: to teach and to learn. However good the teaching may be, it cannot succeed without the learning. We cannot have the one without the other, a reminder that I find helpful to students in recognizing the share of the burden of education which they must carry. All education is pain, in more ways than students are likely to realize until they are no longer students in the limited sense of the word.

In all movement from grade to grade in the teaching of composition there ought to be the sense of the spiral of learning, of the continuous movement up and around, but up and around rather than simply up, for in going around we touch upon the same topics that we have enclosed in the bottom or the top of our spiral, whichever way we may wish to picture this kind of cone made of the flexible steel wire of English composition. Such repetition is one of the exceptions and conditions which I mentioned when I began. It would be fatal, it seems to me, to attempt to build a program which assumed that at the seventh grade such-and-such a thing had been "learned," on the assumption that that matter was over for good and for all and that we could move on to new things. With the great fear of being misunderstood, I should say that surely I mean we should move on, we should move on with the recognition of what we are building on, and of the partial learning which students certainly have. If the partial learning were not so, we might well wonder why we bother to have a grade scale at all. And if our 60 percents and 80 percents are valid grades, then we have said, we have documented, we have put on the record that the total learning has not been encompassed.

The juggling act that I mentioned the teaching of English to be allows me to make a quick jump myself, a jump to a few remarks about book reports. In what I now consider my innocence, I had thought that book reports had all but disappeared from the land, with neither a sigh nor a tear. But I find again and again, distressingly enough, that book reports are still very much with us. My own point of view is that we ought to abandon the requirement of a written book report for reading which the students have in return been required to do. Nothing can more readily dampen the delight in reading, the ardor for reading, the interest in what the book has to say or to tell than the ever-present awareness that, come the last page, a report must be written. Literary criticism is extraordinarily difficult for adults to write, and to expect the book report from the seventh grader or the eighth grader or—heavens knows, even older students—is asking a great deal. I would appeal for reading that allows the student to say he has read the book, to make some oral comment about it. At the most, we might ask for a paper written in class on some specific aspect of the book just read. The sword has been removed, the curse has been taken away, when the report, written as homework, is eliminated. Students do not mind writing papers in class: this is one of the standard requirements they are familiar with over the years. If we have to have some written comment, why not let it come as a brief class exercise, and thereby all the demands will be satisfied.

We can make our best guess as to whether the book was read, we can get some sense of what the student is thinking and feeling, and we can get one more look at the way in which the student puts his ideas, puts his sentences, together. Such papers can very readily be based on a single general question, What was the incident in that book most interesting to you? Who was the character you were most concerned about? And try to tell what it was that gave you that concern. Was there a new thing about people which this book showed you? If not, what one or two things that you already knew about people were brought to your attention again? On occasion we can, of course, furnish these questions in the form of a simple topic sentence, and oftentimes one sentence will do for all of the books which a class may have read. If one will not do, we surely can be prepared to furnish several. Or we can retreat into that sometimes very effective question—asking the student to tell why the idea of this sentence is not one which relates to the book he has read. So much for book reports, though as you can see I could not resist the temptation to try to make another statement against what I have felt has been so discouraging to the enthusiasm and excitement for reading that we might otherwise develop.

Writing in class, whether for book reports or for other purposes, can reveal something else to us about which we may discover we have a surprising ignorance. How long does it take a seventh-grader to write a paragraph—call it half a page? What happens, then, to the seventh-grader or the older student when we ask for relatively long papers? Have we placed upon him a burden in time, in energy, in effort beyond the limits of the physical, let alone the mental, resources which he has? This will in turn make us question very much the value in recopying, for its use of time and its use of energy and the slim results which so often come from it. Revision is, after all, a skill of maturity, a skill we can apply only when we know where to look for help and guidance, only after we know what may be the traps and pitfalls into which we may unwarily, unthinkingly have fallen.

My final word on planning and organization in our composition program turns to ourselves as teachers. If you approve what I have called "fooling around" with words and sentences, if you approve what the members of the committee report, then I urge you to try it yourself, preferably before, or, at least, as your students are trying it. Whether we are pleased with what we produce for our own eyes or shocked by it, we can humble or comfort ourselves with what has been thought to be Chaucer's personal farewell to his work, with what Theodore Morrison has called "a motto for all writing founded on simplicity and worldly good sense":

> No, Scogan, no! I beg off. I refuse
> For any rhyme—so help me God, I pray!—
> Ever again to wake my sleeping muse
> That in her sheath rusts peacefully away.
> While I was young I put her in the fray,
> But all shall pass that men write, prose or rhyme.
> Take every man his turn for his own time!
>
>> ["Lenvoy de Chaucer a Scogan"]

THE BEGINNING STEPS OF WRITING

a committee report

JOHN RAGLE
Chairman, Springfield, Vermont, High School
GARY BURGARD
Hamden, Connecticut, High School
JOHN J. JOSEPH
The Choate School, Wallingford, Connecticut
MARY LANIGAN
Newton, Massachusetts, High School
HENRY F. OLDS, JR.
Harvard Graduate School of Education

"Put down the book and pick up the baby." This is the sage advice of a veteran grandmother to her youngest daughter and her young husband, caught scrambling through the already worn pages of their "baby care" book, desperately seeking a solution to their infant's plaintive but persistent wailing. The baby can't identify what it wants, much less communicate its desire. The parents are experiencing no better success in their perusal of a text. When the inexperienced young couple makes its approach directly to the child, however, its crying ceases.

This committee might, perhaps, have legitimate claim to indulgence if it had sought answers in the same way that the young parents did, scrambling through the research since none of us has had much direct experience with the problem. All of us have done the preponderance of our teaching and supervision in the upper grades of secondary school. None of us has worked with twelve-year-olds for more than a short time.

Perhaps the analogy may be carried one step further. If asked what he needs in order to write better, it is doubtful that the twelve-year-old could either identify or express accurately the answer any more than the baby could recognize or communicate its needs. By extension, the advice of the veteran grandmother may here again be pertinent. Not all future instances of the baby's crying were solved by picking it up once, but the beginning steps toward solving the problem were thus taken. Rather than to start by examining the research, we, too, may best begin by directly taking up the problem of the twelve-year-old who has something to say in writing.

In doing so, our lack of firsthand experience, though a handicap in some respects, is on two grounds, at least, an asset: first, and perhaps the less important of the two, we may view the case from the perspective of having dealt extensively with the plaintiff three, four, or five years later, the erstwhile twelve-year-old, now grown, but still plagued by problems in writing (problems ranging from mechanical incorrectness to chaotic thinking); second, we must as relative amateurs approach our task with thoughtful self-examination at each juncture and with honest humility.

Why have we chosen specifically and primarily to deal with twelve-year-olds when our problem is to work out the beginning steps in teaching writing? To some small degree the answer may lie in the fact that it is at this level that children first enter the early grades of secondary school, and we are secondary school teachers. Primarily, however, it is because whereas generally speaking seventh-graders do not express themselves well in writing, it is at this stage that the need to do so begins to make itself strongly felt. To this point in his school career the child's writing has been largely imitative and the nature of his opportunities to write limited.

It must here be clearly understood that in talking about the "seventh-grader," the committee means the "seventh-grader," (in terms of intellectual maturity and skill) wherever he may be found: in the ninth-grade classroom, for there can be no question but that some children are late in achieving the readiness of the average twelve-year-old; even in the twelfth grade. Every teacher must recognize that in certain classroom situations there will be some children who neither can nor should be expected to accomplish what the majority of the group is learning. Indeed, there are youngsters in the earlier grades who are seventh-graders in capacity and readiness long *before* they reach their twelfth birthdays. In summary, we shall be talking about teaching the beginning steps of writing in the seventh grade, all the time keeping in mind that there are "seventh-graders" almost all the way up and down the scale.

Before we can focus specifically on the teaching of writing, one more conviction of the committee should be understood: namely, that the writing skills and understandings to be learned are common to both junior and senior high school. The senior high school teacher should neither want nor expect the seventh- and eighth-grade teachers to concentrate on grammar, or mechanics, so that he can teach "creative writing." The fundamental elements—among them selection of a subject, awareness of the audience, recognition of a purpose, the need for accuracy, for organization, for correctness—these elements are important in the twelfth grade, as they are in the seventh. The difference lies in immediacy and in degree, as will be seen. The teaching of one or another of the elements must not be restricted to any one point in the curriculum; nevertheless, for learning to take place effectively it is important that the emphasis at any one time should be limited: the class may be asked to focus upon one skill at a time, though not to the exclusion of the others.

Up to now this report has offered little except ground rules and, on behalf of the committee, a devious alibi calculated, it might appear, to release us from any obligation to make any valid contribution. A moment's review, however, proves that already certain facts have been collected. First, the normal seventh-grader will more and more frequently recognize a need to say something in writing. (The teacher must, in turn, recognize that a felt need is a necessary part of the motivation to write.) Second, the seventh-grader, to say nothing of his older brothers and sisters, too often writes ineffectively. Before we go any further, however, and lest we be caught at this early stage in a serious fallacy, few are the twelve-year-olds who cannot communicate at all in writing. To borrow a thought from Louis Zahner's challenging contribution to the first Yale Conference, in teaching the language arts, ". . . we are dealing with our students *as if* certain principles and theories were true,": as if, to resort to an unhappy example, English were an inflected language, like Latin. We cannot afford to teach the formal beginning steps of writing *as if* our students have never written at all.

Aware, then, that the children can put words together on paper so as to represent, at least temporarily and for themselves, an idea, the teacher of writing must first make a diagnostic writing assignment. This is *the* beginning step in the teaching of writing, not so much because the teacher must know each year anew the problems he faces (though if he is to help every individual this must always be to some degree true), but particularly because the students must be brought to see where they succeed and where they fail: this they can best see in terms of their own attempts to write about something.

According to teachers of seventh-grade youngsters, these children are best able to write about personal experiences and their own reactions to the world around them.

In the seventh grade students should be given a subject limited only in the most general way. One of the members of the committee likes simply to write on the chalkboard the word "worms," or perhaps "luck," and, following some preparatory discussion, to turn a class of twelve-year-olds loose on that. The length of the paper should be limited, both because little is to be accomplished by a long assignment and the teacher's time is, as always, a factor. Little will be gained by assigning "a paragraph"; seventh graders will be more successfully limited by "a third of a page" or "half a page." Many junior high school teachers like to have their students keep journals, which may, indeed, have constructive uses; for these teachers the diagnostic assignment may be among the earliest journal entries of the year.

Once the teacher has read this first set of papers, he may determine his next step. In the seventh grade this is not likely to be in terms of *the paragraph,* but rather of *the sentence,* for it is here that the problems of most twelve-year-olds begin.

Seventh-graders commonly fail in their attempts to say accurately what they have seen, felt, or thought. Let us consider an exercise which might well grow out of the diagnostic situation. The teacher holds up between the thumb and forefinger of his right hand a small fragment of white chalk. In clear view of the class, he drops it on the top of his desk. It bounces against a book, where it rests. The students write down what they have seen. What they write may range, ideally, from a perfect recital of the act just described onward to such statements as "The

teacher dropped a piece of white chalk on the desk" down to
"He dropped it," "He dropped something," and "Something was
dropped" (or even, "It drop," the "ed" ending of the past tense
having been, as is so often the case, cheerfully overlooked). Let
us assume that one student has been sent from the room and,
upon returning, is asked to describe, from his reading of what
one of his classmates has written, the act which was performed
in his absence. The student reads, "He dropped it."

Here beginneth the lesson.

In order to enlighten their puzzled colleague, the youngsters
must see their task in terms of two specific problems: first, that
concerning the teacher's action, certain particular facts hold true;
second, that the writer must take into consideration a person,
specifically a reader, who is completely unaware of these facts
and for whom they must be described accurately. Underlying all
else, the students themselves must initially have *observed accurately;* for, indeed, a large part of the stuff of good writing
consists in a completed awareness of that which is to be said. The
class must see that they must tell what "it" is in the sentence
"He dropped it." They must recognize that "a piece of chalk"
is better than "it"; "a piece of white chalk" is still better; "a
small piece of white chalk," better yet. ("A small *fragment* of
white chalk" is most precise, but such preciseness may not be our
aim at this stage.) Then, who is "he"? In what way did "he" drop
the chalk? Where did it land? How? (Certainly consideration of
the ungrammatical "It drop" should be postponed, probably to
be taken up with the offending individual alone when the basic
awareness has been accomplished).

In brief, the beginning step in teaching writing is to have
the students write for diagnostic purposes. Second, and growing
out of the diagnostic assignment, the students must be brought
to see both their strengths and where the most basic of their
weaknesses lie. We think that this insight must comprehend two
facts: first, that the writer must know clearly what it is he wants
to say; second, that the writer must bear in mind a reader, who
cannot know what the writer wants to say until he has said it,
and then only to the degree that he has said it accurately. We
must convince the student that to write well he must first know,
and then say, what he means.

We have talked about the fundamental elements in writing and alluded to the fact that they are common to the whole continuum, grades seven to twelve. Though all of them may require attention at each level, yet only one (or two that are closely related) can productively receive emphasis at the start. The exercise involving dropping the chalk focuses upon two elements; the importance of thorough observation or knowledge and the essential need for accuracy in reporting what has been seen, felt, or known. Comprehended in these is the obligation of the student to whatever audience is involved (the general reader, the teacher, or even himself alone). Here would seem to be the focus for the seventh grade, first in terms of the sentence, later in terms of the paragraph in its simplest role.

From the outset, of course, the organization of the youngster's ideas on paper will receive attention. So will it be, also, with point of view, style, diction, and grammar. These will enter into the discussion, however, only insofar as a given situation (a specific paper being discussed with a class, for example) demands. As time passes and students strengthen their control over basic skills, each more advanced discipline will come into focus in its own right.

From the very start the student must be required to adhere to certain simple conventions concerning the mechanics and structure of the language. English is an analytic language. In an inflected language, like Latin, the word carries the idea; in English, it is the word group. The seventh-grader must know, for example, correct basic word form and usage, the significant word orders and patterns, and the uses of all these to convey his experience in the world as he knows it. He must recognize that "I will take him" or "Will I take him" are meaningful in order, form, and sense; that "Will him take I," though acceptable in order, is wrong in form; and that "Will take him I" is unacceptable in all three respects. The more intricate facts of language structure can be learned as the student develops the need of them in his writing, to introduce variety of sentence structure, for example.

The committee has felt it important to make more than simply a general reference to the efficacy of emphasizing specific disciplines at certain stages in the students' growth in writing. The initial emphasis has been determined because junior high school teachers say that the greatest area of need, for their students, is in observation and accuracy of reporting, first of all in terms of the sentence. Looking further, it appears that by the time he is in the eighth grade the student is easily interested in words, their histories, their associations, their connotations. Here, clearly, is the point at which to expand his vocabulary and to encourage experimentation.

Twelve-year-olds approach organization in the most rudimentary ways, chronologically or spatially, for example. The ninth-grader, however, is capable of selecting a point of view, which can then control the build-up of his ideas. These facts suggest a productive pattern of approach for the classroom.

Whereas the eighth-grader is excited by words, his implementation of them is often clumsy or limited. It is at about the tenth grade that emphasis can profitably be placed upon precision in word selection.

The refinements of style may well wait until grade twelve.

These divisions reflect the experience of members of the committee or of teachers with whom they have talked. At the risk of being repetitious, I must point out once more that each element is essential at each level, grades seven to twelve. The twelve-year-old requires organization in the expression of his ideas, as does the seventeen-year-old. What consideration each element is to receive at any level is a question of immediacy and of degree.

Let us now return to the process of teaching the beginning steps to the seventh-grader. The diagnostic assignment has been written; basic lessons have been carefully drawn from the "chalk-dropping" exercise. Next each student should give his attention to his own paper, which the teacher will have read particularly in view of the emphasis made in class. (It is important to note that, as has already been suggested, the diagnostic assignment has as its purpose not alone to lay bare the child's weaknesses in writing, but, and of equal importance, his strengths. In writing comments on a paper, the teacher is well advised to emphasize first of all its good points. Otherwise, he is liable to expose his students to the stultifying effects of "red-pencilitis.")

In reviewing his own paper, the student should have two purposes: to see where he himself may have failed to understand or to convey clearly his ideas; to note whatever other major weaknesses (and the teacher will have limited himself to indicating only the major ones) have seriously detracted from the desired effect. Now is the time to bring to the attention of the student his habitual errors so that he may begin immediately to break the habits and establish right ones.

The moment has come for another assignment in writing. Robert Frost was fond of saying that the way to learn to read a poem is not by reading the New Critics, but by reading another poem. In the last analysis, the way to learn to write is by writing. If the busy teacher will prepare the class carefully for each assignment and, particularly at the seventh grade, limit the length of the assignments, he will save himself burdensome correcting and derive the best "mileage" from each effort.

Of course, in the new assignment emphasis will remain (as, indeed, it should throughout the year) upon accuracy of observation and of reporting. But a new, secondary emphasis may now be made, as well. Saying successfully what one means does not depend entirely upon knowing clearly what he wants to say, and to whom, together with the accurate words with which to say it. The ideas must be presented in some sort of comprehensible order. The intricacies of organization can wait, but its importance should be established from the outset. Perhaps the student is remembering (in "a third of a page") his first speedboat ride, or the strange new world of his grandfather's farm. He can be shown that the simplest mechanical patterns of organization will, for the reader, give meaning to what is otherwise a blur of unrelated impressions. The impressions aroused by the speedboat ride can be described in chronological order; the use of spatial relationships can lend structure to the visit at the farm. To illustrate such basic means of organization, the teacher, working with the class, can plan on the chalkboard a description of the impressions which a stranger might receive upon first walking into the school library.

Out of a continuing sequence of such assignments, interspersed with carefully developed class discussion and exercise, can grow a sure feeling for the writer's obligation to his purpose and his reader. Out of it can grow the concept of order in writing and, as the year goes on, an understanding of what a paragraph represents. Then assignments may be made in terms not of "a third of a page" or "half a page," but of a paragraph.

Later in the year we may very occasionally allow the seventh-grader to write at greater length. Since he is still most at home with his personal experiences and reactions, he may describe his family's trip to Washington, D.C. For the teacher reading over his paper, the focus remains the same: Does the student know what he wants to say? Has he said what he means? Has he given some order to his ideas? Has he proofread carefully to spot and correct habitual errors?

What about the same student a year later? Every teacher should recognize the danger of redundancy and unimaginativeness in the making of assignments; but for the sake of our discussion, assume that the student has again written about his trip to the capital. Certainly the paper will be read for the same elements as were important the year before. New emphasis may be made in the course of the year, however. For example, advantage may be taken of the eighth-grader's interest in words. He can be shown that mere faithfulness of reporting may not do justice to his experience. As a seventh-grader he may have had a "great" time on his trip. As an eighth-grader he should be shown that "great" may imply "exciting" to his best friend, but "restful" to his grandmother or, indeed, to his harried teacher.

The seventh- and eighth-graders are likely to describe their trips as they unfolded, in chronological order. The ninth-grader (and, again, we should remind ourselves that we are talking about the "ninth-grader" at whatever level we may encounter him) is better able to assume a point of view—dictated by the purpose of his trip or, perhaps, its highlight—and employ an organization which is basically rhetorical, for example, rather than mechanical. Thus, it may be seen that the teaching of writing must be cumulative. It is not like learning to swim, where the first step may be to master the dog paddle; for the accomplished swimmer seldom reverts to the dog paddle. In writing, what is learned in the seventh grade is an integral part of all else that is learned along the way; so that the twelfth-grader has not merely moved from one stepping stone to another but brought each new stone along with him to form part of the whole foundation of his ultimate skill as a writer.

It would be pleasant for the teacher if he could assume that each of the students under his tutelage will progress at the same pace. But from the beginning of the learning process this is not so. Some will sprint ahead, seeming to absorb each new concept upon contact; some will plod along, slowly, sometimes painfully slowly, eventually grasping the basic lessons. In these facts lies the need for new diagnostic assignments each year, by each teacher, at every level. Herein, too, lies the importance of flexibility in teaching, in assignments, whether the classes be heterogeneously or homogeneously arranged.

In discussing the teaching of writing, one other fact deserves mention, one which has too long gone unrecognized. In theory the old goal of having every teacher in a system a teacher of English is an admirable one, indeed. In practice, however, it too seldom works out. The teachers in other subject areas are often as heavily burdened with numbers of students and activities as are the English teachers; and these other teachers are not trained to teach English. To be sure, they should be encouraged to have concern for the students' use of the language and of language skills in their classes. Yet almost always the best bet is overlooked —the student himself.

That English teacher will win his goal most decisively who succeeds in convincing his students that everything they write down on paper is an exercise in thinking and writing: the sentence written in the course of a chemistry assignment, the paragraph constructed as part of a unit in social studies or history, the note written on a memorandum pad to remind himself of an errand, the casual letter to a friend, the evening's entry in a diary. If the student can be convinced that growth in his ability to write will compound itself through thoughtful attention to each circumstance involving writing, then the aim of having every teacher a teacher of English, finding a ready target, may bring some reward.

In advance of a brief review of the committee's suggestions, one final fact demands notice. Although it is becoming more common for experienced teachers to devote themselves to teaching at the junior high school level, this is still far too often the exception rather than the rule. Elementary school teachers devote themselves in a professional way to the instructing of young children. Teachers in the upper years of high school, likewise, tend to think of themselves as settled and to approach their work with conviction. It is rarely the fault of the junior high school teacher that he is liable to consider himself "in transit." Too often school administrators think of promotion in terms of moving teachers upward in grade level, or into supervisory capacities; the teacher cannot help but be affected by this viewpoint. Too often young and inexperienced teachers are given junior high school classes, either until an opening develops in the senior high school or because of, in the case of young women, the likelihood that they will soon be lost into marriage.

The committee feels strongly the necessity of developing professional personnel in the junior high school, men and women who are honestly interested in working with youngsters at this stage in their development. Those of us who are so fortunate as to have and know such teachers in our systems are acutely aware of their importance, of their key importance. English department heads and school administrative and supervisory personnel are urged to develop and encourage professional junior high school teachers.

We know that in focusing upon the beginning steps in the teaching of writing we have left stones unturned. In our two meetings together and our letters back and forth, we have determined much that is satisfying to us; we have, we feel, isolated a number of significant truths. We leave the job unfinished, the ground to be cultivated and harvested by those whose hands are practiced and sure.

These, we think, are the beginning steps in teaching writing:

1. In order to determine for the student his strengths and weaknesses, and for the teacher his best next step—a *diagnostic assignment in writing.*

2. In order to help the student to see and to accomplish his purpose, to convince him that he must first know and then say accurately what he means, and in order to make him aware of his obligation to a reader—*such class demonstrations as the "chalk-dropping" exercise.*

3. In order to permit proper growth in terms both of pupil readiness and of efficiency—*recognition of the fact that emphasis upon one or two elements of writing at a time is necessary;* but, by the same token,

4. in order to insure the strengthening of writing skills in a reasonable and productive manner—*teaching plans based on the knowledge that the important writing skills and understandings are common to every stage throughout junior and senior high school.*

5. And, finally, that thoughtful planning and focusing by the teacher will reduce the burden of correcting to a minimum, but that, after all else has been conscientiously said and done, *the best way to teach writing is by assigning writing.*

SELECTED BIBLIOGRAPHY

BAKER, WILLIAM D., "The Natural Method of Language Teaching," *The English Journal*, April 1958, XLVII, 212

> "Invoking a plague on both their houses [the structural linguists and the traditional grammarians], this article calls for a natural method in teaching students to express themselves effectively!"

DUSEL, WILLIAM J., The English Journal, May 1957, XLVI, 5

> Discusses first why student writing must be judged and the psychological aspects of judging students' work; secondly, the standards of evaluation of student work in regard to neatness and accuracy, honesty, originality, expression, and style; and thirdly, evaluation of writing by the individual, the group, and the instructor.

English Journal, The, "A Realistic Pattern for Writing Assignments," February 1957, XLVI, 2

> "In Baltimore, too, English teachers are helping each other to develop more effective programs. Several teachers of the Forest Park High School who have enjoyed outstanding success in teaching writing presented [a] discussion to all of the teachers of the city."

————, "They All Can Learn to Write," November 1956, 456

> "if wise, she [the teacher] can instruct . . . and not take the student's mind off what he has to say."

English Leaflet, The, "Composition Issue" (New England Association of Teachers of English publication), Fall 1960, LIX, 5

> Contains eight pertinent analyses of phases of the teaching of writing, including "Writing: The Fourth Art," by Lou LaBrant; "The Positive Approach to Language Success," by Edwin Sauer; "Prepositions and Propositions," by Harold Martin; and "Notes on Writing a Descriptive Paragraph," by Edward Gordon.

EVANS, BERTRAND, "Writing and Composing," *The English Journal,* January 1959, VIII, No. 1, 12–20

> This article brings out the importance of and some approaches to teaching composing along with writing in the schools. The author refers to composing not especially in the form of poems, short stories, novels, dramas, and operas, but more in the form of expository essays and paragraphs.

GIRR, FRANCIS X., JR., "Group Paragraph Revision," *The English Journal,* December 1960, XLIX, 9

> A structural approach to class or individual evaluation of written assignments. Especially good in promoting recognition and correction of many basic student errors.

GORDON, EDWARD J., AND EDWARD S. NOYES, EDS., *Essays on the Teaching of English: Reports of the Yale Conference on the Teaching of English,* National Council of the Teachers of English (New York, 1960)

> This collection of materials from the Yale Conference contains some excellent articles on the study of language and the teaching of writing. The different approaches presented will stimulate thought about how one might teach writing, and the bibliographies provided will suggest opportunities for further study.

GROSE, LOIS M., "Teaching Writing in the Junior High School," *The English Journal,* February 1960, XLIX, 2

> A thoughtful attempt at a basic definition of the teaching of writing in the junior high school, this compact article successfully presents both an overview and specific detail. A good reference.

HAMILTON, MARY GLENN, "A Creative Approach to Writing," Reader's Digest Services, Inc., Bulletin EB-2

> A careful explication of a constructive approach to student writing, based on the keeping of writing notebooks for motivational and source material. Contains a thorough and useful discussion of the elements of writing and procedures for teaching them.

JOHNSON, ERIC W., "Stimulating and Improving Writing in the Junior High School," *The English Journal,* February 1958, XLVII, 68–76

> Presents specific suggestions for stimulating and improving writing, and also includes timesavers for those who teach writing.

KINNICK, B. JO, "Creative Writing," *The English Journal,* February 1957, XLVI, 2

> The introduction of creative writing to junior and senior high students.

LA BRANT, LOU, "Writing Is More Than Structure," *The English Journal,* May 1957, XLVI, 7

> A criticism of the practice of teaching merely sentence structure, with comments on aspects of "the full experience of translating ideas into the English word," including the purpose of a piece, selection of focus, writing with the reader in mind, unity and organization, and moral responsibility in writing.

MAERTINS, GRACE DALY, "Organizing the Class to Care for Individual Needs," *The English Journal,* October 1958, XLVII, 414

MARTIN, HAROLD C., "How the American Boy Learns to Write," *The English Leaflet* (New England Association of Teachers of English), March 1955, LIV, 3

MCCAFFERTY, JOHN, "Beginning Composition in the Senior High School," *The English Journal,* December 1960, XLIX, 9

A step-by-step evaluation schedule designed for teachers in regard to correcting beginning themes. Although outlined for high school programs, it is easily applicable to similar advanced junior high writing units. Exceptionally valuable as a method of coordinating grammar work and composition exercises.

POOLEY, ROBERT C., "What Grammar Should I Teach?" *The English Journal,* September 1958, XLVII, 327

The value of grammar in beginning writing to produce as an end result clear, compact, interesting writing.

PORTER, NORMA, "Fiction Writing—Eighth Grade Style," *The English Journal,* May 1958, XLVII, 292

A personal experience essay explaining how to interest the student and keep his interest in writing.

REEVES, RUTH E., "The W in RWS," *The English Journal,* April 1960, XLIX, 256–258

Deals with the possibilities of adopting the English system of keeping a composition notebook with daily entries, especially subjects to write about.

ROSENSON, JULIUS S., "An Oral Approach to Sentence Sense," *The English Journal,* October 1958, XLVII, 425

Stresses the importance of correct sentences in both oral and written expression.

SAUER, EDWIN H., *English in the Secondary School* (New York, 1961)

An exciting book, full of excellent ideas and techniques for the teaching of composition and literature in the secondary school. Of particular interest is a sequential program for the teaching of writing in grades seven through twelve.

SMITH, DORA V., "Re-establishing Guidelines for the English Curriculum," *The English Journal,* September 1958, XLVII, 317

"This is teaching the process of composition—how to select and organize ideas, how to choose words appropriate to the theme."

——, "Teaching Language as Communication," *The English Journal,* March 1960, XLIX, 167

Speaks particularly of necessity of teaching organization of materials; also speaks of "showing by concrete example" how to bring one's experiences alive for others.

STOCKING, FRED H., "The Two Jobs of English Teachers," *The English Journal,* March 1961, L, 3

A commentary by a prominent college professor on the subject of teacher responsibility, giving certain insight into the importance of a balanced program between structural correctness and creative promise. Possible value lies in excerpts regarding the maintenance of that balance and the views on the instruction of composition from a college standpoint.

TOVATT, ANTHONY J., "This World of English," *The English Journal,* March 1957, XLVI, 3

With a section containing recommendations on the teaching of composition writing at any stage of development.

WERTHEIMER, MAX, *Productive Thinking* (New York: Harper & Row, Publishers, Inc., 1945)

This book does not discuss specifically the problem of teaching writing, but in its discussion of what we mean by productive thinking and of how we might help students to think productively there are implications which may be of help as we try to get productive writing.

WEST, WILLIAM W., "How to Avoid Work," *The English Journal,* December 1956, XLV, 9

A teacher reviews his methods and purposes in teaching high school composition.

THE
SUBJECT
MATTER
OF WRITING

HART LEAVITT
Phillips Academy, Andover, Massachusetts

Several years ago a large foundation invested $50,000 to discover the reasons for academic failure. When the interviews were over, the questionnaires filled out, and the information classified, it was revealed that many students committing poor work were boys who didn't get along with their fathers.

This is serious; in such cases we have an important diagnosis, demanding help above and beyond the regular administration; and psychological fact is the basis for progress, and mercy.

For daily education, however, it is too mixed up with esoteric philosophy and long-range reconstruction of character. Also, too many teachers are unable, or perhaps unwilling, to cope with such matters, so that on both counts this peculiar knowledge is irrelevant to the classroom.

On the other hand, there are pragmatic reasons for poor work which have nothing to do with complexes or syndromes, which, in truth, afflict thousands of American students otherwise secure and normal. No special schooling is required to understand them, as in psychology and psychiatry; and no backward progress is indicated to cure them, as in the resurrection of old grammatical rites. What is needed is an awakening, a recognition of a first cause rarely mentioned in the textbooks: students do poor work because they can't think. To put it metaphorically, poor work comes from failure to use the muscles of the mind.

What is worse, the bottom half of the class usually doesn't even know that these muscles exist; consequently, when they try a word problem, or approach the character of Captain Ahab, or consider the Treaty of Versailles, it is as if a boy tried to play hockey who couldn't skate.

This analogy can be carried out to the last decimal point. A good player learns to control important muscles, and at first does it quite self-consciously: as in tennis, where the beginner concentrates on controlling his wrist, so that he can serve, volley, and lob; or in hockey, where a young skater, wobbling around, tries to discipline his leg muscles so that he can stop dead and race back the other way, full speed.

Similarly in schoolwork, there are specific muscles required for superior accomplishment, and this essay aims to define them and describe their relationships to reading and writing, so that they can be practiced, developed, and played for keeps. Without such rehearsing, students go through life on their undirected own, firmly developing certain weaknesses in thinking which in time become permanent and unteachable habits.

Relative Ignorance

The first weakness is grandfather to them all: ignorance. I do not mean regulation ignorance—the fact that math students don't know their common denominators. I mean relative ignorance—the fact that few students know anything in one course they can use in another. They never use the musical ideas of "theme and variations" in English; or the mathematical device of "proportion" in English; or the "English" way with metaphor in history. To be specific, how many boys and girls faced with a "theme for Monday" and crying "What am I going to write on?" think of using material from history? How many, asked to write a satire, would think of doing to French textbooks what Stephen Leacock did to word problems? Or, to be minutely specific and not quite serious, how many see such combinations as the basic laws of physics, and complex problems in personality? "For every action there is an equal and opposite reaction" is a clear clue to most of the characters in *The Mayor of Casterbridge*.

Most students, however, take nothing from one classroom to another. Last year, discovering that my seniors were also studying *Death of a Salesman* in religion, I assigned a free essay on the play. It was not an innocent assignment. I wanted to find out how many would put two and two together without being told to.

Not one. Instead, they turned in the usual character sketches of Willy Loman and satires on delayed adolescents. When I said pointedly that under the circumstances they could have chosen much better topics, they said, "What do you mean?" I then mentioned the religion course, and asked why, among other prolific comparisons, no one had thought of relating the school minister's approach to the play with mine.

"Well, for heaven's sake, why didn't you tell us!" sputtered one boy, missing the point.

A successful use of material from another department occurred last year at our school when essays in English were assigned on an exhibit in the art gallery: a visual history of the way artists have seen reality. Rarely have such exciting papers been written, and rarely have so many students been so exercised about *how* to write. For an English teacher, this was Nirvana. Furthermore, for the first time, many boys were faced with having too much to say, so that they had serious problems in cutting. Deciding *which* subject to choose, or *which* phase of *which* subject, was a dramatic experience for those who in the past had never been able to find *enough* to say.

I should like to pay tribute here to an ingenious assignment devised at the Sudbury Regional High School. As a guest at one of their regular English department meetings, I described using photographs as a device for inducing specific detail, color, and brevity. At Sudbury they carry this method two steps further. Compositions about pictures are sent to an art class, where young Picassos draw or paint interpretations of what the English students say they have seen. Then, the pictures, with the essays, are compared to the original photographs. In some cases there are recognizable relationships; but in others, the two pictures appear to have only the most imaginative connection. Inevitably arises the problem of language, both as perception and observation, so that the experiment supplies food for thought and writing for many days.

This juggling of the spheres of thought is an excellent example of what I call exercising the sinews of intellect, so that new responses are awakened, and then cultivated. By this means, students find new sources of good subject matter; they learn how to find "something to say" that is important and interesting. The results of such inventive assignments emphasize the point, often neglected in textbooks, that poor writing is almost always the result of poor subject matter.

As English teachers, we should start this cooperative movement, because there are so many theme subjects in other courses,
because the assignments involve personal and intellectual attitudes—our particular province—and because we are freer to experiment with such liberal programs. But the others should help,
too; it isn't fair for the history department to say to a failing
student: "Well, of course we can't help it if they don't teach any
punctuation in that English department over there!"

Ignorance in Depth

Another great weakness of the teenage mind is what might
be called ignorance in depth, a condition particularly noticeable
in mediocre students. Their general average of 67 results simply
from the fact that they know a few things about a lot of things,
but really not very much about anything. In contrast, among
good students, it will be found that high performance in one
field is often matched by high performance in another, with the
performance in direct proportion to the knowledge. What is most
interesting is that often these achievements are in apparently unrelated areas: among *cum laude* candidates, some are good
athletes, some good writers, some good actors, and some fine musicians. It seems that from one field to another there is a powerful
carry-over of the absorption and flexibility that produces mastery.

In my English classes I see more clearly every year that the
most impressive recitations and compositions come from students
who know philosophy or biography or history or one of the arts.
The same thing seems to be true in other academic disciplines: a
boy in our school who achieved 99 in German also won prizes in
literary contests, played the piano with professional skill, and
wrote music for the school production of *Hamlet;* a boy who got
100 on his math final was also high scorer on the hockey team
and played the lead in the annual musical comedy; another, one
of the most brilliant students I've ever known, who has just received his Ph.D. in history, is a composer of popular songs, an
actor, a writer, a designer of scenery, and a master of after-dinner
storytelling.

None of this should be interpreted as a plug for that popular
hero, the "well-rounded" boy. By any other name, he is still a
square. What I am describing is excellence: the student who is
captain of the football team and wins prizes for painting, and the

student who plays Hamlet and earns double 5's on the English Advance Placement exam.

All of these illustrate the truth that excellence is just as contagious as mediocrity and failure. To put it in the terms of my basic metaphor, there is a general muscle of excellence, a kind of all-purpose sinew, which is good anywhere; and the only way to develop it for the highest advancement of one's education is to stretch one's brain to gain an excellent working knowledge of several subjects.

Several I say, because too many students have been scared by the old boogie man of one thing at a time. If ever there were a place in history when man should learn double, triple, and quadruple mastery, this is it. Students in academic trouble should be told not only to go on attacking subject weaknesses but to go outside the classroom and learn something else thoroughly— almost anything really, as long as it has an intellectual, artistic, or emotional basis. Normally such matters are within the curriculum; but they don't have to be; let boys and girls explore an "oddball" world like the history of American musical comedy. What is important is full, rich, knowledge, which gives a student the "feel" of authority and excellence, and makes him recognized both by his contemporaries and by adults.

As a conclusion to this section, let me say I do not mean knowledge of statistical hobbies, like batting averages and automobile parts and hairdos, for these are only substitutes for thinking. These are great fun—I am an authority on the names of jazz musicians—but they do not carry over into schoolwork, any more than knowledge of punctuation rules makes a good writer. Such data are merely collected and piled, high and static, in the minds of grinds.

The Power of Analogy

The mental electricity generated in mastering several fields of knowledge almost automatically insures that another power of the mind will begin to grow: the muscle of analogy. Most teen agers have never heard of it, and those who have do not know how to use it; whereas anyone who has done great or successful work in any important area of human experience shows this striking ability, strikingly. It makes no difference whether he is an athletic coach, a poet, an industrial giant, or a comedian; all strive deliberately to find likenesses, or recognize them by instinct, or else lie fallow in a hammock waiting for comparisons to drift in over a tall glass.

Consider these accomplishments: the two most artistic and successful musical shows of our time—*My Fair Lady* and *West Side Story*—were based on analogies, the former with George Bernard Shaw's *Pygmalion* (which in turn was based on an earlier analogy with a Greek myth), the latter with Shakespeare's *Romeo and Juliet.* A scientist at the A.D. Little Company of Cambridge revolutionized a dangerous steel-making process after noticing a similarity between an artillery weapon and an ice cream cone. Flexing a more whimsical tendon, Walter Winchell once remarked that the girls were out on the beach in their "baiting suits." And Nazi generals made their early successes possible by studying the American Civil War.

To paraphrase Robert Frost, the ability of boys and girls is another thing. The capacity to compare is so undernourished that in their high school composition it is likely that only a few will ever use a simile, a metaphor, or an analogy to develop ideas, emphasize knowledge, or tell a story. Though I speak primarily of English, history should be included, for the same weakness appears in essays for that course. Also I understand from colleagues in the math department that it contributes to failure in coping with spatial relationships. Certainly in foreign language study, poor workmanship would follow inability to compare sound, spelling, and idiom.

Furthermore, this inability to see likeness is the general father of triteness, one of the worst habits of young minds. The reason boys and girls write "calm and collected," "pretty good," "that's terrible," and "sick as a dog" is that they think that way; as Madison Avenue might put it, they "think little." Also, they see little. As they observe the world, they see in a narrow alley of cliches.

I should like to cite two examples of superior student writing to show that their superiority is in part due to noticing what "things are like." Such thoughts rarely appear in failing work, and never in merely moderate work.

> As I grew older, night was not so frightening as it was mysterious. I now listened not for the rasping of bloody claws on my window sill, but for other real things. On warm nights, when the

window was open, the sounds of faint music would sometimes play about me, and laughing, murmuring sounds would drift to my ears.

Most fun of all are the jackets on the new rock 'n roll records. Here we see the "J.D.s," a bright pack of harmonizing young red-bloods. The picture is invariably a close-up, so we may not miss the fine make-up job on their pock-marks and their astounding hair-do's, in which each hair is treated separately, as if it had an immortal soul.

A somewhat grotesque picture of their lack of practice in analogy may be seen in students' first efforts to find similarities. The following sentences come from an assignment to express, via comparison, something seen in a photograph.

1. The tired doctor is like a can sitting in a junkyard, worn out by use.
2. The soldier's eyes looked as if he had seen into Hell itself.
3. The snow kept falling like dandruff from heaven.

Nor are the effects much better in descriptions of what students have actually seen.

1. The jet left a perforated vapor trail like a Brand X pen skipping through butter.
2. The iron dribbled over the smelting pot.
3. The stream of water ran and frolicked down the side of the road like the Mighty Mississippi.

To weed out such natural corn, students should be exercised for four years, and in all courses, in the arts and techniques of comparative thinking. A few drills here and there are not enough, for resistance to comparing is so great that after the first exercises, student thinking trots right back into all the old familiar paces.

As a blessing to teachers, exercises in analogy stir up recitations that are more imaginative and colorful than the abstract ideas restated in terms of other abstract ideas, which most adolescents produce when they are supposed to be thinking. Also, as a basis for judging student understanding, comparisons are often more revealing than bald exposition. I urge, for example, constant exercise in that most fundamental aspect of English, discussion of character. Write one sentence answering "What is Hamlet like?" or "What does Babbitt's escapade with Tanis

Judique resemble?" or develop an extended comparison about Captain Ahab, beginning, "It is as if he had. . . ."

The Natural Parts of an Idea

Adolescent blindness to similarities is like their blindness to other logical relationships: both are caused by lack of exercise. Consequently, the one major connection they make without hesitation is addition, which accounts for the barrage of "and's" laid down whenever boys and girls begin to write. They may not be very good in addition in mathematics, but they are old salts in composition, where a ninth-grader can write like this without even trying:

> One thing I did not like about this skating rink was that there were too many professionals. I think we were the only novices there. One thing I noticed was that the better skaters were very obliging. They would help you around corners. One of the fellows showed me how to take the corners. Some of the skaters were excellent. One person was outstanding. He was a rather foolish looking person but could skate like the wind. We left about ten o'clock. We had been there two and a half hours. I did not have much fun, as I felt kind of foolish among these other skaters.

And a twelfth-grader can write like this, even though he *may* be trying:

> There is occurring at this moment a universal revolutionary movement which dwarfs all others. The people involved are the world's people. The forces of simplicity are massing against the forces of complexity. There is conflict on every quarter. Yet no blood has been shed; nor will it be shed. The ideals of the revolution are simplicity, primitivity, and practicality. They favor a return to Eden. Victory is not in sight or even around the corner. An impasse is hoped for but will never be reached. The revolution is young.

It may be that such students do not understand any other relationship than addition, or it may be that they just do not use any other, for lack of practice. Either way, this "rock-n-roll" type prose leaves an impression that someone is suffering from a bad case of monotonous mind.

Instead, boys and girls should be so disciplined in secondary school that when an idea is mentioned, an intellectual chain reaction takes place which produces waves and waves of new ideas.

In a sense, too, since ideas resemble opponents, a student should be prepared like a boxer, who no sooner sees his opponent move than he moves in other directions, perhaps several at once. To put it in terms of physics, for every intellectual action there should be equal and unequal and automatic reactions. For the student this would mean exploring a problem, instead of just repeating it.

To cure the monotonous mind, and thus discover intellectual variety, students should learn how to take an idea apart—not just exactly as if it were an engine, but somewhat like an engine. Suppose, for example, an English class has been asked to write on "A Complicated Situation in Actual Experience." Suppose one student has the good idea of describing the conflicts in a family with natural and adopted children. However, suppose he can't think of more than a page or two of material, and "that horrible teacher" has very suggestively been talking about 1000 words. There is one solution applicable not only to this English student but to students with essays to write in history, philosophy, or religion: What are the parts of the subject, and how are they related?

Here are the major ones for the topic under consideration, and I don't think it's any exaggeration to say that as a whole, they would be good for 15,000 words.

1. Definition of the problem of natural as against adopted children
2. Contrasting attitudes within the family
3. Results of these contrasts
4. Kinds of contrasts that lead to open conflict
5. Resolutions of conflict
6. Hypothetical cases where conflict would be insoluble
7. Comparisons with other families
8. Time when adoption takes place
9. Conditions in the neighborhood
10. History of adoption problems
11. Concessions required by the facts of life
12. Analogies with similar problems
13. Changes within the family
14. Paradoxes in children's character

The first word in each category is a label for what I have called the natural parts of an idea. The intellectual ability to separate them and combine them should, through vigorous exercising, be available to all secondary school graduates, for this is the basic conditioned reflex upon which all college work depends. This is true for good students who know a lot about their subjects, for the dividing and relating enables them to arrange the best material in emphatic order; but it is especially valuable for those with little knowledge, the ones throughout history who have asked "But what am I going to write about?" Only by such an approach can they realize how little they know, and how much they must discover before writing anything worth reading. Their only alternative, as themes grow longer, is to puff up and repeat and string out to the end, where they then say, "Thus we see. . . ."

As a special part of this program to ignite the discovery of intellectual relationships, I should like to pay particular tribute to the power of paradox. It awakens the most astonishing and profitable possibilities of thought, the reason being that students are so bewildered to find what a paradox really is that they never forget. There is great discipline not only in working out the right sentence form for the paradox—Chesterton is a good model —but in trying to develop a paragraph idea that is a real paradox, not just a simple contrast. Trying to distinguish the two is just the kind of mental wrestling that gives a student a sense of the intangibles, of what is meant by "overtones of meaning"—a quality in their writing more honored in the breach than the observance. Consider the following incident retold by Bennett Cerf:

> Mrs. Harrison Williams, frequently voted the "best dressed woman in the United States," once bought a hat from a Paris milliner for a staggering sum, but with the assurance that the model would not be duplicated.
>
> The very night she returned to America, however, as she was dancing at The Stork Club, she saw another woman wearing an identical hat.
>
> Mrs. Williams was indignant for a moment, but then realized that the other must have been fooled, too. When they passed close to each other on the dance floor, Mrs. Williams pointed first to her own hat, and then to the other's, and then smiled. The lady looked straight through her.
>
> "Maybe she didn't understand," said Mrs. Williams to her partner. "Dance me over next to her again."
>
> This time her gestures were so broad that no misunderstanding was possible. She pointed to both hats, shook her head, and laughed out loud.

The woman cut her dead.

Mrs. Williams was pretty angry about stupid egotism until she went into the powder room and looked into the mirror.

She was wearing a different hat.

In trying to produce something like this, my students had no luck whatever until they realized that they had to suggest a meaning, rather than lay it out in lavender prose.

In addition to such words and ideas as "concession," "hypothesis," and "paradox," there is a special group whose meanings symbolize necessary intellectual exercise: these are the four pairs analysis-synthesis, induction-deduction, content-context, and definition-characterization. Any student who hopes to do good work must master these concepts by constant practice, since they are important to every course in the curriculum.

Most students, however, just do not know the ideas and distinctions involved. Ask a teenager what detectives do, and he'll probably say "*de*duce"; normally, they don't: they *in*duce. Ask another to define intolerance, and he may say it's a horrible thing. It certainly is, but that's not what it means. Ask a student to define any word, and he will probably give a dictionary definition; but ask him what it means in a particular passage, and he may be puzzled, since he has not learned to relate a word to its environment, to see how its general meaning is restricted by context.

To conclude this section, I have a modern instance in hand. Early in my teaching career, I customarily began class discussion of books with the question, What do you think the writer means? If the answer was "I don't know," I went on to the next boy. One day, in the face of widespread ignorance, I thought of a new question: Do you know how to find a writer's meaning? The students' "Hunh?" were a great shock to me, especially since these students had had three years of good secondary education.

The work in question was a short story by Katherine Mansfield, and I insisted that in this literary form the reader could generally find the meaning in the final paragraph, since the main idea is usually suggested there. Quick students saw the point without much trouble.

Moderate minds took longer, since they needed another clue: relate the first paragraph to the last. Then they began to come close to Miss Mansfield's hint.

As for the dullest students, nothing percolated at all until they were instructed to find logical connections between the beginning and ending, and at least four other important passages in the story.

Those who never did understand the story continually failed to understand its interrelationships, especially those designated here as "the natural parts of an idea": contrast, analogy, causation, and result. Poor students always look at a word, a sentence, a paragraph, or an incident, and start answering questions before observing how these smaller units are related to the whole structure. Many young persons struggling with Hamlet's character, for example, are bewildered when they first read the "wisecracks" he makes to Ophelia; they do not see how such vulgarity can be reconciled with other facets of his nature. Likewise in history, students cannot explain the significance of specific events because they don't connect them to trends, policies, ideas, and other specific events. Whereas, distinguished work in the amateur world of school, and the professional world of adult life, is founded, always, on what Shakespeare called "understood relations."

Finally, distinguished work comes from students who as the professionals put it, "have something to say," just as poor and mediocre work comes from students who have little or nothing to say and say it with all the rules observed. Undoubtedly there are other ways to discover something to say, but one of the clearest and most accessible to students is to learn how to recognize and develop the logical relationships discussed in this section.

Subjectivity and Objectivity

Dull and incomplete work often suggests lack of exercise in the intellectual areas so far discussed. The next dilemma does receive some attention: the distinction between reacting subjectively and objectively. Athletics may make an impression, as in the curing of prima donnas; and mathematics can be effective, since numerical precision is the enemy of too much personality. But in the humanities, which are still far more important as education, too many older students are still doing poor and merely moderate work because they have not been drilled to distinguish between what is private opinion and what is public, impersonal, and factual.

I want to analyze this dilemma from the point of view of composition, especially composition about books, for in spite of the delights of discussion, it is writing that develops the sinews of intellect, and it is on writing about books that students are most significantly judged.

As early as possible in high school, students should know that writing about books is a very different proposition from writing about personal experience. There are special difficulties for teenagers in discussing literature on paper, and until these prickly and unfamiliar obstacles are clarified and the right approaches practiced, boys and girls will continue to flounder. Unhappily, too, they will probably think the trouble is mechanical.

First of all, a book can be produced in class and its evidence set face to face with any opinion, with the result that adolescent conclusions are powerless unless bolstered by the text. This is not true of experience. The student who writes a sketch of his nasty neighbor—the one who keeps taking away his football—cannot be asked to produce his subject in class for confirmation. Hence he may write much more freely than if he is explaining a character in a novel, or an event in history. If he feels irritable and sardonic about his neighbor, he may describe these emotions, and if they are controlled, a good composition may result. But when boys and girls face the facts of life in books, they must take another intellectual position, where new and complex responses are demanded; they must be humble and objective, and stop deciding merely on what they *like,* or on the unnatural premise of *ought.*

Teacher: Why does this character act the way he does?
Student: Pretty stupid thing to do, I thought.
Teacher: Why is this ending perfectly logical, after what has gone before?
Student: Oh, I was terribly disappointed.

One of my greatest favorites is this conclusion to a book report: "This is the best book of this kind I've ever read"— whereupon the teacher discovers the student can't name any other books of "this kind."

Intense subjectivity always makes it difficult for students to cope with complex reading. One boy failed a paper on *A Streetcar Named Desire* because he summarized the main character: "I hated that Blanche DuBois so much I couldn't wait to get through the lousy play!" Many teachers, too, must have struggled with failure to understand the climax of *The Admirable Crichton* because the student wants Lady Mary to marry that butler, wishfully forgetting that Crichton thought other things were more important. Or, as with *Hamlet*, how many young people can't get by their own superficial feeling that the central character "ought to have his head examined."

These egotistical misinterpretations show another difficulty in explaining literature: inability to cope with abstractions. Reality in a book is based on words, and words are abstractions whose meanings depend on an imaginative or intellectual act by the reader. Few students can think this way unless they have been born with the capacity or have developed it through exercise; and this is why so many young people, thoroughly congenial with the facts of their own lives, fall apart in discussions about books. After the imagery of childhood, the time of the teens is a vast sponge of literal fads: boys with their sparkplugs and earned-run averages, girls with their hairdos and cute skirts. Small wonder they cannot imagine how

> . . . pity, like a naked new-born babe,
> Striding the blast, or heaven's cherubin, hors'd
> Upon the sightless couriers of the air,
> Shall blow the horrid deed in every eye,
> That tears shall drown the wind.
> [*Macbeth*, I, vii, 21–25]

And there is more trouble for them: the unfamiliarity of literary material. Almost anyone would do badly the first time he tried to cope with unrecognizable ideas and characters. Where in their suburban lives have they ever seen anybody like Lady Macbeth or Charles Strickland, or any thing like a "skimmington ride" or "the slough of despond," or an idea like the Protestant Reformation?

This frustration by the unknown was dramatized this year by one student's instant answer to a question. Describe how actors would say their lines in the clubroom scene in Galsworthy's *Loyalties*. "How *can* I!" protested a boy: "I've never seen a play in my life!"

What do we do about such special "literary" problems? What exercises will help? In the next section, a number of drills are suggested, but here I want to stress the conviction that what many high school students need, first of all, is a new attitude. They need to know that they fail in "book learning" because they do not understand the opposition: those strange and powerful forces of objectivity and abstraction. When problems of form, character, style, philosophy, and mood appear, they've got to change their signs; it isn't just like reading any old book.

I sometimes wonder, though this may be too simple, if students would benefit by approaching their written work with the idea that there are only two kinds of writing: objective and subjective. If the former, the student must expect that the material will be found largely outside himself, and therefore he is restricted; if the latter, as in personal essays and narratives, he has much more license to say what he likes, for the substance comes from within. In an exposition about town government, he should look at his writing as if it were done by someone else; in a claim that "Fabian Can Sing Better Than Frank Sinatra," it doesn't make much difference. Interpreting a poem by Robert Frost depends not on what students think the words mean but on meaning as controlled by other parts of the poem. Fundamentally, in almost any writing about books, students must realize that objective and abstract realities are involved, from which they must divorce their private humors. Whereas in a story about a personal experience with a girl, the whole tale requires developing just such intimate feelings.

Is it too much to ask boys and girls to cope with such "literary" problems? Is man too ornery and private to change? Here are two cases for optimism: one, a student who near the end of the year, remarked of a poem, "This is pretty corny stuff, but then . . . I just don't happen to like what the author likes"; and the other, a boy who summed up *The Late George Apley:* "I really think this is a stupid book, but I don't suppose I know what I'm talking about."

General and Specific

Though it would be appropriate for the next area of exercise, I doubt that it's really necessary to illustrate what teachers mean by "vague generalization," or "be specific." These are our occupational theme songs—or perhaps "torch songs" would be better—and you are probably rehearsing your favorites at the mention of the words. More interesting are the reasons *why* adolescents find it so hard to *be specific,* why they are so governed by what might be called the general mind. We should know the causes before we can battle this devastating weakness in student thinking and writing.

It is partly a change of life. In childhood, boys and girls live in a world of visual and specific images, where they see precisely and originally: "Mummy, look! I'm whispering my shoes." But in high school, they move into a world of lumps. They begin to think in clouds, vaguely. They squint through filters that neutralize all specifics. Look back at their hackneyed language, which is a clear mirror of their minds. For the teenager, almost anything becomes "neat" and "cute"; anybody over forty, an "old guy"; ideological complications, "deals" and "bits" and "kicks"—"Eddie was up in my room last night getting off his religious bit"—and all forms of opposition, "stupid."

Also, in high school, they move in a searing hurry which cauterizes their capacity to observe, so that they never see what a thing is really like, what its peculiar individuality is. It would not be impossible for them to see such details, except that, as they are fond of saying, "Oh yuh. . . . I've been over that once already."

And then there is the mass mesmerizing that takes place in high school, where whole classes are sicklied o'er with the pale cast of general thought. By the end of the eleventh grade, this affliction is an epidemic in which all but a few oddballs mimic the daily platitude. It's not unnatural, and we have to be understanding, for group power is great, and the embarrassment of thinking too precisely on any event is almost irresistible, just as it is disconcerting for one adult to look too specifically at another.

Now and then a student breaks through the prevailing moldy thinking with a dart of accurate thought, like "My roommate is a prisoner of his own cliches" . . . and what happens? Up stand the vociferous stereotypes to make a big production out of it, in reverse: "Hey, man, aren't we smart!" . . . "Didja hear the big deal from Schultz here?" . . . or, "Too bad we can't all be Einsteins!" . . . with the result that next time the speaker protects his image behind a lace curtain of cliches.

Another obstacle is time: it takes so long to learn to see and think specifically. Normally, one year of exercise is merely a start.

What students need, to counteract their regular tendency to go general, is four straight years of emphasis on picking out precise meanings from the mass.

All these personal reasons are important, but sometimes our teaching practice is at fault. If the "magic" words "be specific" are merely uttered as a kind of charm, or are just left up on the chalkboard all year long, like "go slow" highway signs, not much is accomplished. Students must have their minds exercised so that they respond naturally with specific images. They must also do more than write expository essays. Though this conventional assignment may teach some things—such as organization—it is a dubious device for pointing up specific and concrete language. The trouble is that exposition is an exercise in abstraction: it calls for specific material, not as a way of thinking but only as assistant detail in an otherwise general discussion.

In order to seriously undermine the habit of vague generalizing, and to lead students into a routine of sharper thought, I should like to propose the following exercises. I commend them particularly to frustrated teachers with too-large classes, for these drills are short.

1. In two or three sentences, describe an action that stands for an abstract idea.
2. Begin the above with simple ideas like anger and "being snowed," and work up to more difficult concepts like antithesis, thoughtfulness, and conservatism.
3. Do the same thing in half a page of dialogue, with no exposition.
4. Take a general word like "man" and make a chart dividing its meaning steadily downward until a specific point is reached, like Leonard Bernstein.
5. Start with a specific individual like Holden Caulfield, and generalize upward to the most comprehensive abstraction possible.
6. Write a generalization followed merely by an example, and then another followed by proof.
7. Describe a scene or a person known to the class. Do it without direct identification, but so accurately that none is needed.
8. Describe a building or a "place" by photographic details so chosen that the subject has a clearly recognizable quality.
9. Describe something by a cliche, and then by precise words revealing an original observation.

10. Describe or characterize something—a person, an action, a scene—by a suggestive analogy.

11. Select a passage from a book, and then describe its style or mood by a discussion of actual words and phrases. Explain how these words and phrases have a different quality from others that might have been used about the same subject.

12. Select a passage of writing that sounds as if it had been written by a particular kind of person; by referring to specific words and phrases, describe this person.

Finally, as an unusual device to focus student thinking on specific images, here is an experiment that, judging by student reaction, at least has a high coefficient of shock value. Several years ago, frustrated by a slow class of seniors who were not responding to more conventional procedures, I decided to see what would happen if the scientific method of induction were applied to writing problems. Using a paragraph by Chesterton, and giving no prescriptive instructions, I asked for a concentrated synthesis of sentence structure, to see how many general principles of style they could find illustrated in Chesterton's prose.

One or two students found one or two principles, like punctuation of independent clauses; but the majority couldn't discover anything else important, despite Chesterton's continual use of parallelism, subordination, and the proper placement of which-clauses. This failure seems significant, for it suggests there is something lopsided in educational procedures. Shouldn't students be able to find examples of the very principles being explained to them? The trouble is inadequate exercise in the almighty habit of thinking specifically. Perhaps teenagers suffering from low grades should take a year off at a school for detectives, where they would learn the importance of details. Certainly something is indicated, especially in homework drills, that is more startling than what is provided by routine education.

Visual Perception

One of the most important reasons why adolescents fail at anything is that they do not see very clearly, even with glasses. During the course of a school day, they make this perfectly obvious by the number of times they bump into people.

It is no wonder. While smothering them with blankets of isms, abstract principles, and programs, education has not taught them to use their eyes, in spite of the fact that man's life is determined by how much and how accurately he sees. Therefore, and with some hesitation, I suggest that a student who wants to improve his standing in general, and his literary composition in particular, should buy a cheap camera and take a course entitled "How To See"; not "How To Use a Light Meter," but *how to see:* how to look at the world structurally, symbolically, selectively, and emotionally. As a teacher I don't suppose I should talk like a huckster, but I would almost guarantee that anyone who learns to see human experience with such control will not only do better work, but will live a more enticing existence.

In an essay on the lessons of her blindness, Helen Keller declares that "If I were the president of a university, I should establish a compulsory course in 'How to Use Your Eyes.' The professor would try to show his pupils how they could add joy to their lives by really seeing what passes unnoticed before them: He would try to awaken their dormant and sluggish faculties."

We have such a course at our school, and from time to time I talk with the instructor about common problems of seeing. Last year his photographers began making pictures around the campus of good subject matter, with the idea that eventually English students would write about the same things. Then the pictures and the words would be brought together to discuss accuracy, effectiveness, imagination, cliches, incompleteness, and malarkey.

In a statement of the purpose of its course, our art department declares that

> Photography is an educational experience that possesses the advantage of rapidly training a pupil's capacity to observe, perceive, and invent. Simple problems such as "find a broken rhythm," "produce an arresting contrast," "discover a subtle image," succeed each other in such a way as to induce students to look at the world with fresh imagination.

The phrase "arresting contrast," reflecting my earlier point about fundamental relationships, and the conclusion "with fresh imagination," suggest two ways in which the objectives of one course can be used to dramatize the aims of another. They indicate too how closely related the kind of vision that makes a good photographer is to the kind of vision that makes a good writer.

If students receive no training in the art of seeing, they grow up into adults who see the world square, and the kind of writing they did in high school becomes the kind of photography they do for the family album. Think of all those pictures where the main subject—say a pretty girl—is framed with uncomplimentary objects like fire hydrants and tail fins. Think of those where one lumpish "thing" like a telephone pole has been photographed head-on without any contributing images. And remember all those "shots" without feeling or spirit—sister standing dead-pan by an open automobile door in the driveway —what are all these but the same lack of selection, failure of subordination, and insensitivity to mood that make students write dull themes about "A Trip I Took Last Summer," or put together such a silly combination of ideas as this, in a report on outside reading:

> The author talks about some new shapes of French bread that will make it not only edible, but useful. He suggests a walking stick loaf, and a ladder loaf and many other equally ridiculous ideas. He tells about the time he guarded Elizabeth Taylor from Italian pinchers during the 1960 Olympics.

The conclusion is clear: students, like people, produce jumbled work because they see jumbled images and think jumbled thoughts. Or, when the problem is one of having *nothing* to say, the reason is often that they have seen nothing. They need some kind of dramatic experience to show how closely related saying is to seeing, and it is this need which prompts the perhaps curious idea of putting a camera into the hands of poor English students.

This analogy between scholarship and photography is not a new principle: it is a modern application of a technique used by Chaucer, Shakespeare, Dickens, and Conrad. It was perfectly redefined last year by Archibald MacLeish, who said that what students today need most is the ability to "see feelingly." Remember the "Wyfe of Bath"? . . . . and Hotspur's description of "a certain lord, perfumed like a milliner"? . . . . and Cratchet's Christmas dinner? . . . . and the sinking of Lord Jim's ship?

Certainly we are not in the business of making little Shakespeares and Conrads; but we ought to try, with new exercises, to make students who can see and think in some of the ways of great writers.

Some teachers send students to walk the streets for theme subjects, and I have tried it; but if the child does not know what to observe, or how to select, he will return, as many have done, saying: "But there wasn't anything to see." He probably looked for subject matter the way children look for popsicle sticks.

As English teachers, we must naturally continue to communicate abstract ideas and mechanical technique; but in view of the quality of student writing, we must realize that the time has come to add something new: visual perception—what Jacques Barzun called "the concrete imagination." We must realize that a new kind of help is needed for the thousands of boys and girls who have so far been untouchables, within conventional programs of education.

Conclusion

Throughout the long metaphor in this essay, I have urged that one approach to outstanding work is a new set of exercises, which will develop the muscles of the mind. In this way, students will be capable of many more responses than have previously been dreamed of in their philosophies. At first these responses must be self-conscious; but then, through practice, they may become automatic.

In his long essay "Independence," Rudyard Kipling dramatized the same idea in a similarly extended analogy: for a man to be strong, so that he can do his own work by himself and successfully, he must have what Kipling called "his rations," a full supply of spiritual, intellectual, and physical disciplines. These, said Kipling, are the necessary weapons and armor against the opposition; without them, a man should stay home and join committees.

I have cited other professional authorities: Helen Keller, Igor Stravinsky, and Shakespeare. Here at the end I want to return to our reasons for existence: the students. It is not often they know what they have done to produce excellence; but now and then an articulate teenager comes along with his eyes open, his "rations" in hand, and his motives sharp. Consider the following passage, written by a senior to develop an idea by means of an analogy:

> I read books for the same reason Hilary climbs mountains: just because they are there. Books stand before me in mental challenge, and I assault these monuments of creativity with all the necessary equipment and passion of an explorer. My ability to read serves as the guidelines and picks that bring me chapter by chapter, ledge by ledge, to the summit. Of course, reading, like climbing, isn't an easy undertaking. The mind slips along difficult paths of meaning and purpose while ideas are rolling, sometimes unseen, continuously towards you. Sharp winds of emotion may tug at your heart; the terrain may become too rough and force you back. Many times only determination and desire to know the unknown keep a man climbing higher; but when he does reach his summit, the feeling common to climber and reader, of conquest, of having met and defeated a challenge, strengthen the mind, the body, and the spirit.

As his style suggests, this boy is not brilliant; there is too much careful discipline. What he accomplishes he does by hard intellectual work, not special genius. But it is just such hard intellectual work that is necessary to overcome the limitations of a fairly good mind, so that the student can do outstanding work. I doubt that this boy, without the attitude he has toward books, could have achieved the honor grades that distinguish his career.

The student with the "fairly good mind," with moderate ability, with competence, who, in that damning phrase of the music critic, is "adequate to the occasion"—he also needs our attention, as much as the brilliant student. The latter will learn anyway, no matter what kind of assignments; but the adequate types, the ones known in the state of Maine as "mod'rit," they will go right through life being mediocre unless their schools do something drastic. For them, actual experience is a bad teacher, since they do not know what to learn from, being without curiosity. They are the ones who get 67 in English for four straight years, and in this world of fierce competition that is not very good.

For them—*and* the failures—there is an educational policy suggested in *Hamlet,* when Polonius says, "And thus do we . . .

by indirections find directions out." I have suggested, for example, that a weak student may do better work in English by
learning the history of musical comedy; and I have recommended
a course in photography which, by inducing better ways of seeing,
can be beneficial in many areas. These are but two instances of
the conviction that the causes of poor work and ordinary work
are not always what routine pedagogy assumes, and that in the
face of adolescent boredom and opposition to reading, thinking,
and writing, we must be new, fanciful, subliminal, and wily.

TO WRITE
OR
NOT TO WRITE:
AND HOW?

HART LEAVITT
Phillips Academy, Andover, Massachusetts

When I first began to teach English, I can remember being
bothered by the criticism of professional writers. I wondered
whether something ought to be done about it, especially when the
criticism was aimed at methods of teaching teenagers how to
write. My particular concern arose from a personal interest in
writing—since I have constantly composed stories and essays in
my spare time—and from a conviction that, for my students,
writing is more important than talking.

Fortunately for my own peace of mind, at the beginning of
my career, I saw only an occasional professional condemnation,
none of my colleagues ever mentioned such opposition, and I

never read any pedagogical essays on the problem—so that for a number of years I went on about my business relatively undismayed.

Lately, however, I have seen an increasing number of these subversive remarks, and they come from such a variety of literary philosophers that I don't believe the criticism is coincidental. Nor do I believe that these established writers are simply trying to work off a personal grievance against unhappy teachers. The criticism is so consistent that I think the professionals have something against us which ought to be causing intelligent pains —particularly in the field of composition.

The earlier, occasional remarks of men like Yeats and Sinclair Lewis are now being amplified by contemperary critics, poets, essayists, and novelists. In her otherwise delightful book of essays, *The Province of the Heart,* Phyllis McGinley describes what she didn't learn about writing; and at the beginning of a new critical work on Hemingway, Janet Lewis Winters, a poet and a teacher, and the wife of critic Yvor Winters, is quoted as asking: "What does one learn about writing in high school? You are lucky if you're not taught to write badly."

Leon Uris, author of *Exodus* and *Battlecry,* recently admitted that he flunked English three times. What is more important, he thinks the failures are "merely academic," for he said, "It's a good thing English has nothing to do with writing."

In more peaceful times when teaching was a private affair, these criticisms were embarrassing enough; but now their disturbance has been heightened and enlarged into public significance by the conclusion of Dr. Conant's recent national study of high school education: "Every student should spend half his regular English course learning to write."

This is very puzzling. Are these two men speaking of the same English language?

It will be easy, of course, to say that Mr. Uris is a minor writer; but is it so easy to dismiss Winston Churchill's poor showing in schoolboy English, or his sometimes tart comments on the relationship between teaching and good writing?

Instead of rationalizing with the comforting idea that Mr. Churchill is a genius, we should, I believe, consider that we have been warned to start our own critical self-investigation before someone we don't like does it for us. In this essay, I should like to begin such an investigation with the following three major premises:

> 1. Much of our pedagogy is so alien to the disciplines of professional writing that their criticism is no wonder.
> 2. This alienation causes much of bad writing done in secondary school.
> 3. Therefore, we ought to hold our students up to as many professional standards as they can reach for without being deluded into dreams of immediate publication.

I know that such a statement will start a rustle of philosophic red pencils. Many teachers will argue that boys and girls cannot be taught this way. "Teenagers," they will say, "do not know enough—they have not had enough experience—to write short fiction." I think that we ought to try to teach them. Other teachers will suggest that there is something immoral about writing: I remember one man who remarked vehemently, "I hear Fred Simpson is doing a lot of special work in writing. Good thing; maybe he'll get it out of his system." I think perhaps he ought to get it in.

Such opposition becomes specious when considered against the fact that routine exercises in mechanics have failed to show a whole generation how to write anything worth reading. Some can, of course—those few who have learned to follow some of the aims and devices of the professional; but I am worried about the other thousands, those poor boys and girls who spend four years writing such stuff as only bad dreams are made on, whose only natural destiny is the wastebasket.

These teenagers make up a national legion, too; in twenty-five years of teaching English in a large independent school that draws its students from all over the country, I have seen a representative enough sampling to observe that their habits arise from general practice among textbooks and teachers. The same errors appear anywhere, and in every grade.

Part of the trouble is that for a good many years we have been lugging along, with our sound fundamentals, a lot of heavy baggage left over from Caesar's Gallic Wars. Much of it is too easy, or out of date, or unsuited to English. Hence we are giving ordinary minds a minimum, and we are far behind our best students. We need new aims and techniques. Why, for example, should teachers in science monopolize experiments? Adolescents are in as desperate need of new meanings and intentions when they write as when they work in a laboratory.

Now I suspect that in a large gathering of English teachers, many would be sure they knew what they meant by "learning how to write"; but if they itemized their methods, the results would be chaotic. The letter-men would be against the fill-out-a-form men, the analysis-men would be against the fiction-men, and the short-paper men would be against the long ones; and they would also discover that courses in English straddle "business English," Greek literature, and a-year-off-to-work-on-the-school-yearbook, for credit.

I believe in Dr. Conant's idea, despite the appalling burden it would involve in correcting papers; but I also believe the problem is a complex one, and a human one, so that before we leap off into any crash programs, we must face a difficult question: "Spend half their regular time learning to write *what?*"

To prevent certain misconceptions, I should make it clear that I am not proposing to turn the classroom into a farm system for prospective novelists. Rather, I suggest we take a look at what we have been doing. I suggest that we have led many of our students into what I call the Seven Deadly Sins of teenage writing, all of which were long ago exorcised from professional prose:

1. Pretentious Diction
2. Clumsy Idiom
3. Dead-end Sentences
4. Poor Relations
5. No Contest
6. Padding
7. The Big Think

To illustrate the first of these evils, let me quote a group of sentences taken from student compositions. The first two came from seniors:

1. Modern mountain climbers plan walks that are not commensurate with their stamina.

2. After a smoke, I usually berate myself for having so indulged.

3. The rest of the fellows wanted me to go for another ride on the roller coaster, but I quickly turned aside their offer.

On being required to rewrite this delicate piece of verbiage, the boy wrote:

> I hastily disregarded their offer.

> 4. A youth may feel severity of depression at being scorned because his tie is not of the latest fashion.

Many teenagers have impressive reading vocabularies, but in composition the words fall out of phase into a clutter of total impropriety and frightened English. Somewhere these young writers have been so scared out of their wits that they sound as if they were assisting at a rebirth of euphemism. The language appears to be written by boys and girls trying to escape the century-old revolution in letters which has produced so much directness and honesty.

Words like "berate," "commensurate," and "severity of depression" sound an overtone of writing done for the wrong reason. Apparently, teenagers are trying to impress somebody, and the impression they are after is "niceness" and "culture."

The falsity of such diction—with its underlying cause—must be assaulted with the idea that good writing results only when students try to do what the professional does: express ideas and feelings about realistic, specific human experience. For the teacher's part, there must be an end to the cleavage that divides writing into two kinds: that done by professionals, which goes into articles, short stories, and novels; and that done by students, which goes into the mark book. Hundreds of "themes" I have corrected in the last twenty-five years suggest that the writers have never been taught to connect the two.

The result has been a kind of "homework" style of composition, rooted in abstract, Latinate, genteel terminology. It is false to the meaning, false to the age, laughable to any realistic impulse, and utterly impersonal. A phrase like "commensurate with their stamina" stops the flow of thought when no stop is indicated. If the ideas were complex, such language might be excusable; but they aren't. Furthermore, "berate myself for having so indulged" is a very nice phrase whose atmosphere wholly contradicts the fact that we are not living in a nice age.

Perhaps it is this romanticism which makes students hate writing; they instinctively distrust arranging words in a vacuum.

It seems to me their attitude begins to change when they are asked to search for physical, emotional words for physical, emotional meanings in the world of 1960. And as soon as the teacher makes it clear they are not expected to achieve professional competence for a long time, they are ready to accept comparisons between the bite of established writers and their own soft words.

There is a spiritual kinship between Victorian diction and the deadly sin of ungainly and idiot idiom. Where, in Shakespeare's name, do boys and girls find the awkward combinations of words which discolor their writing like unmatched socks?

1. Peter couldn't see how he could bear leaving a man whom he had until then lived to be near to and to talk to.

2. The American soldiers fighting today are the cause of actual participation in church affairs taking a serious slide downwards, and church membership, of that generation, showing a sharp cut.

3. A half day's wagon trip from the nearest settlement is Jody Baxter's home in the scrub-oak and pine-backwoods section of Florida.

4. Bad behavior pertaining to hospitality was shown against Odysseus.

5. The one-eyed Cyclops is evil by his devouring of Odysseus' men.

The most depressing characteristic of these sentences is their perfect grammar: every construction is exactly right, and frighteningly wrong. It is for this reason that I cannot jump on the bandwagon back "to good old-fashioned fundamentals." My years of teaching yield too little evidence that grammatical knowledge has anything to do with good writing. On the contrary, students often write well despite a startling ignorance of grammar, whereas others, though they make 90's on tests in mechanics, write sentences of incredible awkwardness.

As a professional teacher, I am not trying to swing the pendulum over into any cloudland where writing can be fun. It isn't; it requires discipline and exercises. But there must be something wrong with the discipline we have been exacting if it still allows boys and girls to write such stuff after three years in high school.

One of the difficulties is time; it takes hours and hours of rewriting and rewriting to iron out ridges in style. Any professional, however, will say this is precisely what has to be done, since the first revisions may be no better than the original. One device, which, incidentally, saves the teacher's time, is to require a student to rewrite two of his worst sentences until they express, tersely and imaginatively, just what he wanted to say, even if it takes three weeks.

Another device grows out of complete lack of ear-training. Teenagers should read their work aloud, and they should hear it read aloud, in class, for by constant listening they will begin to "hear" the clumsiness of sounds in lumpy combinations of consonants.

One textbook exercise should be extinguished: the long lists of bad sentences which students are asked to correct. Hours of drudgery spent recasting these atrocious sentences leads, by osmosis, to imitation of the atrocity. What boys and girls should do is imitate the tone and structure of the best professional sentences a teacher can find, so that his students, again by osmosis, will adopt fluency.

There is an analogy here with music. No good teacher ever asked a young player to practice exercises based on bad phrasing, or bad substance. Only the best music is assigned, and what is corrected is bad playing of good musical literature. Students are told constantly not to listen to records of men who play badly—like some former jazz musicians trying to play the classics—lest poor habits develop, unconsciously. To ask a student to practice "corny" music is like asking a young writer to model his style on *Silas Marner.*

The third deadly sin of teenage composition is the burnt-out ends of their sentences-in-reverse. Boys and girls do not, with any regularity, know what to do when they have finished their independent clauses, and, in their ignorance, tack onto the end trivial and apologetic phrases.

1. Conformity is the result of either laziness, or ignorance of its occurrence, on the part of those who partake of it.

2. Human prejudice is a terrible thing, it seems to me.

3. In a thunderstorm, the caveman was terrified; he could not help but address some one thing.

4. In my childhood, when life bothered me, I blamed the people around me for my miserable condition. Now I understand *life;* I follow the "Golden Rule," and value all my ideals.

5. When the end of term arrived, I decided to study for my exams, which was a good thing to do.

6. This girl friend of mine has a peculiar habit which I don't know what it means.

These sentences illustrate a variety of mistakes in timing, but the last two are the worst, and, with their ugly *witch*-clauses showing, symbolize the entire problem of climax. In their tormented phrasing, they expose a great failure in education: although students have been drilled to recognize nonrestrictive and restrictive clauses, they have not discovered where to put them.

Student writers could find a sharp little truth on the pages of Hemingway, Maugham, and Conrad: rarely a nonrestrictive modifier at the end of any sentence, and almost never a which-clause, even if restrictive. At his most florid style in the essays, Robert Louis Stevenson observes the same unwritten law. He saves up until the finish line, and even after an elongated sentence of one hundred words, achieves that final sound of "So there!" which distinguishes all good sentence structure.

Students can do it just as soon as they learn to save their strength for the last period:

1. How many times have you held onto a dream until it burned out like a match? [12th grade]

2. For as long as I can remember, night has aroused in me many emotions: from fear at three to ecstasy at fifteen. [12th]

3. Springs make brooks which break and splash from rock to rock as they tumble down the slope. [10th]

4. "The Huntington Ravine" was on the other side of a field littered with tremendous boulders as big as good-sized rooms. [9th]

So far I have been discussing the sins of the individual sentence. Now we must explore devious paths into larger infernal regions: the interconnections between sentences, paragraphs, and beginnings and endings. Many a student ends up with a set of very poor relations when he tries to assemble his material into a closely knit family of thought.

Technically, we give students many exercises in recognizing transitional expressions, but for some reason they have great difficulty in using these intelligently. One obstacle is their failure to understand that certain words and phrases can only be used at certain times; another is their ignorance of the logical relationships of the very ideas they express.

The first dilemma may be illustrated by the connective "however," which students often use to relate ideas between which there is no contrast.

> Martin Arrowsmith is the main character in Sinclair Lewis' novel. He has, however, several faults.

Confusion also follows in the wake of the little word "even."

> My best friend is a very good football player. He even says he likes to study.

Rhetorical handbooks would be more helpful if, instead of merely carrying mechanical lists of transitional expressions, they explained thoroughly, with professional examples, just what logical relationships each word may appropriately emphasize.

The problem of what might be called "overtones of relationship" becomes even more important within the larger framework of a whole paragraph. As long as students are unaware of such overtones, they will write paragraphs like this opening one from a long essay on debutante parties in Paris.

> At the Palace of Versailles, the happy debs danced in their fine evening gowns, for after all when a girl is introduced to society, she can't just wear any old rag, now can she? One of the delighted debs exclaimed in a moment of pure rapture, "I want to meet a French Caballero!" The party must have turned into a rather ridiculous affair when 600 uninvited guests were received after showing calling cards with noble names.

It took a special conference with this boy, a twelfth-grader, to expose himself to himself, fully and clearly, so that he knew what he was trying to do. "Oh, I see," he said finally, "all those details are supposed to show how futile deb parties are." Then we began the hunt for transitional phrases to express this relationship emphatically.

An even more complex difficulty appears in the relation between the first and last paragraphs of a theme. Most students are incapable of sustaining their work from start to finish, and then concluding on the strongest pitch of meaning and intensity. Often even the best boys see only a 1–2–3–4 connection between these parts, so that the whole thing is a kind of patchwork quilt of thought.

The cause of this loose-jointed writing is too little discussion of whole themes, with the student alone, and before the entire class. Too much time is devoted to details for their own sake. What adolescents need is four years of stress on the fact that nothing—whether it is a fact, a feeling, or a finale—should be included unless it adds to the purpose of the whole piece, necessarily and dramatically. Let us, for example, have no more examples when one is plenty. Let us have reasons and contrasts and comparisons and definitions and hypotheses and detail and imagination, all arranged in ascending importance.

Let students, too, come to feel the heft of the whole theme so that they know, factually and intuitively, what it means to write 900 words, as against 200. Over a period of months this can be done by focusing attention on one entire composition mimeographed on one piece of paper—800 words can be contained in single space. For many teenagers, the effect is like seeing a complete personality at once, and the single visual unit makes it quicker for them to see how the parts relate to the main idea. Sometimes the result is so startling as to suggest an ideal textbook composed of nothing but 300 pages of whole compositions from all grades of high school. It would certainly reveal, with immediate efficiency, how important any single paragraph was in relation to others, especially those some distance away.

Another way to make students recognize poor relations is to require an outline *after* corrections. One boy was devastated to find what his skeleton looked like, stripped of all that flattering nice white paper, blue ink, and red ruled lines. His topic was "The Beauty and Foreboding of Autumn."

Paragraph 1   "Autumn is a beautiful season filled with regret." Then after incidental remarks, he wrote: "The foliage is magnificent."

2   Here he described chipmunks, and so on, preparing for winter.

3 He began: "All this beauty is a forerunner of winter," and then elaborated on the contrast.

4 This was devoted to the idea, with comments from coaches, that autumn is wonderful weather for football.

5 The amazing contrast between Spring and Fall.

6 Last sentence: "Autumn, like all seasons, must end sometime, but unfortunately the ending of autumn brings on the dreary season of winter."

Since this boy is in the first year, I decided to prod him quick and early: to make him see that since there is no natural, clear, necessary relationship between "regret," "chipmunks," and "football," he must write it in, on purpose. I like to emphasize the concept of good relations—rather than our old symbol U; it's too negative—because I want to whittle their thinking to the point where they add material only for constructive reasons, where they can actually name a relationship between what they have done here, and then there.

If a student has reasonably good material to start with, he can dress it attractively with the right transitional colors; when the subject matter, on the other hand, is useless and dull, then we simply cannot create any silk purses. We have to start sowing all over again.

In the teaching of secondary writing, one of the most neglected subjects—as in the professional world it is the most cultivated—is pure substance. It must be neglected: there are just as many students crying, in their own wilderness, ". . . . but I don't know *what* to say!" as there were when I was in the other end of the woods thirty years ago. And yet, away they have to go, writing "themes" when they have nothing to say, a sin which professionals would certainly be caught dead withal.

The result? *No contest.*

Two other results: the chairman of our department passed by this morning, muttering; "If I have to read another of those dull, lugubrious themes. . . ." His predecessor passed by, some years ago, lamenting: "Am I going to spend the rest of my life putting little red marks on paper?"

I realize I'm going to oversimplify, but I am convinced that it is such an important oversimplification that only a few very conscientious objectors will object. Student composition will continue to be dull, fruitless, and mechanical until students learn that good writing, whether it be exposition, story, or familiar essay, must be based in conflict. Without it, there is no reason to read further, for the reader does not wonder how it will come out. More important, without conflict within the student's mind, there is nothing for him to resolve; there is really no reason to write a theme one way or the other. Themes, consequently, are much like package deals: a lot of stuff is tossed in which otherwise could not be gotten rid of.

When boys and girls find nothing inside themselves to write out, they must look elsewhere. In textbooks, they find lists of topics which are so devoid of interest—and I mean conflict—that no professional would ever look at them once.

1. How Our School Safeguards Health
2. A Summary of a Speech
3. My Favorite Picnic Spot
4. Our Vegetable Man
5. What I Would Like To Be When I Grow Up
6. People in Glass Houses Shouldn't Throw Stones

It was in these subjects that William Butler Yeats found such a deadly impersonality that he chose other material, from his own life, and thereby antagonized his teacher. I am sure Yeats would have disapproved of our modern practice of demanding almost nothing but analytical themes, with the result that we are producing a nation of writers of reports. Our students take apart Hamlet's character, the need for a new gymnasium, and the values of a small college until there is no life in them. This is not to say that such discipline should be eliminated, but that it should be lessened in favor of learning the discipline of writing about more personal, dramatic material.

I have always wanted to be chairman of a committee for the permanent elimination of theme topics, and my first move would be the burying of "School Food," "And Then I Woke Up," "How I Hate to Write Themes," "Six Kinds of Handshakes I Dislike," and "A Trip I Took Last Summer." Such "topics" provide no genuine human or literary motive for writing; nor is there any real audience for them. No professional writes without human or literary reason, nor without an audience. We will obtain better writing when we make students compose, not for us alone, but for their contemporaries. No boy or girl should ever write a theme he would be ashamed to read before a class.

The best compositions I have ever had were not on *topics* at all but on complete ideas based in conflict: a student athlete tempted to give up the life of muscle for romance, but pulled back again because he liked games better than girls; the dramatic tensions felt by a boy as he adjusted to the dark; a fictitious dialogue between Hamlet and Hedda Gabler about their troubles; and the gradual loss of a boy's Roman Catholic integrity when he found it was unpopular in a secular community.

I have just finished correcting a long essay on the dubious philosophy that seniors in a large independent school ought to have dates with college freshmen rather than high school girls. It was full of far-reaching abstractions about maturity, background, relative intelligence, and mutual attendance at lecture courses. Only in the vaguest hints was there any perception of the dramatic conflicts implicit in the subject. The boy would have written much more effectively if he had described one scene in which a student who had gone away to school tried to return home for a date, but stuttered and suffered through an embarrassingly realistic failure of togetherness.

Instead, he meandered through a tangle of generalities until he arrived at this heavily wooded conclusion:

> There are other ways in which the boy and girl may profit from this relationship. The couple has the opportunity to show their greater maturity. They will have little chaperonage, and their parents are also likely to be lenient about reporting times. It is an evidence of their maturity if they are able to utilize these and other privileges without betraying the trust granted them.

Nowhere is the "No Contest" sign hung out more visibly than in such an ending. Here comes the triumphal march of the dull, the obvious, and the moral. There is often such a lack of contest between writer and reader that the teacher can supply the actual words of the ending before he lugs his red pencil up to it: "As we trudged back from our mountain, anyone could see that we were utterly tired, but happy over the day's exciting exploits."

What can the teacher do about the lack of overtones, the lack of those "inner meanings" which students are so constantly asked to find in their reading? I think it might be profitable to try imitating the "surprise" in O. Henry's endings, as long as the corn was avoided. I am sure the thus-we-see summary should be abolished. Final statements should be rewritten and rewritten until the last sentence says something which leaves something unsaid. And finally, at the close of a good subject, like "Teen-age Arrogance in a Sailing Race," there should be one sentence which contains a concrete, human action that sums up the entire composition, in one clash of the symbol.

It certainly can be done. A ninth-grader wrote a dramatic tale of his escape from drowning when, while practicing swimming under water, he suddenly came up under a large float where there was no head room. His first ending was:

> Then my hand hit a bumper which I knew outlined all the outside of the float. Desperately grasping it, I yanked myself to the surface. Taking the most precious breath of air in my life, I looked around and thought, I guess this is the way other people feel who escape death.

After class discussion, in which he was instructed to dramatize his feelings by a suggestion of conflict, he wrote:

> I yanked myself to the surface. I literally gulped the precious breaths of wonderful air. After I got my breath I looked around for my friend, and sure enough I spotted him swimming toward me. As he came within hearing distance, he stopped long enough to say, "You know Bill, you should be careful, you might have come up under the float."

When I asked him why he made such a substantial change, he said, "While I was rewriting the ending, I realized that what I really wanted to emphasize was the conflict between the way I felt and nobody else knowing what I had just been through."

The sixth sin is the fattest: too many words.

The standard symbols are "Rep," and "W," but these are really too nice for the fault—and—for the students' own word for it. In my classes, the new sign is "W. C." (For an *explication de texte,* see your local New Englander.)

1. The caveman had no mind developed enough to offer a solution as to why the natural elements were acting as they were. [12th]

2. To me the purpose of Robert Louis Stevenson in his writing was to put into words his impressions of people and places. [11th]

3. Is it not true that one judges a book not by what is in it in regard to style or information, but whether it expresses the opinion of your chosen "side" or not? [10th]

4. Tending to agree with modern psychologists (nice of me, isn't it?) I believe that the negative approach to the correction of defects in the personalities of adolescents is for the most part ineffective. [12th]

Such sinful flatulence has a terrifying relationship to adult writing. Once upon a time I used to believe that bureaucratic doubletalk was an occupational disease of later life; but look more closely at 4. Already this boy is ripe for his first governmental directive: "Underprivileged preadolescents are allocated minimal opportunities for the implementation of cultural objectives."

The causes for such padding lie partly in the failures discussed under poor relations, and no contest. Much more important, though, is small writing: for most assignments, the national maximum is probably 400 words, if that. When a student who has never graduated from this limit is suddenly required to write 900 words, he must, as he will quickly admit, begin "to throw it." Some teachers use this very fact as evidence against long compositions—but this is bad education; it becomes worse when after one summer of let-up, high school graduates must shift into writing anywhere from 4000 to 10,000 words. Hence, our great duty as we teach writing is to show students how to discover subject matter, not how to avoid "like" as a conjunction.

The worst cause of bad writing is bad thought; and the worst thought is "The Big Think." It is not limited to teenagers, either: many adults never outgrow the habit. In fact, it is such an instinctive custom of the mind that its control should be a major aim of education, for if controlled, it is man's greatest strength and leads to philosophy; out of control, it breeds dictators.

1. Public schools are better than private ones.
2. Lynching will continue to run rampant in the South unless our Washington politicians formulate Federal laws to prevent lynching.
3. Technicolor movies are in every way better than black and white.
4. There are always some students around who are "different"; they ought to have their heads examined.

One of the teacher's greatest frustrations is trying to stop students from making such statements, or to document them. Since neither can be done convincingly the teacher must try to lead his charges into different patterns of thought. The standard generalization-followed-by-example is usable, but there is a variation on this rhetorical theme which helps certain students, particularly good ones. This is the "generalized examples," used by professionals. It says more, it requires more thought, it tells the teacher the students know what they're talking about, and it is a great enemy of big thinking.

> We are accustomed nowadays to be scientific about human personality. We trace effects to a variety of causes—to economic conditions, to heredity, to ductless glands, to the nervous system, to the operation of natural laws.

In phrases like "economic conditions," the writer Elizabeth Drew generalizes but also points up her ideas with succinct reference to many examples. The abstract adolescent would have said "certain parts of life" for "economic conditions," and then used the mechanical example: "For example, if a boy is brought up in a slum condition and has no playground, he will probably turn into a delinquent and end up in a fight somewhere and be jailed and have to miss life's great opportunities."

This is not bad, but the following passages from exceptional students are better:

> 1. Long-playing record jackets are a new American art form, with their lurid blotches of color, bubbling glasses of champagne, and blondes sprawled on fields of mink.

> 2. The mystery of the night still called to me. . . . Sometimes I sneaked from the apartment. . . . Things scuttled into the shadows when I approached.

3. We caused some trouble. We shocked the neighbors, and even some of our friends. We set tongues wagging and wise folk preaching. We were meaty subjects for the gossip crows in the faculty of a certain high school.

To write the "generalized example," a student must first use all his senses, acutely and imaginatively, and he must use them in many places. Phrases like "blondes sprawled on fields of mink," "things scuttled into the shadows," and "wise folk preaching" show these students had watched and listened carefully, many times, so that they could communicate in depth. Here, I think, is our real objective: not devices and rules and tricks of writing— but the boy and girl behind them. For a long time we have been guilty of the same myopia as the doctor who covers a rash with salve and ignores the cause.

"The Big Think" is, in a way, a symptom of the almost total failure of adolescents to use their senses and their sense of relationships. Since they don't see anything, they don't say anything, and the poor cliche we therefore always have with us.

1. I stood on the high diving board not feeling very good about the whole idea.

2. Our trip was not too bad until we came to a long hill that was a different matter.

Somehow we must make them slow down and begin to develop the sensitivity without which no professional would ever sell a thing. For small students, there is good shock value in Helen Keller's writing: some never recover, fortunately, from the precise and sensuous words she uses to describe a world she cannot see or hear—because she is blind and deaf—a world others also cannot see or hear because they are blind and deaf in another sense.

No teenager should be allowed to grow up without reading, four or five times, Miss Keller's essay "Three Days to See," and every English classroom should have her advice printed around the walls:

I who am blind can give one hint to those who see—one admonition to those who would make full use of the gift of sight: Use your eyes as if tomorrow you would be stricken blind.

Her extraordinary thought is reflected in a new textbook by Walker Gibson of New York University, who requires his students to blindfold themselves and then write about their experiences with the other senses.

For the past five years I have been working on a book explaining the process of using photographs as a classroom aid to the teaching of composition. It will come to about 100 pages, so that I cannot hope to explain the complete idea in a few minutes. I should like, however, to give you several concrete examples of how the process works.

You may remember the photograph of Albert Einstein and Robert Oppenheimer which appeared in *Life* several years ago. I distribute copies to each student and ask them to write one sentence describing what they see. Their incomplete, unemphatic, and vaguely general powers of observation may be illustrated by this sentence:

> There is a great contrast between the two men's physical appearance.

To attack such a slovenly use of the eye and the mind, I require the student to study the picture, on an overnight assignment, until he eventually writes something like this:

> Einstein's expression is that of a teenager who takes life as it comes, in contrast to Oppenheimer, who is like an ambitious scholar eager to learn more and more.

In a short time, this boy learned something positive about the art of seeing and writing; and it is my conviction that four years of such visual discipline would make adolescents look so precisely at human experience that they would find much more interesting subject matter to write about.

There are prominent writers, of course, who argue that descriptive writing is antiquated; and I do not advocate a return to purple prose. But there are also many successful and admired professionals whose writing is lively partly because of their sharp eyes. Conrad and Stevenson are two striking examples; and yet even Hemingway, who has advised young writers to throw away their adjectives, writes photographically of what he has seen. The following four sentences are from his story "The Three-Day Blow":

> The road came out of the orchard on to the top of the hill.
> There was the cottage, the porch bare, smoke coming from the
> chimney. In back was the garage, the chicken coop and the second-
> growth timber like a hedge against the woods behind. The big
> trees swayed far over in the wind. . . .

The photographic device is merciless to the cliché. I showed
one boy a picture of a soldier back from the Korean front, and he
said it showed "the ravages of war." It didn't at all, for though
the warrior's face was dirty, his eyes sparkled and his almost
arrogant pose suggested he had just won the war. After a general
assault by the whole class on this boy's hackneyed abstraction, he
finally confessed, in embarrassment, "I guess I didn't even look
at the picture."

This boy's fuzzy observation was emphasized by a remark of
my teenager daughter the other day. She was listening to her
mother and father describing a friend who did not look well: we
used words like "pale," "bored," "sitting heavy in her chair," and
"dark under the eyes."

"You older people," said Judy, "you're always saying things
like that. I never notice how people look."

When my book is finished, I'm going to make her read it—
that is, I'm going to try.

As you all know, teenagers almost never try to express their
written ideas in metaphor, for they have never learned that one
talent of an educated and interesting mind is the ability to see
how things are alike. The device of the photograph is an excellent one for arousing this ability; and then, when the first images
are stimulated, the picture serves as a dramatic symbol of the real
meaning of the word "connotation," that quality of words which
is so difficult and foreign to boys and girls. There is nothing so
medicinal, for example, as the contrast between a photograph of a
weary, bewildered surgeon whose patient has just died, and the
following sentence written by a boy trying to use figurative
language about the picture:

> The doctor is relaxing over a cup of coffee which has become
> tepid as old dishwater while cigarette ashes form stagnant clots
> in the black puddle.

A great variety of exercises can be devised to use photographs as an aid in teaching effective language, and many of

them have the virtue of being short. The following are among those that have been effective in my classroom experiments:

1. Find one word which accurately suggests a peculiar shape, such as a cloud, a mountain, a jaw, or a rhinoceros.
2. Describe one object so that it appears to be a symbol of the atmosphere of a picture.
3. Write one sentence to express character, as it is caught in a revealing moment.
4. Explain the essence of a conflict as it is conveyed in a photograph.

All of these reverse the usual process, for they send students out to find subject matter first, and then stimulate the search for words to express it. Ideally, we ought to send boys and girls out to view "life," but since this plan will remain impractical until the curriculum is revised, we must resort to methods which come close to bringing human experience into the classroom, like photographs. If one selects only the greatest of pictures, he enables his students to study important subject matter, so that in the long run they may understand, by contrast and comparison, why many of the subjects they might like to write about are not worth the effort.

Finally, in the face of almost all secondary school practice, I urge the writing of short fiction as the most effective and the most interesting discipline for sharpening students' minds and observation. By short fiction I mean the story which the professionals call the "short-short," for it is distinctly within the capabilities of young writers.

There are many, many things to be said for this exercise, but I will focus on just two big ones. In the first place, to come even close to success, the student must be more specific than in any other kind of writing: the short-short requires the utmost narrowing down to tight limits of character, setting, dialogue, idea, and diction. There is no greater cure for one who suffers from the sickness of the big think.

The boy who used to say, "When I was little I used to be really scared," may eventually write, "I can recall lying in bed at the age of five, expecting horrible monsters to come creeping over the window sill"; and the one who once said, "I used to put on an awful act in front of older people," may eventually imagine himself wearing a mask, "with eyebrows arched over wide innocent eyes, and the mouth pursed in a judicious ellipse."

To be minutely specific about this assignment, I require students to spend a long time composing the first sentence, since most of them are by nature likely to begin with vague generalizations. They need to be broken of the habit of fooling around with scenery, exposition, and philosophical abstractions, for the short-short requires that the central conflict be started within the first two or three lines of the story.

One boy came to me this year with a good idea about a conflict between a boy and a girl, and I told him to write the first two pages. When they were finished, they were filled with the usual wanderings through fields of "life," "love," and "the pursuit of happiness"; not until the end of the second page did he begin to focus down to emphatic detail. I told him to throw out the first 500 words, and begin at the precise, specific moment of struggle. He must have understood, for his second version began:

> "Let's go park."
> "What! Again?"

This, of course, was just the beginning. From here on, the student writer had to work out a mosaic of precise details illuminating an intimate personal conflict between his central character and his girl.

His problem illustrates the other major purpose in having boys and girls write short fiction: the exploration of character, ideas, and conflict from their own lives. Students should never be allowed to write about murder, dope addicts, psychiatry, or battle fatigue. For teenagers, writing should be one primary means of helping them develop a comprehensive, and private, vision of human experience, and only of that kind of experience which is important in their lives. Then, too, when they have begun to understand what sort of experience is important, they should be challenged with the task of finding the best words to express their vision of that experience. This constant process of interrelating life with language is, for me, the best possible kind of education.

Some of you may be wondering whether, in pursuing this kind of work, I ever use that sentimental expression: "creative writing." No . . . . for I am wholly sympathetic to those who dislike it. I try to avoid all such pedagogical lingo. Rather, I attempt constantly to emphasize the ideas suggested by the word "identification," for no fiction can be done well without some spiritual and emotional identification between writer and subject matter. Exposition can be done very successfully without this sympathy: history papers, book reports, sales reports, and "projects"—only the intellect is needed. For teenagers, the heart must be committed to write well.

This year, after I had wiped all the "drayma" out of their minds, my seniors responded by writing such subjects as their parents' social ambitions, their own fears about college admission, conflicts arising out of racial snobbery, the desire to rebel against convention, and the irritability of a spoiled only child.

Over and over again, great writers and great photographers have maintained that the exploration of such subjects was the primary function of their art: to name only one extraordinary example, Joseph Conrad spent an entire lifetime following this goal.

Only when professional writers discover that we have stopped giving such assignments will they stop declaring that "English has nothing to do with writing."

Only when student writers stop complaining, "But I don't know *what* to say," and ask instead, "But, how do I do that?," can we bring out our mechanical weapons. Then will be the time to swoop down, armed with prepositional phrases, subordinate clauses, and the right word to split an infinitive with!

THE
ORGANIZATION
OF WRITING

EDWARD B. IRVING, JR.
University of Pennsylvania

How do we teach our students to organize their writing? Perhaps it would be more accurate to say that "organization" is a word I shall use from time to time in the course of these heterogeneous and probably inconclusive remarks, for I have some doubts as to whether my talk will exhibit any of the virtues of its subject. Only when one begins to reflect seriously for any length of time on the problem of organization in writing does he come to experience true disorganization. For "organization" is not a concept that will stay small and neat and easily handled. If you take it in any larger sense, it is the goal of all our efforts, it is all we really want our students to learn, not only in English courses but in the whole process of education.

Some random questions may perhaps serve to put us in the appropriate disorganized state of mind for the contemplation of our subject.

What are the principles of organization?
Are there handy formulas for organization which we ought to require our students to learn?
Do these formulas apply to every piece of writing?
Does it do the student any good if he knows them?
What is the relationship of the study of other people's writing to the organization of one's own writing?
How important is "outlining"?
Is it possible to have bad but well-organized student themes?
Is it possible to say: "There is absolutely nothing wrong with this theme but its poor organization"?
Do we spend enough time talking about organization?
Do we spend too much time talking about organization?
How is organization related to comprehension?
How is it related to logic?
How is it related to the processes of thought?

77

Such are some of the questions which we English teachers may occasionally ask ourselves, when we are not too busy to have time to worry about such matters. Perhaps luckily, we are almost always too busy, and the questions often seem remote from the dust and heat of the classroom. Indeed, I consider it something of an achievement on my part to have found time to pose these questions; if you insist on answers to them as well, I can only regard you as unreasonable and ungrateful. But since I am here tied to the stake, and since this is not a seminar where I might retire gracefully behind a cloud of pipe smoke while you struggle with my questions, I shall continue.

Let us begin in a practical way by looking at the problem as it exists in our hot and dusty classrooms, by looking at some student writing. I shall read two one-page themes written by freshmen in a "slow" division, assigned on a Monday to be handed in on a Wednesday. We were at the beginning of the part of the course devoted to the study of poetry, and the assignment was for them to read Dylan Thomas' poem "Fern Hill" and to state in a page or less what they considered to be the essential meaning of the poem.

First, Student Able:

"FERN HILL" BY DYLAN THOMAS

In this poem, the poet is reflecting on youth and arrives at the idea that only during this innocent state in life is the person carefree and able to fully enjoy nature. Youth is not plagued by the awareness of time. Childhood is the golden part of life. Time marches on; it has implicit within itself both life and death. To the youth, the enigmatic night provides whatever chill of death he experiences. With the birth of a new day, though, all anxieties are erased and the youth basks in nature, only cognizant of the present. Each day to the child is a fresh start: a new interval in which to roam. The youth is not aware of and does not care about what will be made manifest in time: how he will be removed from his timeless void and placed in the moving stream of life, never able to halt the march of time, powerless to impede approaching death.

Now let us see what Student Baker has to say on the same poem:

THE MEMORIES OF AN OLD MAN

In the poem "Fern Hill" Dylan Thomas tells us about his childhood. The poet tells us that he lived on a farm when he was a little boy. In a very colorful description he gives us a very good picture of the place where he used to live. For example, he tells us that the farm was surrounded [by] green grass and green trees, that there always was blue sky and that during the daytime one could hear the foxes bark and at night one could hear the jaring [sic] of the owls.

In a somewhat sentimental way Thomas also tells us that as a little boy he was able to live a more careless life than he could live as a grown up. He remembers the days when he used to roam around in the country and when he did whatever he pleased to do. Thomas also recalls the places where he was playing [as] a little boy; for example, he recalls that sometimes he was sitting under an apple tree or at other times was running around among the barns. In those days, the poet remembers, he didn't even think about the fact that one day he no longer would be a young boy but an old man.

But Dylan Thomas also remembers the peacefulness that existed around the farm. At night he recalls it was always very quiet; the only thing that one could hear now and then was the jaring [sic] of the owl.

Neither paper is perfect, but I believe we could all agree that the first paper, by Student Able, is a good deal better. And I think we could also say that it is better organized. What do we mean when we say this?

If we look first at Student Baker's paper, it is clear that it is very badly organized. The details cited from the poem are sprinkled in what appears to be random order through the three paragraphs (although actually a rather feeble skeleton is discernible on a second reading). There is little indication that some statements may be more important than others. What we might call the key sentence—almost the only one that shows comprehension of the poem—is this one: "In those days, the poet remembers, he didn't even think about the fact that one day he no longer would be a young boy but an old man." But it is thrown away, buried almost out of sight at the end of the second paragraph, and robbed of all emphasis by the needless and anticlimactic third paragraph.

No, in these terms it is not well organized. But what comment would a teacher write on the paper? "Poor organization"? But how do we separate "poor organization" from the other deficiencies of the paper—notably the generally childish level of thought and style? Should one write "You don't understand the poem very well"? If he does not understand the poem any better, will it help to tell him to rewrite his paper in a more organized form? Can he do this properly by just looking at his paper and not at the poem? Is there much point in reminding him of "unity, coherence, emphasis" or telling him to put his most important point at the beginning or at the end or in asking him to subordinate properly all the less important aspects of the problem? He doesn't really seem to *know* what his most important point is and would no doubt be ready enough to subordinate the whole problem clean out of sight.

What distinguishes Student Able's paper from Student Baker's? For one thing, it is remarkable for the power of abstraction evident in it. He understands the basic theme of the poem well enough to rephrase it over and over in his own words; indeed the ideas are generalized to the point of sounding a little too much like proverbs ("time marches on"). We may also note that where Baker offers us the primitive and lifeless, "for example, the poet tells us that," Able presents some of the poet's words in the more sophisticated form of allusion. "Childhood is the golden part of life" *alludes* to Thomas's repeated use of the word "golden" in the poem, an elementary kind of allusion, to be sure, but something that Baker is not capable of. Finally, it is important to see that Able's "proverbial" restating of the ideas in the poem does not seriously oversimplify it; he has his eye on the poem, for his paper is given its structure by being a running interpretative paraphrase. The last sentence of his paper is a rather close paraphrase of the final stanza and a half of Thomas's poem and succeeds in suggesting, with some rhetorical skill, the intense nostalgic focus on a vanished part.

I seem to have wandered far from the subject of organization, but, as I warned you in the beginning, it is a subject of considerable complexity. In any case, one point which I have been trying to make in this comparison is by now no doubt clear enough. Student Able has given close attention to the poem and has responded imaginatively to it; Student Baker has not. Student Able's own imagination is an integral part of his paper.

In facing the practical problem, it may be that the best way to try to help Baker in his struggles with organization is simply to continue the study of poetry so that he eventually comes to have a better knowledge of what things to look for in poems and what kind of things to say about them. All that he reads, all that he picks up from class discussions, all that I can teach him directly may help him. That he will ever write very well about poetry is doubtful, but he ought to come to be somewhat better at it.

Knowledge of one's subject, or, better, understanding of one's subject, is certainly related then to organization. What is chaotic in the head is not going to come out neatly arranged on paper. One need only turn to essay questions on examinations for some prime and painful examples of disorganized writing; but I will spare you these, for you all know the kind I mean. The student wallows in disorganization, but it is the disorganization of despair; he doesn't know what he is talking about.

Organization is also related, most unmistakably, to logic. If we look at the marginal comments (apart from the purely mechanical corrections) which we write over and over again on our students' themes, we will probably find that many of them, if not most of them, are ultimately criticisms in terms of logic. "How does this follow?" "You've left something out." "Do you have any evidence for this?" "How can you come up with this conclusion?" Or even that most frequent comment of all, "not clear," very often means "not *logically* clear."

Many English courses, particularly on the college level, are partly or entirely courses in logical thinking. Speakers at this conference in previous years have described such courses, as some of you may recall, and I refer you to their descriptions of them. Mr. C. G. Waterston in 1956, for example, suggested the systematic use of the syllogism as the basis for organization of students' themes. Last year Professor Harold Martin of Harvard presented a memorable demonstration of his own method of teaching composition by what he called "scrupulous attention to the rigors of ordered thinking." In his classroom the very process of thinking, of defining clearly, of ordering, is dramatized by the intensive use of the Socratic method.

It is clear that an organized student theme is the result of ordered thinking. It represents the operation of the human mind and the human imagination on a set of facts. Where facts appear that are not thought about, not related to the order of the paper, we write in the margins "irrelevant," "what's this doing here?" or "are you planning to *use* this?" A freshman struggling with a sonnet by Shakespeare informs me that "Shakespeare uses quite a lot of metaphor in this sonnet but may I add that at no time does there appear any simile." A mature critic might show us that the absence of simile was of significance, but my freshman staggers on to something else, leaving this undigested crumb of fact to mark his winding path.

Where is my winding path leading me, you might well ask at this point. Down from this rather shaky plateau of truisms, you will be glad to hear, and back to the dusty classroom. I have told you nothing very new up to this point. We are all aware of the particular relationships I have been describing, and we deal with them in our different ways. We try to help our students understand what they are asked to write about; we try to give them topics they *can* write about. Whether or not we teach them logic in any direct way, we exercise a constant pressure on them through our reactions and comments directed toward making them conscious of the necessity of thinking logically.

But now let us turn to the question of how organization is in fact taught in secondary schools. By this I mean not the complex process I have been describing, but organization by itself, the paragraph which might appear in a teaching plan under the heading "Organization of Writing: six weeks" or whatever it may be (six years, possibly!). Here I am in great ignorance, not having taught in a secondary school. I have only some fantastic impressions based on what I have observed of my freshmen's work or on conversations with them about their preparation in school. Most unreliable evidence, but it may amuse you to see yourselves in this cracked mirror. And perhaps new vistas may open up.

Most students are taught something called "outlining," a word they mention sometimes with awe and sometimes with horror. Those whose teachers were fanatics about outlining apparently found little time to write any papers; everything they turned in bristled with numbers and letters and elaborate systems of indentation. There may be some truth in this. If I manage to get some of them to stop putting "III. A. 6" in the margin, they still begin paragraphs with sentences like this: "Having dealt with the third of my eight above-mentioned points, I shall now proceed to the fourth, under which there are two subdivisions." If I suggest that this is a rather dull way to start a paragraph, they give me looks of pity. Here is an English teacher who has probably never had outlining. People either have had outlining or they haven't, in which case there isn't much point in explaining.

Another way in which they are taught organization, they tell me, is through completing a tremendous project in senior year comparable only to the building of the pyramids—the research paper. These papers are several hundred pages in length and on such subjects as "Democracy" or "The United States" or "The Cold War." Writing a PhD thesis could only come as an anticlimax to these people. Months are spent writing and revising outlines (at least seventeen of them), filling cards with facts, writing footnotes, interviewing experts in the field, sharpening pencils. It is small wonder that there are snickers from these heroes when I tell them to write me a paragraph for their first assignment.

But seriously I do indeed recognize the value of outlining in making them conscious of the fact that what they write has, or should have, a kind of structure. A very competent junior at Yale who had been subjected to such rigorous training in outlining in high school told me that he had been herded into a room for three hours with some other students and told to write an essay on an assigned topic for a prize contest. "I was helpless," he told me. "All I had ever learned how to do was outline, so I worked on an outline for two and a half hours and then dashed the thing off." He won the prize of course. So sometimes in our examinations here we deliberately withhold the blue books in which the students are to write for the first half-hour of a three-hour exam. They are not permitted to write; they can only outline, or think, which is about the same thing.

Yet, on second thought, to equate outlining and thinking has meaning in only a limited sense. While the written work of most of my students is no doubt the better for this kind of training, I sometimes wonder whether some of them have not been given a false sense of security, whether they have not been encouraged to believe that making a clear plan of what you are to do is not merely half the battle, but all the battle.

In any case, I think most of you would recognize a species of student paper which we might call "the mere outline." The student has made a preliminary analysis of his subject and has set out the topics to be discussed in a commendably orderly fashion; the only fault in the paper is that they are simply not discussed. A typical paragraph may consist of elegant variations on the topic sentence:

> Before we can discuss the problem of social conformity, we should first define the kind of society to which the individual must conform. Not every society is the same. The problem of conformity varies greatly depending on which society we are studying. What might be said about one society might not be true about another society. Societies differ so much that it is difficult to generalize. It is, however, very important that we know what kind of society we are dealing with.

And so on, as long as you like. But the second point is not a definition of the society he is examining, but something else. We may imagine that point 1 on his outline read: "Importance of Defining Society." But what the student may do is repeat "defining society is important" in as many ways as he can.

Another unfortunate, if less serious, result of this kind of training is what we might call "the bony outline," of the kind I was parodying a few moments ago, where the outline structure is so prominent that the reader is distracted from what the student is talking about. Where the student is thinking clearly, the problem of course becomes one of rhetoric rather than of logic; we must teach him to put some flesh on his bones, to add a little grace to his transitions or show a little grace to his readers. I think that the study of models of professional writing may be very useful here. We can try to bring him to see how good writers do have a plan—we can make outlines or précis of their essays—but it is really a plan that we feel rather than see in nearly every sentence of their well-muscled prose. In our study of these essays, we should take care to give as much attention to the flesh, to the texture, as we do to the bones.

What might be called the Procrustean outline always offers some trouble to college teachers. A student has committed some simple formula to memory and forces whatever subject he is asked to handle into the mold. He comes in for a conference.

"A badly organized paper," I say to him. "The first three paragraphs are all right, but in the fourth you have enough stuff for two more themes, all jammed together. Why don't you break that down and talk about it properly?"

He looks at me nervously. "You mean . . . write *another* paragraph?"

"Sure," I say. "At least another paragraph. More likely three more."

His world is obviously tottering. He has been told, it turns out, that a theme consists of an opening paragraph, three paragraphs of development, and a concluding paragraph. All themes, on all subjects. He confesses that he loses a lot of sleep sometimes trying to push things around into this pattern, but it has to be done.

This does really happen occasionally, although not always in such an extreme form. Sometimes I make what seems to the student the hilarious suggestion that he write down what he thinks first and *then* make an outline of it. This sometimes helps them. I think that some students are very seriously inhibited from writing well by the mistaken belief that the form must be decided on in all its details before a single complete sentence is set down on paper. The notion that ideas will ever *take* form as you write them down has never occurred to them.

Some students have picked up and distorted the idea that all expository writing is essentially polemic, or dialectic, or argumentative. There may be some truth in this, but what we often get in fact are papers written in a shockingly rancorous tone for no good reason and students who are prolific in the creation of straw men to argue with. Their themes will begin with this kind of preposterous remark: "Most readers will probably feel that *Hamlet* is a bad play, but this is by no means the case, as I will now proceed to show." Such phantom readers have not even the solidity of straw. A real point of view is an essential to good and well-organized writing, but the mechanical creation of an obviously synthetic one is a perversion of the principle and a fertile source of bad papers.

I mentioned the research paper a moment ago as another means by which students are taught something about organization. I think, perhaps somewhat fancifully, that a research paper may have some value in dramatizing the process of organization. Can anyone who has ever had the experience easily forget the table piled with little filing cards and the slow process of sorting, of making piles, of shifting those tangible facts from pile to pile and *seeing* a kind of order being imposed on chaos? It may well be that we learn kinesthetically something of the mental process that should accompany all good writing, just as we may learn more about science in a few hours spent with a microscope or a beaker in our hands than in many hours of lectures.

But, if a speaker on my topic may be allowed a mild digression, I have some serious reservations about the advisability of devoting so much time to the research paper. I realize that the colleges sometimes exert a great deal of pressure on the schools to furnish this sort of training, but I doubt if much of the pressure comes from English departments in colleges. I am not an official spokesman, but I know that other college teachers share my opinions. Some of us believe very strongly that the *mechanics* of the research paper—documentation, footnotes, and so on—can be taught in a relatively brief period, that few secondary school students are mature enough to do anything like real research anyway (and should perhaps not be encouraged to think that they are), and, most important of all, that the vast amount of time often given to the research paper could be much better spent in doing more writing of shorter papers on a variety of topics, or, in the terms we have been using, in learning to handle various problems of organization.

I suspect that by now some of you may have detected a subtle bias in my remarks. I have been conscientiously speaking of technical problems and disciplines, but it is clear enough (you will say) that my heart is not really in such matters. I have paid lip-service to their value but I have been mainly stressing their shortcomings.

These suspicions are perfectly justified. I believe that at least as much harm as good is done by the formalistic approach to writing which in making the student excessively or exclusively conscious of rules and form often effectively cripples his expression. I would not deny that we still have the chaotic writer and the formless theme, but it is relatively easy to deal with them. But even more common now and much harder to deal with is the overtrained boy who comes armed with his Procrustean outline and his complacency, who turns in a long bleak series of perfectly organized themes signifying nothing, who resists doggedly any attempt to subvert either his organization or his opinions, and who may go on to write the excruciatingly dull editorials in the *Yale Daily News*.

Several years ago at this conference Professor Richard Sewall of Yale divided teachers of English into the formalists, those "who believe that a student must know how to say something before he is in a position to say it," and those who believe that, "if a student has something to say and wants to say it, he will learn with a minimum of technical guidance *how* to say it." He placed himself very firmly with the latter group and it is perhaps not surprising, since he was my first mentor in the art of teaching some ten years ago, that I should place myself there too. Everything I have learned in ten years confirms me in my choice. And I agree on the whole with Professor Sewall when he says:

> Quite frankly, the student writing that I see, except for the products of a few noble but isolated experimental programs, strikes me as little short of appalling. It is dull and lifeless, stultifying to the imagination, and blighting to the spirit. The old disciplines are perilously near bankruptcy.

But now I am talking about writing as a whole and not about organization. But how can they ever be separated? Isn't there a point when we must stop concentrating on the parts and deal with writing as a whole—have them do writing as a whole? Yes, we must teach them the fundamentals; but surely sooner or later—and *before* they come to college—they must write, write as a whole, write *about* something worth writing about with their attention on their subject, not on their form. They can be kept sensitive to the problem of form through our comments and our conferences, but even there I believe our attention should be on what they have to say and the way in which bad grammar and poor planning gets in the way of it, comes between writer and reader. If they are interested, if what they are writing about is genuinely important, if they are really thinking about it, the only organization worth anything will come.

I am trying to learn how to figure skate, in my spare moments, at the new hockey rink here. I can buy books on figure skating; I can look at pictures in *Sports Illustrated;* I can watch good skaters for hours on end. I do, and I learn a great deal. Everything in fact except how to skate, which I will learn painfully (if I ever learn) by skating, and falling down and getting up, and skating. Perhaps some day my muscles will become organized.

I realize, of course, that any program which demands a sizable increase in the amount of student writing may put a crushing burden on the teacher. It is a sufficient strain on college teachers, even though they may often teach under conditions that may seem to you utopian—sixteen to eighteen students in the average section, with some time for conference. How a high-school teacher with well over a hundred students can handle all this, I confess I do not know. If we are to improve our schools, to my mind the item of top priority is the reduction of the teaching load of English teachers, who are likely to work harder for less thanks than anyone else, and whose job is of the highest importance. We may wait a long time for this improvement, but unless we believe it to be important and make our convictions known, we will wait forever.

But even in our present situation I think there are some things we can do. There is one area in particular, which, incidentally, the committee on which I served here last year tried to deal with, to which I might direct your attention—the choice of topics on which the students are to write. It is all too often the case that we forget to spend much time thinking about topics; standing at the chalkboard, chalk in hand, we will invent something or other for Monday's paper, on the assumption that it really doesn't make much difference what they write about. I am more and more convinced that it makes a great deal of difference. We should keep up as high a level of stimulating thought as possible in the classroom, but this is hardly separable from the obligation to give them subjects to write about which—whatever they are, and they can be quite various—have one thing in common: they must make the student think.

Nor is this problem at all remote from the problem of organization. If real organization has a great deal to do with real thinking, then the higher the "thought-pressure" registered in a paper, the better organized it may be. And this is true in spite of —or is it really because of—the fact that a good topic is often planned to disorganize, insofar as it suggests a new idea, and the student cannot readily reply to it by anything he has memorized, or said before, or heard somewhere.

All too often in our assignments we give the student a carte blanche to offer us a cold batch of clichés or we invite him to pour out in tedious hour-by-hour detail the events of his vacation or his weekend in New York or we expect him to deal with a large subject without providing him with any standpoint or opening wedge and we get weak generalities.

We can apply these standards for good topics to the various kinds of papers we ask our students to write. Instead of asking for their views on democracy, surely we can make the effort to find an interesting instance, an iconoclastic remark, a difficult problem in definition, a novel point of view, a paradox. Or we can ask them for a series of attacks on the same problem as their initial approach is affected and modified by what they read or what they discuss in class.

We can do much to make the papers they write on literature challenging and interesting. The analysis of brief passages can be used to make them think; there is no escape, they are boxed in and have to give their attention to what is before them. Or we can give them widely divergent critical opinions about a work they have read and ask them to reflect on them, to reconcile them, or make a choice between them.

Even the "personal experience" essay can be made thought provoking and interesting. Sometimes we can help by providing them with a purpose or with a kind of ready-made frame for their own experiences. I had surprising success recently with a topic of this kind. The students had just read E. B. White's essay "Once More to the Lake," in which, you may recall, White describes his return with his young son to the summer resort where he had gone as a boy. I explained carefully that I wanted them to describe a "place revisited" in their own experience, where they came to a sudden insight into change, not an objective change in the place (that would be too easy), but a change in themselves. Whether it was because they liked the model or because I had emphasized that this was a very hard thing to do successfully (they could choose other topics) or because I had suggested a kind of artistic purpose to their reminiscences, I shall never know; but I know that all the papers were interesting, and two of them were really excellent, from students who seemed to rise far above their usual level of writing.

But now it is time to bring these remarks to a close. Even if you disagree entirely with what I have said, it may seem a welcome relief from all the frenzied screams for "more grammar" that you have been hearing from the colleges and the alumni and the PTA. I am convinced that this is no solution. I know that every fall it is a pleasure to see the light come into the eyes of a student who discovers that I am at least as interested in his ideas as in his paragraphing, and who begins to see dimly the point of writing well, and who may begin to try for the first time.

In his essay on "The Aims of Education," Alfred North Whitehead attacks as "one of the most fatal, erroneous, and dangerous conceptions ever introduced into the theory of education" the notion that "the mind is an instrument, you first sharpen it and then use it." "The mind is never passive," he insists.

> It is a perpetual activity, delicate, receptive, responsive to stimulus. You cannot postpone its life until you have sharpened it. Whatever interest attaches to your subject-matter must be evoked here and now; whatever powers you are strengthening in the pupil, must be exercised here and now; whatever possibilities of mental life your teaching should impart, must be exhibited here and now. That is the golden rule of education, and a very difficult rule to follow.

HOW DO WE READ COMPOSITIONS?

FRED GODSHALK
Educational Testing Service

Language As Metaphor

Language is inescapably ambiguous, metaphoric, euphemistic in a broad sense, and heavily redundant. That it has these characteristics can be shown, and that they are all necessary and, in varying degree, all advantageous can be logically derived and concluded. That, whether for good or ill, the characteristics are of proportionately greater occurrence in a "rich" language than in a primitive or a controlled one can also be inferred. English is a bountiful language of luxuriant growth, and it both benefits and suffers from the exuberance of these four attributes of language.

By way of introduction to a discussion of student writing, let us examine the characteristics called ambiguity, metaphor, euphemism, and redundancy. Our focus is upon the English language, of course, and our view is that these characteristics are inherent in language, unavoidable, and all to some extent useful, without exception of the writer's bugbears, ambiguity and redundancy. We can make our points rather simply, I think, for they are matters largely of redefining the obvious, without recourse to the scholarly or the profound. Let us begin with metaphor.

All language is metaphor; not *contains* or *uses,* but *is.* Words are not things, but symbolic sounds and corresponding marks. We do not in any way *depict* an object or an idea by the speaking or writing of a word. Though Dick and Jane may quickly recognize *l o o k* because the double-*o* suggest a pair of eyes, they would have an impossible task of sight-reading if they interpreted every *o* as a literal peering eye, as in "cook took a book to a secluded nook," "Look, Dick. Look, Jane. Look, look look!"

Language uses symbols for ideas. In the relaxed days of a less sophisticated era, a textbook writer was so misguided or brash as to write for children: "An *idea* is a *mind-picture.* A *word* is the spoken or written *sign* of an idea. A sentence is a *group of words* expressing a *complete thought.*" I quote from memory. This was in the halcyon years of about 30 to 35 B.L. (Before Linguistics). I figure that the present date is roughly A.S.L. 13, or the thirteenth year of linguistic science. (I use the word "science" loosely.)

Though we may quibble over the word "word," possibly we will agree that in some way it stands for the smallest bit of "meaning" that can be separated conceptually from the confused jumble in our heads. Its function is to convey that meaning or, as we say, to "express" it so that other human and subhuman jumbles of intellect will react to this stimulus in some appropriate fashion.

Now the process of communication through symbols is an extremely complex one. The "code" by which a sign of meaning is "interpreted" differs from mind to mind, and differs *intra* mind

from time to time and from context to context. It is a code intricately created by experience and put into variant operation by
variant proximate (or concurrent) experiences. These experiences
constitute the specific environment of each use of, or encounter
with, a certain symbol or its source of reference and meaning, or
both simultaneously. For example, the "dog" in my mind today
is not the "dog" in yours, and never was nor will be. Furthermore,
the "dog" in my mind today is not the "dog" of yesterday, last
week, or last year, for my concept of "dog" alters continually,
affected by my reading, hearing, thinking, writing, and speaking
of dogs and my experiences with dogs. Further, if neither the real
nor the ideational or mental dog has affected me since yesterday,
the "dog" of today differs by a slight decrease in specific character
and not quite a corresponding increase in generalized attributes.
In a word, today's dog is vaguer.

There is little need to expand this point, for it is a familiar
one. We have illustrated the idea that language is the symbolic
generalization of experience, and that it can be no more exact
than experiences can be and are exactly duplicated. Rather obviously, if so simple and almost universal a word, or linguistic
symbol, as "dog" must have such a complexity of coding and
decoding, it follows that words for the abstractions of thought
and discourse are almost infinitely varied, both *inter-* and *intra-*
mind. For this reason, whenever a speaker or writer attempts anything more complex than a description of an object or an exposition of simple process, we may be amused to have critics and
teachers comment: "People should learn to say what they mean."
Upon analysis, this criticism from the layman is naïve, and from
the teacher, useless. Language is an approximation of thought,
and we do not "say" meanings; we make use of amorphous symbols to code and interpret protean meanings. We are "matching"
the symbols, insofar as we can, with various likenesses created by
experience in mind and memory.

Language is possible because the mind can generalize experience and put labels upon it. The labels suggest interpretable
likenesses from experience to experience, and from mind to mind.
It is in this sense that language is metaphor, a "carrying over"
of similarity by means of symbol. We can neither say what we
mean nor say what we think. We can merely suggest that certain

similarities of experience be brought to bear, be used, to re-create in the mind of hearer or reader something similar to the picture, the idea, the concept, the congeries of concepts in our own mind.

It may be objected at about this point that we have taken liberties with the word "metaphor" in the attempt to conclude that all language *is* metaphor. To this hypothetical and, I trust, merely rhetorical, objection there are two answers: first, the discussion of metaphor was prefaced with the statement that we should like to make certain points by redefining the obvious, and second, our context and construction have been consistently directed to "metaphor," a generic term, as differentiated from the specific "a metaphor" or "the metaphors."

However, we have no wish to weasel out of (note the metaphor) a possible vote of "no confidence," even though our fears of it are based upon a purely visionary sour note aimed at undermining our position. That it is possible to put into one sentence a half-dozen or more incongruous examples of *the* metaphor, and still to convey meaning, has just been demonstrated. As a matter of fact, *ten* words or phrases have been used in senses that are suggestive, illustrative, derived, figurative—in senses that are not included in the definition of "literal" as "conveying the primary meaning." Some of them, such as "based," "aimed," and "undermining," have the character of the "dead" metaphor (Fowler's term), while others, at least because of their juxtaposition, are very much alive (*purely visionary sour note*). These four related words combine a primary reference to physical quality, "purely," shifted to suggested amount or degree, and primary references to matters interpreted by the senses of sight, taste, and hearing, so arranged as to suggest that we look at a sound that has a flavor on the tongue.

This exaggerated example of the use of metaphors (plural, specific) has been given to drive home the point that, while all language is metaphor, much more of it than we notice consists of metaphors. We are not conscious of the derivative meanings that we attach to many well-used words, very common words, unless the incongruity of their use calls them to our attention. Of course we see, though many students do not, that such blind-flying oratory as this is elaborate and unhappy metaphor:

We are indeed bereft at the impending departure of Mr. Askitt, who has so far piloted us well through the shoals of our fund-raising tour. We feel, I hope temporarily only, somewhat rudder-less as he leaves us for fields of wider usefulness. But as we continue to toil up our hill of difficulty, let us be resolved to knock upon all gates boldly, forgetting that we must be for a time sheep without a shepherd.

This is pure fiction, of course, but not unlike the production numbers staged by many people with a talent for the big and brassy.

On the other hand, the following gem of purest ray is just subtle enough to escape notice, even in print and especially in, or on, newsprint. It comes from a brief report of a Washington's Birthday speech at a Cincinnati conference on international affairs. The speaker, a highly placed official of the Federal government, was reported indirectly as saying that the United States would continue to press for peaceful agreements with Moscow, because we believe that the leaders of the Soviet Union want to avoid what he called, with great originality, a "nuclear holocaust." He went on as follows: "We believe that, objectively considered, they have a common interest with other nations in putting a ceiling upon the arms race and in finding ways to turn that dangerous spiral downward."

Apart from wondering what a Russian student of English would make of races run on arms, in dangerous spirals, upward to the ceiling, we may find in these scrambled metaphors a hint of language in the process of creation. Taken separately, the literal meanings in clear context become a convenient shorthand for common abstractions. We have an arms race and a space race, a ceiling on the national debt and a ceiling to be hoped for on the competition in armaments, the spiral of inflation and the spiral of competitive preparation for nuclear war. The race, the ceiling, the spiral have become in these common uses dead metaphors—dead at least in Foggy Bottom and Wall Street, Madison Avenue and Times Square, though perhaps only moribund in the clearer atmosphere of Cambridge, New Haven, and Princeton.

Incidentally, since we are interested in the competent use of language, it may be noted that "a spiral" is probably an inaccurate metaphor for the economic inflation which it commonly describes. The path of a point moving spirally in a single plane, represented visually by a flat watch spring, is a spiral. The path of a point moving both around an imaginary cylinder and forward, represented by a corkscrew or a circular staircase, is properly a helix. Hence the "rising spiral" of inflation is a spiral helix or a helical spiral, the path of a point that would create an imaginary upholsterer's spring. There seems to be no exact word for this, but a very close approximation is "volute." A volute "spring" is, in fact, a combination of the spiral and the helical form; however, though geometry has its "involute" and its "evolute," it stops short of the noun "volute," so far as I can determine.

The "spiral" of economic inflation, then, is presumed to be both a forward or upward motion and a constant expansion, a volute. Perhaps, as we move to conclude this discussion of metaphor, we may suggest that the evolution of language is also an inflation, this dangerous volute, and that in a much more complex way the proponents of the free versus the controlled economy have their counterparts in the field of linguistic philosophy today. The economics of scarcity must give way, say some theorists, to the economics of abundance. When we had too little, it was advantageous to have the entrepreneur take economic risks at his own expense. Now threatened with too much (or, as in agriculture, having too much), we must make terms with social reality despite classic economic theory. We must control and regulate, in the best interests of us all and in anticipation of the future.

But perhaps we are anticipating (no euphemism intended). If there is time, I should like to expand this pregnant analogy. If not, I suggest it as a promising digression (or diversion) that some may wish to pursue (or explore) further. We return to our metaphors with a last illustration.

We used the Cincinnati stereotypes to develop the point that language grows through the use of metaphors, and that in this sense, too, language *is* metaphor. At present, however, the figures of speech of the illustration are still to be easily and usually identified as substitutes, as primary meanings suggesting simple, easy abstractions. We have not yet gone through the process of hyphenation, dropping the hyphen in time, and eventually deriving from "arms race" the single word that it may become in rapid speech. But of evidence of language created by similar neologisms there is no end. Consider *icebound, jackknife, journeyman, keep-*

sake; ladylike, laudable, and *loathsome; magnetize, recreation, psychotherapy, rainbow, subhead.*

Notice in other illustrations of metaphoric adaptation the striking differences between primary meanings and later uses, especially as function changes:

an accident	accidental
a bar	to bar
to bore	a bore
a captive	to captivate
a dial	to dial
a dog	dogged
to dwell in	to dwell upon
to ease	to put at ease
	to be easy
good	goodly
fast	to fasten
	a fastness
to haunt	the haunts

Notice also, as a general rule, that older and simpler words produce the greatest number of variations in function and meaning.

The result, of course, is a "rich" language, varied, allusive, frequently colorful, interesting as language, potentially precise, potentially effective in its rhetoric—but very, very difficult. Like all language, it is conceived in metaphor, is nourished by an unrestricted diet of metaphors, grows to an attractive but overblown maturity in ambiguity, covers its middle-aged deficiencies with garments of hyperbole and the cosmetics of euphemism, and in declining years, unwilling or unable to restrain a gross and unselective appetite and subjected to the conflicting treatments of specialists called into consultation or self-appointed, goes into the ungainly fat of greater and greater redundancy.

But enough. How far along English may be in the fifth age of man's language I leave to your imagination and judgment. That metaphor is necessary and very useful as the stuff of language has been shown, I believe. That it is useful also in a narrow sense goes without saying. It is the language of the poets, of the artists in slang and persiflage, and of the purveyors of Wonderland gobbledygook in business and government.

That it produces ambiguity should be, again, self-evident—and again this ambiguity may be called "useful" because it is the essence of poetry, gives scope to the humorists, guarantees the livelihood of lawyers, advertisers, salesmen, and teachers, and eases the burdens of politicians, labor-relations specialists, administrators, diplomats, and lecturers of various sorts.

The offset of ambiguity is redundancy. As the suggestions of meaning attached to words and word groups by variations in use multiply with use, the careful speaker or writer consciously uses a redundant style, for he accepts redundancy in principle as necessary to accuracy and adequacy. We have seen something of the imperfections of language produced by experiences that are always peculiar to the individual, by variation in the intent of communication and in the nature and quality of the receptive instrument, so to speak, and by the shaping of words, already vague, to new purposes that multiply the possibilities of inaccuracy and misunderstanding. In this light, the paradox of intentional and necessary redundancy (the characteristic, by definition, of using more words than necessary) fades or disappears. For the definition is an abstraction that lacks an operational counterpart. The concept of redundancy, as commonly defined, includes a value judgment, lacks objectivity, and cannot be successfully applied. Language is redundant because language is ambiguous; we risk saying too much in the hope of saying enough. Depending upon purpose and audience, we *must* frequently say "too much" in our desire to be understood by all sorts and conditions of men.

There remains euphemism. The euphemistic character of language has been included to complete the survey of language as metaphor, and to reinforce this point of view with what amounts to simple illustration. The statement at the outset was that "language is inescapably . . . euphemistic in a broad sense"; that is, by its nature it must fall short of any truly graphic depiction of unpleasant reality. However brutal the facts of poverty, disease, cruelty and torture, specific pain, famine and thirst, riot, death by violence, and war, we must usually make do with the eyewitness, "It was awful!" or the banality of "the total destruction of a nuclear holocaust."

Truly we are hemmed in by metaphor and one picture is worth ten thousand words: the full corrective effect of unpleasant experience is denied us by the euphemistic effect of its expression in vague symbols. But it would be hard to say that euphemism is in the main a disadvantage, for in our comings and goings it usually reduces mayhem to muttering and permits the continuation of social intercourse in difficult situations. In the wide aspect, one can conjecture that an inescapably exact and necessarily frank world language would long since have produced utopia or annihilation.

The Teacher's Critical Role

Our effort so far has been directed to a re-examination of language, undertaken because a new perspective may affect critical judgment in salutary ways. More than this, possibly we can derive from our preliminary analysis some set of principles, hardly to be dignified as theory, that will bring into focus the complex and disorderly process of judging student writing.

In any case, I believe we have seen that the concept of metaphor can be useful in the analysis of language. I trust I have made it reasonably clear also, at least by implication, that I regard the English language as neither an analytical one primarily, nor a positional one, but a semantic one—that is, a language in which meaning, not structure in the abstract sense, lies at the center of many variations in pattern, creates far the greatest number of difficulties, and so may well be the basis of the most pertinent and successful critical analysis.

English is a language that because of its history acquired, with its extensive vocabulary and astounding orthography, bits and pieces of the divergent "patterns" or structural characteristics of its source languages. Little enough of logic or order could be the outcome, and that little almost disappeared as the clash of patterns reduced inflections indiscriminately and created variations of pattern unique to special purposes—created idioms, in short. Ours is a language, therefore, in which exact knowledge of idiom, a term used here as a generalization for specific structure and diction in specific semantic situations, is a kind of key to most meaningful and effective use.

In this weedy linguistic garden of ours, then, the finding and use of conventionally acceptable English calls for the recognition and discrimination, from a most disorderly array, of the medicinal herbs, the edible plants, the decorative flowers, and the proliferating flora of useless or dangerous trash. There is no question that English is a living language. It is so much alive that today's slang or malapropism may become tomorrow's barbarism and the colloquialism of the next day ("strictly from Jerksville," "not hardly any," "irregardless"). Thereafter it can go either way: into standard speech becoming standard written English, or substandard impropriety of speech becoming written and finally spoken solecism, which is defined as a violation of the idiom of the language. Perhaps I should make that past tense, for I have no idea what has happened to the word "solecism" in the lexicon of the descriptive linguists.

Needless to say, the teacher of English, particularly the mentor of students supposedly acquiring the skill of written expression, must be a qualified specialist in the vagaries of English idiom at all levels for all purposes. The teacher's critical role, at this time of a new eruption of the constantly smoldering controversy concerning precision in the use of a different language, cannot be overestimated. I use with intent the three-pronged idiomatic form, "teacher's critical role." The English teacher holds a position of crucial importance to the controversy, as a qualified critic of the issues and their advocates, and as a professional critic of the results of instruction. As people who deal with student writing, the teachers of English are all critics—professional critics in the most difficult and unrewarding field of professional criticism. If student compositions are produced, they must be read by teacher critics whose mastery of the language is assumed when they are made responsible for instruction in its use.

Parenthetically, I doubt that many beginning teachers believe that they have a mastery of the language. "Mastery" is one of the loaded metaphoric words. But I question that any English teachers today are unaware of the fact that language changes, and that the canons of taste at any time are determined by the custom of the time. It must, then, infuriate even the least qualified teacher to be "talked down to" as someone whose teaching, presumably through ignorance, disregards matters dignified as "the scientific facts of language."

The task of the teacher of composition is an unenviable one, as members of college departments of English prove by the pressure to move into the less difficult and more rewarding field of expounding literature. To the teacher-critic, the reading of schoolboy compositions is unlikely to be instructive, stimulating, challenging, or entertaining. Nine-tenths of it is undiluted drudgery. But its virtue as a task lies in its enormous usefulness to men and to mankind, in its shaping of the world far beyond our conceiving. For the civilized world is ideas, not things; it takes shape in words. It is fabricated to our civilized and humane purposes and imaginings well—efficiently, enduringly, powerfully, beautifully— if the words of the shaper are written words so contrived that they not only can be but must be understood. The contriving of ideas is at least a noteworthy skill and for most purposes must become an art. To learn or acquire the art of contrivance in writing requires study, practice, the acceptance of direction and criticism, and great pride in workmanship. Transmitting the skill is beyond any question our chief business as teachers of the native tongue. If we are to be effective practitioners, we must share with the student a respect for the task and pride in its accomplishment. We must also know what we are doing, of course.

Do we know what we are doing? In the criticism of compositions for the purpose of instruction, how well do we accomplish the purpose? If the question which heads this paper be interpreted as a question of quality rather than of procedure and practice, I have now reached a point at which I can answer without great offense: "Poorly." The reasons are many, and they are not empty excuses. When the businessman complains to the college teacher, "Why don't you teach them to write?" and the college teacher asks the identical question of the school teacher, the proper answer, I am convinced, is: "If you think you can do it better, try it already!"

One outstanding reason for our not really knowing what we are doing is that we have had to accept merely logical prescriptions of procedure, or devise our own, because the psychological and the verified experimental do not exist. Furthermore, the best concerted efforts of experienced English teachers, researchers, and experts on methods are devoted to the teaching of reading, speaking, the enjoyment of literature, and even listening. Writing is a stepchild. Everyone knows how to teach writing: give themes and mark them. What this country needs is not a good two-for-a-quarter cigar, but a good series on composition teaching: "Psychology and the Teaching of Writing"; "Scientific Short Cuts to Better Themes"; "What Research Has To Say About the Retarded Writer"; "How To Mark Essays Effectively in Only Five Hours a Week"; "The Optimum Use of Teacher-Pupil Writing Conferences." Needless to say, these must all be based upon the most exacting research—and I am entirely serious.

A second reason for our poor accomplishment as critics of writing is that the requirement is a terrifying expenditure of time upon a drab wasteland of the childish, the careless, the ignorant, and the inane. I have yet to meet an English teacher who learns anything of value to him by reading student themes. A common reaction to beginning the reading task is that of the teachers who assist in the group reading of essays used to evaluate work in a national program, such as Advanced Placement English. Orientation to the procedure is extensive, but upon its completion, many teachers are still reluctant to take the plunge. They stick a tentative toe in by retailing "schoolboy howlers" that they come upon in the first ten or twelve papers. (As the chief readers say, "They take a while to get going!") One item from the reading of sample essays to standardize the Cooperative Essay Tests remains in my memory because it suggested another of a much better vintage year, many years before. The newer "blooper" was this: "Women are misunderstood men, but men should know better." There was little doubt that a preposition had been lost in the windy chaos of essay creation, and I was reminded of a student whose knowledge of women, misunderstood by men or not, can never be known, for he himself misunderstood almost everything. We cannot know what he thought he thought, but what he wrote went like this: "Leonardo da Vinci was a great *sculpture*. His most famous painting is in Rome. It was *The Last Virgin*."

As I review the range of the teacher's problem, it occurs to me that *her* role is critical because she must mediate or reconcile the ignorance of men who should know better, and who lack a common language.

Reading Compositions: The Procedure and the Product

I have no illusions about discussing the problems of reading student compositions. They are difficult problems indeed, for writing is the fully creative aspect of communication, stands at the top of the hierarchy of skills, and is the most complex and difficult of them. Of the skills, listening and reading are in the category of the receptive and interpretive. Speaking and writing are productive and expressive—communication initiated by the mind of the individual as a creative unique response to external stimulation.

The speaking reaction, though extremely complex as a process, is acquired with little thought and less guidance. It is almost purely imitative in development and is normally used to deal with the basic needs and commonplace activities of daily life. Listening and speaking are complementary elements of "simple" primary communication, and I repeat that I call it simple because of product, not process. Language is so complex and yet so commonplace that we cannot overemphasize the need of those who use it most to think of it as the essence of the human, at the same time both the tool and the product of human thought and the unique characteristic of man as a species.

How can we visualize the communication process to greatest advantage, to show the writing element in its proper light as we consider integrated communication in its logical, psychological, and practical aspects? Suppose we draw a quadrilateral of lines ending in arrow points to show direction—four arrows, of which the two horizontals are pointed to the right and the two verticals point upward. The lower left corner is marked "listening" and the upper left is "speaking"; listening develops speech by imitation, with speech at the productive higher level. The lower right corner is "reading" and the upper right is "writing"; again there is the association of imitation, with writing on the productive level of communication through written symbols or marks. It will be seen that the diagram makes listening the common source and writing the ultimate product of communication. If you wish to include the normal chronology of development, draw a diagonal arrow from upper left to lower right to produce the sequence of listening, speaking, reading, and writing. The enclosed area may be labeled "thought," if you wish.

This diagram may not please the theorists who make much of the interaction and social significance of the aspects of communication and will question its psychological soundness. Nor yet may it please those who make oral communication the be-all and end-all of language development and even the criterion of linguistic propriety. The latter critics may question its logical soundness, but here we are on firmer ground. The oral point of view may fit into a science of language development, but matters of linguistic propriety are in the realm of human values, with which I understand science has nothing to do. Critics have my permission to draw as many dotted-line arrows in and about the figure as they wish, in any direction. The figure as I have presented it is an attempt to connect the identifiable integers of language as it develops for the individual, chronologically and in its psychological complexity. The verticals denote the chronology of imitative acquisition and the aspects of the receptive versus the productive. The horizontals represent the movement from oral to written symbols and suggest the complexity resulting therefrom.

If we think for a moment of the individual variations in reaction to oral symbols, the further problems of understanding produced by the growth and change of language structure and by metaphoric adaptation, the problems of idiom, the complex step from oral to written symbols, and the creative nature of extended language reactions to stimuli, we may begin to appreciate the complexity of the process of student writing. From the first word, the composition can go literally anywhere (and usually does) and the permutations and combinations of the possible "meaningful" symbols for the writer's purpose have approached infinity before the student has ended a paragraph.

What do we look at, what do we look for when we read student compositions? We look at almost infinite variations of the possible and look *for* some recognizable pattern that can produce a judgment because the pattern at hand is related to other patterns with which we are familiar. We look for patterns of relationship, for identifiable similarities, however gross, and we do so consciously or unconsciously but inevitably because this is the logical basis of human judgment. For each individual, the concept of quality of any sort is based upon a hierarchy of values acquired by his individual experience. If he has, for example, a wide experience of music, an excellent memory, and a keen mind not to be diverted from the business at hand, he can say with considerable assurance: "This is a good performance of the 'Y Concerto.' I believe it is in the top ten percent of such performances. I recall hearing this work done better only once, and that was by X, acclaimed by critics in his day as the outstanding interpreter of Y's music."

What weakness, if any, is there in a comparison of the teacher-critic of the writing done by a student with the professional critic of a musical performance by a professional pianist. There are two major weaknesses, both tending to prove that the teacher's task is far the more difficult one. First, the student produces or creates, while the pianist merely re-creates; the student is a composer. His preparation or practice is general, concerned with procedures and techniques that may be applied to a process of creation; but the pianist need only aim at flawless reproduction and something of personal interpretation of that which another has created. Second, unlike the musician and his critic, the student and his teacher are involved in a problem of intellect, a problem of meaning, vital to the student's performance, theoretically separable from the technique of presentation, but probably not separable in practice. Student and teacher are interested in content or "theme" as a creative effort, hardly to be judged independently of technique, for the expression of thought and the productive use of language are identical, or nearly so. Hence, what is said conditions the mode of saying to the point of almost complete control of technique. This is most likely to invalidate judgments of technical quality if they are divorced from consideration of content, as it also invalidates *comparisons* of technique or form from composition to composition and from writer to writer when comparisons are made without regard to content.

The theoretical point just made is that readings of a composition do not produce valid judgments of the writer's potential as a writer (his technical skill) when form and content are judged independently. If this is more than theory (and we have some evidence to sustain its logic), two practical outcomes might be expected. First, judgments of essays for examination purposes should be more accurate—more fair to the students, if you prefer —when they are made as unitary judgments. Second, the reading of an essay to be used as instruction is of no consequence if the writer really did not know what he was talking about, and all the teacher's marks and comments, all the pupil's efforts at revision, are of so little instructional value as to suggest that the student should throw the paper away and start over, using new material. Verbal tangles, in short, result when we try to find words for that which we know not of. A subject beyond the capacity and experience of the writer produces poor technique or form and is of negative value for its practical purpose, which is practice and critical assistance.

The two applications of theory just suggested are intentionally anticipatory. They belong in the following section of the discussion as matters of the purpose and process of reading, or critical judgment. Theory and applications have been introduced here because they are important to the main theme of this lecture and will provide a focus for much of what follows. How do we propose to support the theory, and what other applications does experimental evidence suggest?

I have said that there is little research evidence that will assist us in analyzing the writing process, its product, or judgments of the product. Analysis must turn to logic and lean hard on theory, as this lecture does. The little evidence that we have comes, with one exception, from "practical" research—findings produced by the effort to make the measurement of writing more accurate. The primary purpose of this section on procedure and product is to describe variations in methods of judgment and the quality of information produced by different methods. Since it is neither a survey of research nor a discussion of measurement, I shall be brief, emphasizing information that may be useful to the teacher critic.

1. When accomplishment in Advanced Placement English was first tested by a single examination, separate grades were reported for literature and for composition. A detailed or "structured" short-answer analysis of a poem and a nonliterary expository essay provided the basic grades for their respective elements. The third question presented a certain problem commonly arising in the critical analysis of literature and asked the student to write an essay explaining the problem, with illustrations from his reading. Grades given for each question ranged from one to fifteen, or were translated to this range. The literary essays provided two grades to be added to the grades for literature and composition from the other questions. Each essay was read independently twice, one reader trying to grade for composition only, and one for knowledge of literature. The result confounded logic, for the relationship of the grade in composition and the grade on the expository essay was low, while the relationship between the two independent grades for different purposes on the same question was high. Readers were experienced, each group was trained for its special task, and the training included grading and discussing samples.

2. On another Advanced Placement examination the composition question made use of a difficult passage from Pascal and

gave students a choice of interpreting the passage in detail or writing what amounted to an illustration from personal experience of its main point, a specific point stated for the student. The average grade of students who chose the interpretation was higher on the rest of the examination, but lower on this question, than corresponding grades of students who chose to write the illustration. This was an expository essay testing composition skill. On the whole, somewhat less able students wrote the better essays if they chose the simpler topic.

3. The topic for the CEEB General Composition Test was presented in great detail, and students were given two hours for the writing. Carefully trained readers used an elaborate manual to grade analytically, giving separate grades on a nine-point scale for mechanics, style, organization, reasoning, and content. Each paper was read independently twice, and a third time if readers disagreed. The results were mediocre. Reader agreement on the five categories varied by category, with reasoning lowest and mechanics highest. The test had low validity as shown by comparison scores of students who wrote a comparable essay in the following year, and by a comparison of essay grades with teacher ratings. Style and mechanics were most consistently rated throughout.

4. The trial run of the Writing Sample topics was a "test" of topics rather than writers. Papers written by college freshmen on ten topics were read very rapidly by experienced readers and marked only *high, average,* and *low.* The training session was thorough, making use of sample papers marked independently, with discussions of differences and the reasons for them. In the actual grading, however, every effort was made to subordinate detail and make unitary judgments—general impressions of the total quality of each paper. Reader agreement or "reading reliability" was evidently high, since the method successfully differentiated topics on the basis of general characteristics that could be analyzed later, logically, as levels of generalization or abstraction. This reading was a first effort to use the simplified criteria of quality and single unified judgments that we have come to call "holistic" reading.

5. Pure research of the reading problem used factor analysis to determine what professional people of various kinds might look for in reading student compositions. Five factors affecting

judgment appeared: ideas, form, flavor, mechanics, and wording. Readers were given no standards or criteria, but were asked to use nine categories or grades and to put not less than four percent of the papers in each. Reader agreement on total quality was slight, with 94 percent of the papers given at least seven of the grades. The qualities of writing affecting the judgments were derived by relating the factors that appeared to a classification of readers' comments on individual papers. College English teachers agreed with one another's judgments better than other groups agreed (lawyers, editors and writers, executives, university scientists, and so on.); in fact; readers in each other field agreed slightly better with the English teachers than with one another. The factors of mechanics and wording were most closely related to each other, but the report of the research makes no direct statement concerning what might be called the best concerted judgment of total quality. Its importance to teachers lies in the information about views of writing competency other than those of the teaching specialist.

6. In the attempt to discover relative validities of kinds of items used in the College Board English Composition Test, student essays were used as the criterion of writing, obviously the only direct or pure criterion. Each of five essays written by each student was read very rapidly by five readers and marked only 3, 2, or 1. The training session made use of sample papers marked independently, with marks compared, but there was no discussion of the reasons for differences. As usual, readers were both school and college teachers of English. Except for comparisons of marks awarded the sample papers, the only other basis for a common standard of quality was information concerning the grade level of the writers, the conditions of the writing, and the topics as the writers saw them. Reader agreement was unusually high, and the reliability of the total essay test was high as shown by the close relationship of the scores of all the essays of each pupil. The agreement of scores on the test questions with total scores on the essays was highest for questions on basic usage (grammar, simple diction, an occasional example of very simple structure) and for questions requiring the discriminative choice of longer sentence patterns: combinations of structure and phrasing that include the inexact, the verbose, the ambiguous, the awkward, and the nonidiomatic.

I believe that most of the findings just reported furnish support for the contention that form and content cannot be successfully separated in the reading or judging of compositions, and probably are not so separated as we read any kind of writing unless our purpose is the critical appreciation of a literary work. Why this is so, or how it may have come about, has been the source of the organization and content, even much of the style, of this paper. My concluding comments will suggest a unifying concept, with some possible applications to the task of teaching writing and reading compositions.

Reading Compositions: Theory, Purpose, and Process

The unifying concept toward which we have been moving is that language is an art. I hesitate to use the word, for it is a rather extreme example of metaphoric adaptation and other loose applicatory use. (Consider, for example, whether "He is an artist" means that he is a painter, a musician, an actor, a designer of bridges, or a trapeze performer.) Further, it seems most probable that I am using "art" in a sense as far removed as possible from the concept that produced the term "the language arts." I take it that this term is some combination of these definitions: "a branch of learning; a science" and "systematic application of knowledge or skill in effecting a desired result." As we look back upon the trend of my remarks and the points supported by speculation and some evidence, it seems unlikely that we can call language a branch of learning, a science, or a matter of the *systematic* application of *knowledge* or skill to a certain purpose.

The art of language that I conceive of is a combination of the following characteristics, which are also definitions. The first is primary, definition number one: "skill in performance, acquired by experience, study, or observation; knack." The second is "application of skill *and taste* to production *according to esthetic principles.*"

It seems hardly necessary to say more. We have stressed the point that language is imitative, that its acquisition and its meanings are highly individualized on the basis of unique experience, and that it is so much the product of variable human influences as to make its successful use a matter of seeing metaphor and having a feeling for idiom. The latter is particularly central to

the concept of language as an art. That taste and esthetic principles govern its use has also been implied, particularly by reference to what I regard as the limitations of descriptive linguistics.

This concept can serve, I believe, at least to provide focus in
the teaching of writing. Whether it is in the broad sense "true"
as we have developed the idea, or merely of pragmatic value,
must depend a great deal upon psychological studies that would
provide a really scientific basis for our teaching practices. I am
here reverting in thought to the idea of language for the individual, for the great average of individuals, as a *unitary* accomplishment of the greatest complexity.

What points of purpose and process in the reading of compositions can we quickly derive from a reasonable conviction that
analysis is not of much use? What does this suggest as to the teaching of composition?

1. Purpose should determine process. That is, we should
make a careful distinction between composition practice and
composition for evaluation.

2. Evaluation, as has been said, seems to be unitary. Mani-
festations of an art are not susceptible to analysis based upon
the idea that the whole is equal to the sum of judgments of partial qualities.

3. Reading compositions for instruction should make use of
only as much analysis as the *individual student* finds useful. Remember that he imitates, and that skill grows with use and
experience.

4. It seems likely that evaluation of *instructional* essays
should not be used as a carrot or a stick. This depends, of course,
upon individual problems of motivation. Ideally, compositions
for practice should receive no grades at all—but I have no idea
as to how this state of affairs might be brought about.

5. Concentration upon detailed error seems to be a defeatist
procedure. Unless the student is constantly guilty of gross care-
lessness, here again development through experience can be
counted upon. Most students need to read and read the best
examples of current expository articles, *not textbooks* in other
subjects, that can be found. Patterns of language are acquired
naturally. Consider speech as a distressing example. (Incidentally,
I suggest that none of us give house room to the bleeding-heart

types who warn against teaching the child speech patterns that would hurt his little psyche because they are different from those of his family and friends.)

6. Almost all practice writing should be expository, or expository-argumentative.

7. Writing assignments should be custom tailored—difficult, but not impossible. Few if any group assignments hit the target for all students. If they do, they are too generalized to produce good writing. Avoid "my experience" essays and "Why I like" matters. When will the student put this practice to use? (But here I am going beyond my territory!)

8. Class work on writing should be frequent, for much or most practical writing is extemporaneous.

9. Brief paragraphs are much better training devices than long compositions. It is likely, from the evidence, that too much is made of problems of organization and logic.

10. The student must have something exact and detailed to say. Writing is not speech; the *and-uhs* show too much. Vagueness of information, paucity of ideas, and fumbling travel in train. This, again, is I suppose a matter of assignment. Writing is not well done in a vacuum of thought.

I limit the list to ten. These points are not new, hardly controversial, and certainly not startling. I intend them as possible initial suggestions for an extensive and detailed list that teachers and departments might develop for themselves. How we use and read the compositions that are all too often the life's blood of student and teacher should be a matter of intelligent and consistent purpose and process. I hope some will find it helpful to put the process upon a base of fairly consistent theoretical principles.

EVALUATING EXPOSITORY WRITING

R. STANLEY PETERSON
New Trier, Illinois, High School

I had been reading the other night in Frazer's *Golden Bough,* as I sometimes do, when I chanced upon this paragraph concerning contagious magic.

> The sympathetic connexion supposed to exist between a man and the weapon which has wounded him is probably founded on the notion that the blood of the weapon continues to feed with the blood in his body. For a like reason the Papuans of Tumleo, an island off New Guinea, are careful to throw into the sea the bloody bandages with which their wounds have been dressed, for they fear that if these rags fell into the hands of an enemy he might injure them magically thereby. Strained and unnatural as this idea may seem to us, it is perhaps less so than the belief that magic sympathy is maintained between a person and his clothes, so that whatever is done to the clothes will be felt by the man himself, even though he may be far away at the time. In the Wotjobaluk tribe of Victoria a wizard would sometimes get hold of a man's opossum rug and roast it slowly in the fire, and as he did so the owner of the rug would fall sick. If the wizard consented to undo the charm, he would give the rug back to the sick man's friends, bidding them put it in water, "so as to wash the fire out." When that happened, the sufferer would feel a refreshing coolness and probably recover.

Of course I made the inevitable connection. I thought of your students and mine and of the blood-letting which our red pencils have caused. From our hands they receive their brain children dripping with gore. Is it any wonder that they shudder and wish to throw the bloody messes into the most convenient trash can sea? Do they not fear that the bloody bandages may fall into the hands of some college admissions officer who is sample

111

hunting? Is it not to be expected that they will resent the injury done to their opossum rug? Would it not be better if the magician consented to undo the charm by removing the offending fire of negative comment so that the sufferer would feel a refreshing coolness and probably recover?

The trouble with grading papers is that the wrong end is most often sought: teachers have to give grades at the end of nine weeks or at the end of the semester—ergo, every composition must have a grade; whereas the end should be the improvement of writing. I would substitute some other method than blood-letting. I would rub out even the red pencil. I would eliminate the grade. I would—but, as Cummings would say:—"listen: there's a hell of a good universe next door; let's go." This is the purpose of the investigation. What would *I* do about evaluating expository compositions?

I have assembled for you four themes written by an average class in eleventh-grade English. They are not the worst papers one could imagine. They are certainly not the best. They illustrate just about all the important faults of expository writing and at least some of the virtues. I have tampered with the manuscripts somewhat, and I hope you will forgive me. I have removed most of the technical errors of spelling and punctuation. I have done so because I have faith that these are not the kinds of errors you wish to talk about today. I wish to remove the obvious faults and concentrate on some of the factors in writing that are harder to evaluate but which are infinitely more important for the student to learn. For as I see the problem, it is this: the aim in evaluating composition is not an ultimate grade but improved writing.

The Assignment

First, let me explain the assignment. The teacher responsible for this composition problem writes as follows:

TRUTH PAPER

The purpose for giving the assignment of writing on truth had as many edges as there are to the topic itself. First, since the students had just finished *The Scarlet Letter* and were about to read *The Crucible*, they were in the midst of the issue of truth. The paper would help them to take the issue from the page and into their immediate life. Second, it was an exercise in *writing*.

The temptations to verbalize and to ride high in the air and forget that their feet were on solid earth were inherent in the topic. The topic was a test of what they might have learned about solid reasoning and solid exposition.

Before assigning the paper, I gave the students four situations which they might face. These situations involved choices between the truth or a lie.

1. The student was told that in the three months since he received his driver's license, he had maneuvered three minor accidents. His parents warned him that if he had a fourth accident within the next three months, he would lose car privileges for a month. A big weekend was approaching and he needed the car. However, a week before the important weekend, he had backed the car into a pole and dented the bumper. Would he go home and tell his parents about the accident, or would he hope they did not discover it until later?

2. Each boy in the class borrowed one of his father's golf clubs. He did not ask permission to use the club because his parents were away. While playing golf, he broke the club. Would he tell his father immediately, or hope that his father would find it and never suspect him?

Each girl in the class borrowed a pair of her mother's earrings to wear to a dance. She did not ask permission because her mother was away. When she arrived home from the dance, the student discovered that she had lost the earrings. Would she tell her mother when her mother came home or would she remain silent?

3. When writing his library theme, the student copied a passage from a source. He did not give credit for the information. When his teacher asked him whether he had plagiarized on purpose, would he admit the plagiarism or say he forgot?

4. Each student in class started his first job six months ago. During that time he learned that his employer was temperamental. Few jobs were safe if the employer was feeling irritable. One afternoon, the student threw a spitball which ricocheted off the wall and hit the back of his employer's neck. The employer flew into a rage and began an inquisition of each person in the room. No one had seen the student throw the spitball. If he confessed, he would lose his job or the raise in pay that was supposed to come soon. Would he admit his "crime" or keep silent?

After the examples were given, the students were asked to write on the reasons *why* people have valued truth so highly. They were to use the examples to determine their own positions on the question and to keep their ponderings in the realm of their own lives.

Analysis of the Assignment

The instructions to the students, incorporated in the last paragraph of the teacher's statement, were clear. They were to write on the reasons why people have valued truth so highly. They were further warned to use examples from their own experience. The teacher's awareness, then, of the dangers implicit in the type of assignment given is clear. She wanted every student to understand the limitations of his subject, to have his intention clearly in mind, and to avoid the loose verbalizing that such a topic as "Truth" might inspire in adolescent writings.

Four situations were spelled out, which involved incidents that might have happened in the lives of most students. One pertained to driving a car, one to borrowed sports equipment, one to school work, and one to part-time work outside of school. The cautious observer raises only one question: How does the student move from particular incidents to generalizations about *why* people have valued truth so highly. It will be interesting to examine the themes themselves to see whether the assignment (or rather the intention of the assignment) was carried out. If the student departed from the avowed intention of the paper, taking upon himself a different aim, what then? Is he to fail because he did not do what the teacher asked him to do, or is he to be evaluated on his own achievement in terms of his own intention? Our analysis of the individual themes may perhaps clarify this problem.

TRUTH (A)

Since I was very small I have been taught that truth is a very important part of life. I have been taught that above all truth is right. Never wishing to be at the wrong end of my father's temper I accepted his judgments. It was not until I was about ten or twelve that I began to think and form my own opinion of truth. It was a trip to Canada that started my questioning my father's definition of truth. We were visiting my uncle, who lives in Minnesota, just across the Rainy River from Canada. We took a ferry boat to visit the small village across from my uncle's. My father is always looking for new novelties and came across an extraordinary tie clip which he bought for fifty cents or so. On our trip home we had to pass customs and declare if we had bought anything during our stay. The ferry was just leaving, with an hour wait before the next one. If we declared the tie clip and took the time to pay two or three cents customs duty, we would miss this ferry. My father told us all to be quiet and we didn't declare the clip, but we did make the ferry.

This upset me at the time, I remember, because it was against the principles I had been taught. What was worse, it was my teacher that went against them. That is neither here nor there but it was cause to wonder. I still wonder about truth as it applies to me. Through my childhood I have come to believe that in all situations truth is my goal. I may put it off or slight it a little, but always it's the truth. For example if I broke my father's golf club sometime I wouldn't say anything right away. I would wait until he asked about it or until I thought it was a good time. I would feel it my duty to replace it out of my own earnings.

Why do I try to tell the truth? I do because I let my conscience be my guide. It depends upon the situation as to how much truth I tell. This is like evading one's income tax I suppose and most likely the government will some day catch up with me. Until then I will continue to do as I do, and I do try to be sincere in all I do.

Analysis of Theme A

I should be looking first for acknowledgment of the teacher's intention for the theme—or for the student's alteration of the intention. I do not see how I can avoid looking for one or the other. The progress in the student's thinking seems to run something like this: the student recognizes a time sequence in her moral development—first, authority; second, fear; third, personal judgment. Then follows an incident about the tie clip which raised the doubt. At this point the theme breaks down. The student cannot generalize from the experience and must fall back upon citing the given example about father's golf clubs. Perhaps it is asking too much of a sixteen-year-old to make this subtle decision. I would suggest omitting most of the paragraph, especially sentences 3 and 5 and the final incident about the golf club.

In the last paragraph the student writer stumbles upon a purpose for his theme: "Why do I try to tell the truth?" The student has already tried to answer this question in the first paragraph but now succeeds only in muddying the waters by talking about income tax, which she obviously knows little about. The almost amoral remarks at the end of the theme are due, I suspect, to confusion of aim rather than to an embittered life.

The primary difficulty in this theme is reflected in the title, which does not provide the student with proper direction. If she had said, "Why I Tell the Truth," she would have avoided most of her difficulty, for then she would have known her intention and avoided proliferations. The theme falls apart when "telling the truth" becomes simply a matter of convenience and does not follow from earlier statements.

The only way in which this theme can be evaluated so that it will become a true learning experience for the student is for the teacher to sit down and work through the logical sequence of ideas, elicit proper transition words, phrases, and clauses that will indicate to the student that writing is a sequence and a consequence of idea and example.

There is hope for this student. Her language is better than average; her sentences are generally acceptable; her mechanics are good. What is wrong with her composition, no amount of red ink in the margin is going to improve. I suspect, too, that the assignment was a little difficult for this mind which was too immature to make generalizations, but the validity of the assignment is indicated by the partial success which this student has achieved.

Shall we attempt some kind of evaluation?

Intention	Fair
Organization	Poor
Language	Better than average
Transitions	Fair

If a grade has to be given, I suspect that most teachers would give this theme a low C. I would prefer to reserve the grade until the student had rewritten the theme, in which case the grade might conceivably be higher.

TRUTH (B)

From babyhood we are faced with the problem of telling the truth. At first our parents may use force to instill in us the importance of the truth. When we are young, we tend to make up "stories" to tell in place of what actually happened. Perhaps we can attribute these little "stories" to a child's vivid imagination. However, if a child is not shown that even a little lie is a bad lie, the results may be tragic. Little fibs and white lies lead to big ugly, black lies. For example, if a child is not punished for lying, his conscience probably will not bother him and he will lie as an adolescent or adult. And, if the conscience is not troubled after telling a lie, what is the point in telling the truth? I feel that a person's conscience should be his guide. If a normal person tells a lie, whether it hurts another person or not, his conscience is likely to bother him. This is true especially if the lie hurts someone else. Thus he is faced with a decision. He can either suffer under the power of his conscience and let the lie live, or clear his conscience by letting the truth of the matter be known. However, a person who has been a chronic liar since childhood will probably have no conscience problem because of lies, even though it may hurt others. Similarly, he will lie to protect himself at the cost of others. The point in these examples is simple. Lying is a matter of conscience. Even though liars are despised, the real punishment lies within one's self. Therefore, truth should stem from a sincere desire to be honest with oneself and others at all times.

Analysis of Theme B

The author of Theme B has a facile pen. The paragraph moves swiftly. The transitions, at first glance, seem appropriate. Technically, the theme is faultless—almost. And yet, this is a very poor theme. In the first place, the author does not follow the assignment; he does not discuss the problem of truth.

If you, as teacher, can find it in your heart to be charitable, at least you can expect a clear statement of the writer's own intention. I take his intention to be the origin and development of conscience. If this is true, the student stumbled upon it in the course of his writing. It is not explicitly stated until the last sentence. It is a good sentence, but unfortunately the path to it is cluttered with generalities. As I see this theme, the writer begins with an historical approach describing how the young mind experiments with truth and untruth. It deals with punishment or the tragedy that may spring from a lack of punishment. Logically the theme should then proceed to the development of conscience and conclude with the effect of conscience in the life of the student.

How can this theme be improved? How can it be evaluated? Only through conference with the student, for no amount of writing on the margins can explain to a student what is wrong here. The problem is again one of failure to express an intention. If the student can just decide where he is going, he will have much less trouble than he has had here. Each sentence has to be traced through logically. Each false start must be checked. Each proliferation must be halted. Note how the person changes, for example, ringing all the changes of the personal pronouns, the voices, and the moods.

Comparatively, is this a better theme than Theme A? Frankly, no. I would not like to give it a grade at all until it is made to say something specific about a subject. I would want the student to get off his generalization kick and write what I can feel is his own.

Intention	Poor
Organization	Poor
Language	Good
Reasoning	Fair

THE IMPORTANCE OF TRUTH (C)

Every day of our lives a decision of some magnitude must be made by everyone, and it is often when a person finds it hard to tell the truth. The importance of telling the truth cannot always be seen by a person because the long range benefits are constantly being hidden. It is much easier to see the consequences at hand, such as the licking which is to come. The long-range benefits are made obscure by fear, and a person does not realize that the physical and mental anguish which is received at the present time because one tells the truth will be much less than the fear compounded in your conscience and your heart afterwards. For a person's own benefits the truth should be told so he can live with himself. The mind is a mighty weapon and when it turns against you it can wreck a violent punishment.

Another reason it is important to tell the truth is that one lie leads to many others. After a person gets away with the first lie, the second lie becomes easier, and the next one easier yet, until they become everyday habits. A person turns to lying as a way of not facing reality, and he always takes the "easy" way out. The "easy" way out, however, does not become easier as one progresses, but it becomes more painful. Pebbles turn to stones and pretty soon a person can become "a nothing" with troubles facing him at every turn. He cannot face life, and his life is worthless because he can do nothing but lie. To do something in life one must, therefore, always tell the truth.

While it would be foolish and idealistic to pretend that truth is all around us we must fight lies to the end. In our newspapers we can see the press misrepresenting statements, and in business we find people who are trying to get ahead in any manner possible. While the truth is not always represented here we must still be true to ourselves and to others. We must try to work toward truth, thereby being a shining light, and we must force truth's virtues into the world with us.

Analysis of Theme C

The author of Theme C is obviously a good student, sensitive to language and to the world around him. He also sees relationships, can argue logically and quite convincingly. He has an occasional lapse in usage, but generally the style is good, though the young man has been frightened at some time or other by a first person pronoun and the trauma has driven him cowering into the passive voice. I am sure that even a short conference could straighten out this major defect of point of view: it shifts from *our* to *a person* to *your* to *one* to *a person* to *one* to *it* to *pebbles* to *he* to *one*—until the poor reader is lost in the confusion and the theme loses vigor. If the first two paragraphs could be rewritten from the original first person point of view, then the last paragraph fits in well and the whole theme will have proper direction and force.

Shall we try to evaluate this theme by means of the categories already set forth?

Intention	Good
Organization	Good
Language	Good
Reasoning	Good
Vigor	Fair
Content	Fair

Most teachers, I think, would be inclined to give this theme a **B** grade. It has the possibilities of excellence in a good revision using a consistent point of view.

TRUTH (D)

Since man is a superior animal, he is better equipped to make the necessary decisions which will shape his destiny. Every day he is constantly faced with many varying decisions, most of which he can make with a minimum of effort, until he is confronted with a decision involving truth. When he is in such a situation, his natural animal instinct of self-preservation takes over. Due to this instinct, he fears that by telling the truth he will only be exposing himself to criticism and physical punishment, while he believes that by lying, he will be escaping reality; however, in this state of mind he fails to realize that by keeping the truth within his heart, he is actually only subjecting himself to a more severe mental thrashing. I feel that the great authors stress truth because they fully realize that the momentary pains of physical punishment are not nearly as agonizing as the constant throbbing of a guilty conscience.

Now the question arises whether the truth really is as important as the authors make it seem. At first it would appear that the truth is far from important, for when one looks about this society he sees only graft and corruption; however, he must realize that dishonesty is only so prominent because the unusual is more highly publicized than the usual. Actually the truth is very important, not only to the person who uses it as a way to relieve his mental anguish but also to the person who hears the truth spoken, for one who knows the value of truth is less liable to become a hypocrite himself.

To think that any one person can be completely true is ridiculously idealistic, because no one is perfect; nevertheless, one must remember that when he lies the first person he deceives is himself.

Analysis of Theme D

The author of Theme D tries to answer the assignment. In paragraph 2 the student raises the question of the importance of truth. He recognizes the fact that dishonesty is prevalent in society, but also that it is publicized more than honesty because it is still "news." Two reasons are offered further: the truth prevents mental anguish and hypocrisy. However, since the assignment asked for examples from their own lives, and since no examples are offered in substantiation of the general statements made, the theme must be rated low in content.

The language of the theme is better than average. It has a smooth, convincing flow and is marred by only an occasional incomplete comparison, an inexact conjunction, or a tired transition phrase, but we might wish that all of our students could use language as well as this student.

The chief fault, as I see it, is the inability of the student to follow out the assignment with specific examples that touch his own life. The theme is verbalizing on a rather high level but without much convincing detail. The theme, as a result, lacks vigor.

Intention	Fair
Organization	Poor
Language	Good
Reasoning	Fair
Vigor	Fair
Content	Poor

Would you like to give this theme a C+, hoping that a revision would do something about the weak final paragraph and the paucity of specific examples?

A System of Evaluation

It seems to me that some system of evaluation must be presented to our students other than a single letter grade. I have at various times experimented with different forms. Some years ago, when the General Composition Test was being prepared for the College Entrance Examination Board, a committee worked out a grading scheme that covered the following points: Content, Organization, Reasoning, Mechanics, and Style. A student could make as much as five points in each category, so that a perfect paper gained 25 points. A's, B's, and C's were adjusted to the scale, and an F would come at that spot where incompetency seemed to be evident.

The University of Illinois in its "Standards in Freshman Rhetoric" suggests a nine-point scale with ratings of Poor, Fair, and Good: Content, Originality, Development, Paragraphing, Diction, Grammar, Sentence Structure, Spelling, and Punctuation. This method of evaluating themes has much in its favor, though I sense too great emphasis on mechanics and not enough on the constructive aspects of the teaching of composition.

I shall attempt a third rating scale (and there must be a hundred or more in existence) which I believe can be adapted to secondary school teaching, to individual teachers, and to individual classroom assignments.

> *Intention*   Does the student know and demonstrate that he has a purpose in this theme? Does his title suggest his intention? Does he give the reader some indication at the very beginning? Does the theme end with a direct or implied statement of the intention?
>
> *Content*   Does the student have the required information, recognizable in his use of example, illustration, analogy, comparison, or contrast?
>
> *Reasoning*   Is there some flow in idea and argument, made clear and vigorous by proper logic and accurate transitions?
>
> *Language*   Does he use language with precision and clarity, with effectiveness, and some attention to pleasing sound and rhythm? Does he observe standard grammatical forms?
>
> *Manuscript*   Is there neatness in format, in margins and signatures and legibility?
>
> *Effort*   Does this theme represent an honest and worthwhile attempt commensurate with the ability of the student?
>
> *Accuracy*   Does this theme conform to standard practices in punctuation, spelling, and capitalization?

I have found that in each category it is possible to use the simple device of a plus mark, a check, or a minus sign to indicate the degrees of good, fair, or poor.

The list is perhaps too long; yet it is possible for teachers to vary the number of items used for any individual theme. Exercises might conceivably be given that would involve only intention, for example; or content and language. The teacher can judge. If a total picture is desirable, the teacher could use the entire battery. If there is difficulty in remembering all of the items, she may rearrange them starting with mechanics, followed by intention, then reasoning, and so on, so that appropriately she can come up with the acrostic *miracle* to guide her in the search for the perfect theme.

The themes are now evaluated. Conferences follow. The students know where their weaknesses lie, they know where to concentrate their efforts in making the revisions, and the end result is therefore not a grade to put in the grade book but an improved writing ability to apply to the next writing assignment. Let us hope that the Johnnies and the Janes of America of the future will thus be able to write without repression from grades and that the teachers can have all the time they need to evaluate all themes accurately. It is a consummation devoutly to be wished. And as long as I am being so sanguine, I wish for you no more than a total of 80 students in all of your classes, so that you will be able to do the evaluating I have been talking about today.

Lift up that opossum rug from off the fire and bid your students wash it carefully. Throw away your red pencils and sit down on the log and talk things over. The *miracle* can happen.

EVALUATING CREATIVE WRITING

JAMES K. FOLSOM
Yale University

Perhaps the best way of approaching the subject of my talk today is to begin by explaining just exactly what creative writing it is which I am going to evaluate. Being firmly convinced that students—in addition to their other substantial merits—are absolute masters at giving the professor what he wants, a flank attack by way of answering the question of what the professor asked for in the first place may prove illuminating. The professor —in this case myself and three other colleagues—teaches a course in Yale College called, in the catalog and by the course of study committee, "English 77—Daily Themes," and referred to by the members of the undergraduate body, depending on their cynicism at any given moment, either as "Daily Reams" or as "the D.T.'s." In the first term of this course the student is asked to submit a theme of approximately 300 words daily on a subject of his own choosing, as long as that subject is fictional. We do not accept essays, or anything which in our opinion might not be part of a longer fictional work, more particularly of a short story. Should the student submit such a theme, instead of a passing letter grade —A, B, C, and so on—he is given a failing grade of W. Once, with the object of discovering why he was not given an F, I made inquiries as to the exact meaning of the grade of W and was told that it stood for "Waffle." I was not inclined to pursue my inquiries further.

These themes are submitted—five of them a week—from the beginning of the fall term until the beginning of December. The rest of the fall term and all of the spring term are devoted to the writing of short stories. The student, in the spring term, writes one short story of approximately 3000–5000 words every two weeks. This evening I wish to limit my remarks to the shorter daily themes, which are the basis of most students' later writing.

In addition to the writing of themes the students attend two lectures per week where problems in writing are discussed generally as well as a private conference once a week with one of the instructors where their work for the week is criticized specifically. These private conferences represent the most important single feature of English 77, since this is where the student's writing is most closely analyzed. In the course of the term each student moves from one instructor to another, until by its end he has had conferences with each of the instructors in the course. We have found that this rotation of students has one obvious advantage, the fact that every student has the benefit of the criticism of four critics, each of whom will probably pick up some very different aspect of his writing as worthy of comment.

I mention this at such great length since I think the very way this course is set up determines what kinds of writing we will get in the themes which are handed in to us. In the first place, the nondirective approach to the themes—that is, the fact that the student is solely responsible for what he hands in—means that the student himself is encouraged to think up his own artistic "moment" rather than to descant on a subject supplied by the instructor. Therefore, except insofar as the instructor retains the negative control of penalizing papers which he considers entirely uncreative by grading them with a "W," the student himself determines what he will write about. And, as a result of this the instructor's criticism tends always to be pragmatic. We accept the principle that the student's aims are worthwhile, and hence we argue with him about how he has or has not been successful in achieving them. This criticism—and, by extension, the direction of the entire course—then, tends to be practical and specific rather than theoretical and general.

In fact what this means, as we evaluate student writing, is that we try to encourage students to use dialogue as a means of artistic expression while we try to discourage their use of scene painting and description. Theoretically, of course, there is absolutely no reason why a story has to be told in dialogue, as students are quick to point out to us. But, again pragmatically, we find that in student writing description turns only too rapidly into paraphrase, and that the student tends to rely on it too heavily. This, I suppose, is because he is more at home when he is writing description, at least as a beginner, than he is when he writes dialogue. The student's overreliance on description emphasizes, I might mention at this point, the great failing in student writing. Put in its most general terms this is an inability on his part to get inside his situation. He views it always from the outside, and hence its significance escapes both him and his reader.

Before turning specifically to the daily themes themselves, I might mention one other not completely unrelated fact. This is that the quality of student writing in terms of what the students are trying to say is very impressive. The students themselves are usually serious; they do not consciously write "escape" fiction or adventure stories or other kinds of "slick" writing. As a result we do not have to convince them that they are wasting both our time and their own by writing off the tops of their heads. Possibly the very fact that the students *are* so serious is the cause of most of the defects in their stories. They are so overwhelmed with the importance of *what* to say that they tend to assume *how* to say it is unimportant.

To turn specifically now to the daily themes themselves, we might begin by asking what general things go wrong with them. Probably their most common shortcoming is their anecdotal quality. By an "anecdote" I mean a situation which is not developed in a fictional way, even though it might possibly be the basis for fictional treatment. An example is probably a clearer way to explain what I mean than a definition. Some years ago one student wrote an anecdote which is probably the worst of the genre and which may serve to define the idiom. In this theme a man enters a bar in a small Western town. After some conversation with the bartender the twin facts emerge that the visitor is just passing through on his way East and that he is very fond, on first acquaintance, of the little town. The bartender informs the visitor that there will be a rodeo in the town the following day and the visitor is overwhelmed with regrets that he cannot stay to see it. The bartender urges him politely to reconsider, but all attempts at persuasion are vain. The visitor remains immovable in his plans to travel on. At last the bartender, overcome with curiosity, asks him why he cannot stay for the rodeo. The reason, it turns out, is that the visitor's wife has died in California and he is carrying her ashes home to Boston in the trunk of his automobile. He cannot stay for the rodeo because he must be in Boston in three days for the funeral ceremonies.

Well, one might ask, what does one do to correct a theme like this? Obviously practically any particular criticism which one offers misses the point of why the theme is unsatisfactory, which is, put bluntly, because it's silly. Its silliness, however, may prove instructive if we ask ourselves why the student would write something like this in the first place. The reason, I submit, is that the student is so filled with the very grotesqueness of some bizarre circumstance that he forgets to ask himself what its significance is. In such a case probably the best remark is, as one of the other instructors puts it, that it is not necessary to murder your grandmother in a daily theme. But a further question emerges at this point, which is how one manages to keep the student from writing such an anecdote again. Our suggestion here is a completely pragmatic one. We tell them to write only about things they know unless they have good reasons to the contrary. When we tell them this they usually reply that nothing ever happens to them; and we reply to this that that is precisely the point. We are not interested in what happens to them, but in what they make out of it. This, let me emphasize, is the hardest single point to get across to them. They are always convinced somehow that if only they could find the proper strange and exotic experience this would be the key which would unlock the mysteries of artistic success.

After our mythical student has been sent back to his room to write about something in his personal experience, and when he has filed his theme about the rodeo in the wastebasket and is sitting despondently gazing at the blank sheet of paper in his typewriter, filled with good intentions but nonetheless at a loss for ideas, what does he finally do? He writes, not surprisingly, about college life, and quite often about his roommates. The roommate story forms a good part of any student's creative output, and sometimes the stories, growing from the most commonplace of commonplace relationships, are excellent. It is true that the general picture one gets of roommates when surveying the sizable field of roommate literature as a whole is that they are universally the most nasty, unwholesome, stupid and despicable young men ever gathered together in one spot, yet occasional stories rise above personal animus into something which is oftentimes quite good.

Take for example Theme 1 (in the Appendix to this paper). In this very good theme the single most interesting point is the student's rather deft handling of the situation by means of understatement. He avoids the very real temptation to go into irrelevant and unnecessary detail, and yet the story is by no means vague or disorganized. We know, if we read carefully, what has happened, at least insofar as we need to know it. Notice as well how easily this story could have been ruined by the author's stepping in to make the point more obvious. How much worse it would have been had it begun with a sentence such as "Lou had not gotten a letter from his girl that day!"

Throughout this short theme the author has nicely refrained from commenting at all in his own person. Any such comment, I think, would have been unfortunate, and the author has seen this by telling the story almost entirely in terms of dialogue, with description held to a minimum and handled in a perfectly flat and colorless way. The effect of the story, as a result, becomes more profound than it would have been if the author had concentrated on whatever inherent shock value there might be in the situation.

Unlikely as it would seem, the roommate story is probably the best of the stories which deal with college life. Occasionally one gets similar stories which, if not specifically about roommates, nevertheless come from someone's unique experience of student life at Yale. As a general rule when these stories reflect the "official" view of college life they are not worth reading. They are saccharine tales which deal, among other things, with nobility on the football field, with teachers for whose instruction the author is everlastingly grateful, with friends in need who, despite the author's expectations, turn out to be friends indeed, as well as with all the other platitudes about college which ignore its reality. As a generality one might say that bad stories about life in Academia fall into two opposite groups, the cynical and disillusioned story on the one hand and, on the other, the optimistic and happy one. Both types of tale are opposite sides of the same coin insofar as each one represents a refusal to look at the actual facts of life in favor of some facile generalization about it. Whether this generalization is cynical or not is not really very important as far as the merit of any particular story goes.

Theme 2, though not so good as the first one, is perhaps more interesting as a typical case study of where a student theme goes wrong. Very obviously, it seems to me, the first paragraph is the best. The second and third paragraphs, though still acceptable, do not come up to the first, and the rest of the story is not even up to these. What is good about the beginning is, for lack of a better term, its zanyness. We start with an absolutely absurd situation and the impression we get is one of broad humor. The author has nicely handled our attitudes so that we are conscious of the foolishness of the whole affair. The tone, if sarcastic, is still lighthearted and genial. But very soon the student lets his personal animus against the bad food get in the way of his artistic presentation of a grotesque encounter with the bureaucracy. The last sentence gives the whole game away. We discover, to our disappointment, that this is not a story at all but a sermon against bad food, and the zany humor is spoiled by the strident tone of the ending.

Technically another interesting point is raised by this story, which is the author's lapse into paraphrase in the last long paragraph. This is emblematic of the story's weakness. The student can no longer cram into his story all the nasty things he wants to say about the dining hall staff so, in effect, he steps outside the story and tells us plainly, in case we happened to miss the point, just what is wrong with college food.

The question raised by this theme is a major one in evaluating student writing. On its most general level, the weakness of this theme is its inability to combine the author's "ideas" with his means of presenting them. He is unable to say what he wants to say within the confines of a story, with the result that he ultimately lets the story go by the board and speaks to us man-to-man in a kind of polemical sermon. His story, rather than being a believable moment in the life of a fictional character, has turned into an anecdote made to illustrate a point, in this case "Resolved: that college food is terrible."

Generally, as I have mentioned, our daily themes are strong in "ideas" and weak in their presentation, and nowhere is this better illustrated than in the students' universal inability to present believable characters. Too often the student's idea of a fictional character is that he is a mouthpiece for some consistent ideological position. As a result, many stories sound like nothing so much as a pamphlet which has been divided up among the several characters. A good example of what I mean may be seen in Theme 3.

Again the significant fact emerges that the first part of this story is indubitably the best. Ludicrous without being overdone, sarcastic without being cynical, the first four speeches are nothing so much as a modern telling of the fable of the ant and the grasshopper from the grasshopper's point of view. More important is the fact that the picture the author creates—that of someone wasting his life in building a fallout shelter which is ironically supposed to preserve it—has gone a long way toward making his point. The cards are already stacked against the man building the shelter, and whatever our own views of fallout shelters may be, we are willing to accept, fictionally if not in real life, the absurdity of the whole thing. But what happens to the story is that the author does not see how well he has created his scene, and as a result he feels obliged to tell us what the "point" of his theme is. Unlike the last theme, this one does not turn into paraphrase. The dialogue, however, becomes wooden and we see that the characters in the theme are not really characters at all, but mouthpieces for two opposed sets of ideas. Again the story has really turned into propaganda, and its content can be summed up in a proposition for debate: "Resolved: that the American people should not build fallout shelters."

This kind of dialogue, to generalize for a moment, represents a real failing in student writing, and one which students will ask, in all good faith, how to correct. The answer to this is not so simple as would first appear, since what is really wrong with this dialogue is not so much an error in technical presentation as a failure to grasp the implications of the problem raised by the story itself. In the theme we have just discussed what is obviously wrong with the dialogue is that the "conservative" point of view—by which I mean only the point of view of the man building the shelter—is not adequately represented. The good arguments are all on the side of the man with whom the author agrees, and as a result the whole debate is unconvincing since we know from the beginning of the story how it is going to end. This failing, I suppose, is more due to the immaturity of the student than to anything else. Students, like most of us, are unable to abstract themselves from something about which they feel strongly. They cannot make the case for the opposition since they do not feel there is anything to be said on the other side of the issue. They are too inclined to see the world in terms of simple right and wrong to make a convincing case for a point of view in which they themselves do not believe. People as they see them are either "good" or "bad," and a course of action is either "good" or "evil." As a result, their literary characters tend to be drawn in terms of black and white and to turn into stereotypes.

Nowhere is this simplistic view of human character more evident than in a group of themes which I had originally thought would produce the best stories, that is, themes which deal with the relationships between students and their dates. My original assumption was that, since the sexual relationship is probably the student's deepest emotional experience, stories dealing with this relationship would of necessity represent a more profound view of life than stories dealing with other things. I was surprised to find that I was completely in the wrong. When I mentioned this to my colleagues their opinions were the same as mine, that boy-girl themes were generally terrible. The only conclusion that I could draw from this undeniable fact was that though I had been correct in my assumption my conclusion was mistaken. The sexual relationship *is* important to the students—so important that they are unable to abstract themselves from it in order to portray it in realistic human terms. They cannot see what actually happens in the relationship between a boy and a girl because they are too obsessed with various cliches of what should be happening. Consequently boy-girl themes generally fall into two equally bad types. The first of these deals with a boy—or occasionally a girl—innocent beyond belief, high-minded, studious, morally beyond reproach, who for some reason which remains unfathomable, is treated with inhuman cruelty by someone of the opposite sex who, though cunningly disguised as a normal human being, is in actuality heartless, vicious, sadistic and corrupt. The second type details the fortunes of two young people who, through the malevolence of fate—or occasionally the malevolence of someone acting through incomprehensible motives of the purest evil—are separated from each other forever.

Needless to say, I have overstated the badness of these themes, but I have done so not only for the purpose of raising a laugh. For it seems to me that these themes fail more grandly in the same ways in which the themes we have discussed earlier fail. First of all, they deal in cliche. The characters are stereotypes, as are the situations also. Secondly, these stories are not so different from the anecdote I mentioned about the man who, bearing his wife's ashes in sorrow to Boston cannot stop for the rodeo, as would first appear. Don't all these stories depend on some inherent meaning in the situation to make their point? Doesn't the author in each case ask us to observe closely a bizarre and horrible event and from it to draw our own conclusions? And aren't the conclusions themselves oddly propositional and general?: "Resolved: that we should all be nice to one another" or "Resolved: that life is sad." And when we ask for a more particular exemplification of this proposition the author is unable to satisfy us because he cannot see the motivations which must lie behind the event in order to make it interesting.

When, however, the student is able to get behind his material and see its significance, the "boy meets girl" theme is often very good. When the student has maturity enough to see what his material means without losing his feeling for its emotional content, a quite competent and sometimes distinguished theme emerges. I would like to consider next three themes which I received during the last semester which I find quite impressive.

The first of these, Theme 4, is perhaps not really a theme at all, but rather a character study, the raw material of which a theme is made. But behind this character study stands a very significant reason why this is a good theme where others fail. First of all, I think we should note that this story takes off from both types of boy-girl theme I mentioned earlier; it is, ironically considered, a kind of gloss on the idea of how the course of true love never does run smooth. But the author is not merely content with discovering this elementary fact about this situation; though by the end of the tale we are well aware that this particular boy and this particular girl are not meant for each other, the author is not merely content with pointing this out. Rather he asks us to understand what is inherently wrong in the situation that causes the breakup of this relationship.

Technically probably the most interesting single feature of this theme is the handling of the first person narrator. Notice that the narrator himself is a bystander to the action. This enables the author to assume an apparently completely disinterested point of view while actually he is ordering his material to achieve a definite polemic effect. We should notice the very clever way in which the author has turned the situation against George while building up sympathy for his nameless date. The author has let the situation speak for itself. He has avoided stepping into the action with some kind of comment to the effect that "George was always a boor when he had had too much to drink" because he sees perfectly well that the events he is relating make his point without the necessity of authorial comment. Where most students tend to assume that a fictional situation is, as it were, "neutral," this student has realized that this particular fictional situation in its very nature holds George up for contempt and at the same time builds up the reader's sympathy for his date. As a result this student's theme succeeds precisely where some of the earlier ones have failed, because he allows the situation to speak for itself without himself entering the action.

Another significant feature of this theme comes from the ironic mode of perception which its author adopts. This is not to say generally that irony and humor are of necessity good things. Indeed, "humorous" student papers are often very bad, if only because students do not realize the implication of comic writing and tend to assume that comedy reduces itself to a series of bad jokes. The irony in this theme, however, is emblematic of its goodness since it stands as a kind of metaphor of the author's detachment from his material and hence of his control over it.

Detachment rather than irony is, I suppose, the important thing. In Theme 5, irony, in the sense of sarcasm or of bitter humor, is totally lacking, yet the emotional impact of the action comes across because the author remains detached. Again we should notice how close this theme comes to being a cliche without actually turning into one. It teeters on the edge of sentimentality yet never becomes sentimental. The tone of the story, a tone of impersonal detachment, is set in the first sentence and is nicely controlled through the rest of the theme. By picking a commonplace scene—a railroad station—and by depicting in it a commonplace event—a quarrel—the author has succeeded in getting us into the reality which underlies this apparently uneventful happening. The theme lives for us if only because we have the feeling that somehow it applies to us, that we ourselves have been in this situation before but have never realized what it meant.

So far in this discussion I have confined myself to a rather general analysis of student writing. This is frankly because of a feeling of mine that student writing is bad because of general considerations rather than particular ones. Particular technical blunders in style, imagery, bad metaphor and what have you are usually results of a larger failing on the student's part to control his material. In my own experience the best thing to do about stylistic blunders is to ignore them and to concentrate on the more major deficiencies of the themes, hoping that when major faults are corrected minor ones will take care of themselves. If one spends too much time as a critic concentrating on the details of themes the student often gets the completely erroneous idea that some kind of fiddling with the language of his story will automatically turn it into a literary masterpiece.

This is not to say that style, narrowly considered, is unimportant in student writing. On the contrary style is very important, the more so because most students have no conception of it. When you, as critic, tell them that what they say depends on how they choose to say it, they will nod their heads sagely, not understanding a word of what you mean. In the teaching of style I have found that general precepts are almost invariably of no value whatever, and that a student cannot be shown how to do something well by pointing out that he has done something else badly. Most students fail in style because they think of it as a concept completely divorced from the rest of their literary effort. One gets the uneasy impression that the student oftentimes finishes a creditable theme and then goes over it with the express purpose of putting in a little style.

Generally a student's stylistic effort will focus around some kind of symbol. Students are fascinated by symbols, and generally for the wrong reason. Like description, a symbol holds out all kinds of promises to the unwary. It is a handy device, students think, for introducing authorial comment in a subtle fashion while at the same time it serves to make stories more complex. As a result, symbols in student themes are almost always completely divorced from the body of the story as well as being purposely enigmatic for the avowed end of confusing the reader. Students are fascinated by the conspiratorial theory of art—the notion that literature is some sort of puzzle in which the author spreads clues about his work which clever readers will unearth, while the unwary pass blindly by them.

I mention this at such great length by way of prologue to the last feature I would like to point out in the theme we have just discussed. This is the enigmatic figure of the "old woman, with heavy black shoes and ankles as thick as her knees," which appears toward the end of the story. Here again, in my opinion, this theme is excellent in a way where many others fail. The old woman is obviously some kind of metaphor of the situation in the story. We can all see that somehow she symbolizes the girl waiting for her date. Yet the author has not ruined this symbol by insisting on it. Think what the temptation must have been for him to put in something like "Do you see that woman over there, Freddie? That's just what I am to you." Such a comment would, of course, have completely destroyed the symbol by making it too explicit and would have turned the old woman into a mechanical and lifeless restatement of the point of the story. It is very difficult to convince students that the less they attempt to say the more they will actually accomplish. Though they will all theoretically agree that art should reveal the implications of a situation rather than telling us what we ought to think about them, in actual practice their writing tends to be either didactic or vague. If the former, their stories fail because they tell us— often in so many words—what we should think about the action;

if the latter, they fail because the author refuses to control our attitude toward his story, and as a result the story has no implications at all. If we stop to think of the many ways in which this theme might have failed, its success becomes all the more impressive. Its apparent off-handedness should not deceive us into thinking that it is a simple story.

The last of these themes dealing with the relationship between a boy and a girl, Theme 6, is also impressive. Had it not been carefully handled, it too would have been a cliche. One can see how the story could have been cheapened into an ostentatiously profound discussion of the irony of fate. But the author has realized that this is not the ultimate point of his theme. What he is interested in presenting is a meeting between two people, one sick and the other well. He has, very intelligently, seen one point which is only too easy to overlook, that the nature of the girl's illness is beside the point. A poor theme would have concentrated on this aspect of the situation. The girl would have been in the hospital because—as happened in another theme which I received—she had been injured in an automobile accident through the fault of the boy. Similarly, a poor theme would have been explicit about why the boy comes to visit the girl in the first place. He would have been her lover or they would have been engaged. In sum, a poor theme would have failed precisely where this succeeds. It would have been sentimental rather than compassionate.

This is not to say, I should add, that the effect of this theme is vague. The details of the theme can be imprecise because the author is so certain of the particular over-all effect he wishes to achieve. The title of the theme, "The Visit," points this out. The author is interested only in the particular effect of this visit on the two persons concerned, and has eliminated anything which is not in some way relevant to this situation.

The considerations raised by these three last themes might well be reviewed at this point. In the first place, each of them is modest in what it attempts. As a result it achieves a great deal. The nature of this paradox—for it is a paradox—is perhaps ultimately mysterious, but I think we can make a few cautious generalizations about it. It is, first, worthwhile to point out that where these themes we have been analyzing go wrong generally is not because they have too little to say but because they say too much. It is a great help to point out to students, whether or not it is ultimately true, that a writer, like a happy man, is rich in proportion to the number of things he can afford to leave alone, and that the most important tool in literary artistry is not the typewriter but the blue pencil. That a story should have unity of effect is a saying which is so trite that beginners are inclined to forget how true it is. These last three stories might serve to indicate this.

The first of them would have been completely ruined if it had turned into a general description of a picnic where there was too little food and too much liquor. The author was aware—and most student authors are not—that his story was not about a picnic, but about his main character. The second would have been ruined if the author had felt it necessary to tell us any more about these two people than he actually does. He realizes that his concern is not with the background of this unhappy relationship but with the scene of its conclusion. The last story, its author understands, is about a visit to a hospital. It is not about sickness, except insofar as sickness is responsible for one of the characters being in the hospital; it is not about the background of the characters except insofar as this explains why one comes to visit the other; and it is not about hospitals, except insofar as a hospital is important to the characters. In sum, what is right with these stories is clearly seen in terms of what is wrong with the story I mentioned at the very beginning of the hour. The story of the man bringing his wife's ashes home was a story about an event. These stories are stories about people.

We should also notice that because these stories focus on their characters they move away from melodrama. Whatever action there is in each of them has been interpreted in terms of the characters within it. Hence the stories are not "shockers," though the last one at least could very easily have been turned into one. Similarly, just as "action" has been subordinated so has the ideological content of the stories been reduced to a function of the characters. Just as these stories are not about events, so are they not about ideas. Events and ideas are important only as they reveal character. Put as simply as possible, these themes achieve their effect by revelation rather than by exposition; they do not tell us what to think, but rather show us what happened.

By way of summary I would like to consider one final story,

Theme 7. This is probably the best theme I received all term and I think its goodness does not need explication. I would only like to remark the peculiar density and tightness of its structure, the brilliant handling of exposition, every detail of which adds to the total effect, and the deceptive clarity and off-handed quality of its tone. I might add that its effect depends entirely on the author's realization of what profound implications are inherent in the most commonplace events.

I would like to conclude my remarks this evening by considering a problem which, strictly speaking, does not enter into the subject under discussion. This is the problem of whether or not a course in creative writing is a legitimate function of an academic education. At first glance the only justification for such a course would seem to be that it is an amiable way for the students to waste time. If writers are born, not made, how can creative writing legitimately be taught? The answers to this question are not as simple as would first appear, yet the problem itself cannot ultimately be sidestepped. I myself must plead agnosticism of the mysteries of the creative process. I do not pretend to know whether writing can be taught to people who have no inherent gift for it. My own experience in teaching creative writing has been highly ambiguous in this regard. Certainly some students do improve, but whether this is due to constant practice, to the refinement of inherent talent, or to some other cause I am unable to say. On the other hand a great many students do not improve at all, and certainly the average performance of the entire student body is not especially remarkable.

To my mind the most compelling justification for a course in creative writing came to me through a casual remark by one of my students. We had finished our conference on his week's themes—which, I should add, were not particularly distinguished—and, since I had a few moments to spare, he stayed on in my office to chat. "You know," he said, *a propos* of nothing at all, "This is the best course in criticism given in Yale College." I thought the remark rather strange at the time, but on thinking it over I began to see what he meant. I had noticed the same thing myself without having analyzed it. What he meant, as I chose to interpret him, was that the value of "Daily Themes" to him personally was not that it had taught him how to write, but that it had taught him how to read. It had given him an insight into the techniques of literary analysis by making him aware of how other writers had succeeded where he himself had failed. It had taught him by example rather than by precept that the proper question to ask in the interpretation of literature is not "What does the story mean?" but rather "How does the story work?"

APPENDIX: REPRESENTATIVE DAILY THEMES

1

"Here's your mail," Lou said to his roommate, walking into their room. Jeff grinned big. He was lying on the couch reading the sport section of the paper. Lou dropped the letter on the couch and walked back into his room and changed books.

"Listen to this, will ya, Lou? My parents just got a new car!"

"Great," said Lou. He looked through the books in his book-case but didn't see them.

"You sure are overbounding with interest and enthusiasm these days, Lou."

"Sorry." Lou picked up two books and one of lecture notes and walked back through the living room. "I'm going to dinner. Then to the library."

"Writing a paper? Or an hour exam?"

"Neither," said Lou.

"Then why ya' goin' to the library?"

"I like the library," he said. And he let the door bang shut.

2

"According to William Blake," I said, "to limit desire, to re-strain, is to obliterate the chances for progression. Therefore, if I desire string beans with my savory meatloaf, you should give it to me, or else I will not realize my real creative potentialities." She looked across the counter at me wth big brown eyes, cow's eyes, which told me that she had not understood anything that I had said.

"I'm sorry, Sir," she said, "but we are told to give only broccoli with savory meatloaf. The string beans is for the broiled franks. If you want the beans, you'll have to come back for seconds." She stood there with the big spoon in her hand, looking like a steam shovel. I wanted to push my plate at her protruding lower lip. I became conscious of the line building up behind me, and I stepped back, and let a few of them go by me. Then I moved in again.

"What in God's name is the difference whether I have the string beans now or later?" I shouted. She stood there expressionless. "I mean, if I take the stupid broccoli now, and dump it on the table, and then come back and get the beans, what possible difference is it going to make?" She had a large brown gravy spot precisely between her ponderous breasts. My eyes caught it, and I angrily thrust my head back to look at this woman. Her expression, her stance, had not changed one iota.

"If you shout anymore I am going to call Mr. Dean," she said.

I wanted to tell her to go get [him], but I couldn't do it. The idea of arguing for any length of time over some lousy underdone string beans seemed absurd. Besides, the woman still had not made any movement that could indicate any form of life within her. "Ahh, the hell with it," I said, and I moved on down the line. As I picked up some glasses of milk, I looked back at her, holding the big spoon in her fist, putting broccoli on all of the plates with savory meatloaf, and bypassing those with broiled franks. On her face was a smile of contentment. I walked out of the kitchen and ate another delicious lunch, prepared by the members of the Silliman dining hall staff.

3

I was sitting in the backyard enjoying one of the last warm days of early fall. The neighbors were all busily working on a construction of reinforced concrete, cinder blocks, and lead shielding. An unsightly square block was taking shape.

"How's the fallout shelter coming along, Phil?"

"Pretty well. Another couple of weekends and it ought to be done."

"Sure you have that much time?"

"Let's not get defeatist about this thing. I'd just rather have some protection for my family if some jerk pushes the wrong button."

"What kind of a world would you have when you came out of that thing?"

"At least we'd be alive."

"What would you do if I tried to get in after the warning came?"

"Shoot you."

"Sure is a nice kind of mentality this business is breeding. Love thy brother seems to be out of style."

"I guess you haven't heard that this is the post-Christian era. If you want a shelter, build it yourself."

"No thanks. I'll don my civilian fallout suit and go put mad dogs and Englishmen out of their misery."

"You cynical son-of-a-gun. You never take anything seriously."

"You damn fool. You don't know what all this business is doing to everybody. All you care about is your scrawny neck. You remind me of the cartoon where the Neolithic man comes out of the cave and the modern man dives back into his bomb shelter. The goddamn bomb is even making me talk to my neighbor like this."

"Go soak your head. All you flaming liberals are all alike. You make me sick."

4

The thing was, George had the kind of looks, and the attitude, that made people feel obliged to comment on them. Anyway, George's date that night came out with the wrong thing on the way to the picnic. She said he reminded her of an Italian Rock Hudson and, well, George kind of considers himself a good-looking Rock Hudson.

George managed to depress the conversation until he swung his red Fairlane convertible off the road into the picnic grounds. We had barely spread our things out on the warm springy grass, when George began pouring down J & B and water. He usually drank like he was about to face a firing squad, but it was always J & B.

"You know, I have my own theory about good ol' Allen Dulles retiring from the C.I.A. Even though I don't think it was the old bugger's fault, I think Jack wants to get the blame off his back for the Cuba bit. Because, well let's face it, Jack hasn't been too red hot in Laos and Berlin and the U.N., too." George's voice commanded attention. "Well, I don't know, if you're not interested, why doesn't someone tell a joke or something." He filled his glass again, stirring in the water with his little finger. He glanced heavy-eyed around the relaxed group before pouring the liquor into his mouth.

Clearing her throat, George's date explained that Mr. Dulles was at retirement age after many years of faithful public service. George turned to look at her deliberately. "Is that right?" He murmured "Jesus" in his drink.

The girl made another effort. "Oh, it's such a beautiful day, I kind of wish we had gone to the beach."

"I kind of wish you'd gone to the beach, too," George giggled into his drink.

"No, it's lovely here. It's just I love the beach so."

"Jesus, only clams love the beach. Maybe you're a clam, huh? Hey, Neal, my date's a clam, I dug her out of the sand." He rolled backward on his rear end, shaking with silent amusement. Then he struggled up to one elbow and washed down his laughter with warm scotch.

I told him to ease up on the scotch.

5

Footsteps echoed on the cold stone floor of the railroad station waiting room. She recognized them but did not turn toward the sound. He stopped in front of her—grinning. The room was almost empty.

"Have you been waiting long?" he asked.

"Yes."

He stopped smiling and picked up her suitcase. "Ready?" he said, not waiting for an answer but starting toward the large doors leading to the street.

"I'm not going, Fred." He stopped and turned, looking straight and hard into her eyes. "Give me my bag, Fred. I'm going home."

"Oh now, Sweetheart, what's this all about?" he said, walking back to her but not putting down her bag. She looked at the floor.

"I'm tired of this kind of thing, Fred." The last words were almost lost. She opened the little black purse in her lap and took out a package of Kents. He took it from her hands, opened it, and gave her one but did not take one for himself. He knelt down in front of her and lit her cigarette. He waited for her to look at him before he began.

"Okay, Baby, so I'm late . . ."

"An hour late."

"Look, I'm sorry . . . but you know me."

"That's right, Fred. I know you." She looked away and saw an old woman, with heavy black shoes and ankles as thick as her knees, talking to the clerk at one of the ticket windows. "I'm tired of waiting for you, Freddie." She bit her lip hard but started to cry anyway.

He took her chin between his thumb and first finger and with his handkerchief mopped under her eyes. She returned his smile. With a single motion, he stuffed his handkerchief into his hip pocket and stood up.

"Let's go," he said, reaching for her suitcase. But it was in her hand.

"You know where to reach me, Fred." And without looking back, she walked to the lighted ticket window.

6

The Visit

The smell nearly overwhelmed him when he entered the room. The accumulation of odors—cheap flowers, floor polish, antiseptics, and medicines, none quite escaping through the slightly raised window—reminded him so much of illness and death that he was momentarily seized by a claustrophobic desire to escape. He tried to realize the smell was no different from any other hospital room or this particular one on his previous visits, but the freshness and life of the spring day outside prohibited him from accepting the premise.

The teenaged girl was lying on her back, eyes closed. Beside the bed stood a blood transfusion device, not presently in use. Over her head hung a sepia reproduction of Jesus dying on the cross. Thank God she doesn't have to look at that, he thought. He hesitated a moment in the doorway, then approached the bed. Her eyes opened.

"Oh, it's you, Jack," she breathed, raising her frail body on one elbow.

"Sit still," he said. He drew up a chair and sat down beside the bed. "How's my girl today?"

She smiled. (Goddamn it, he thought, why does she have to smile?) "Oh, pretty good," she answered, "I've been a little groggy off and on, and I have to sleep a lot. I guess I was sleeping when you came in. What time is it?"

"Ten till four," he said, not bothering to check his watch. What did accuracy matter?

"Gee," she mused. "I guess I've slept a long time this afternoon. I can't complain, though; it makes the days go fast. It hardly seems like I've been here two months."

Jack forced his widest grin and took her hand, squeezing it. "That's good, Tiger. With all that time behind you, you should be getting out pretty soon."

She smiled plaintively, and he felt the room about to overpower him again. "I don't know, Jack. They've got to get me well first. Dr. Taylor's starting a new treatment Monday."

"He'll get you out of here in no time."

She let go of his hand. "Didn't Sue say there was going to be a dance last night?"

"Oh, yeah—the same old gang sat around and talked. You're the only dancer in the crowd, so you'll *have* to get well in a hurry."

She closed her eyes. "I'll try."

"Are you sleepy?" he asked.

"Just a little tired, Jack," she murmured. "I don't know why I have to sleep all the time."

He said that operations always leave you tired, and then he noticed she was sleeping once more. He stood up, then leaned over the bed and kissed her pale face.

As he left the room, its smell seemed to follow him, spreading out into the hall. Tears came to his eyes, and he ran towards the stairs.

7

Their father had not come home on leave for three years, he was coming now for two weeks. The children were beside themselves. They had all their teeth saved, for tooth money. They had ashtrays, made with the print of a hand in clay, too fragile to send. They had drawings, and spelling papers, and arithmetic papers, and stories their mother, who wrote for women's magazines, was not worthy to read.

In the chill March dawn they sat shivering on the floor, and the boys told their quite-small sister stories of what he would say when he saw their teeth, their drawings, their stories, their papers.

"Is he like the plumber?" Lucy asked. She wished the plumber was her father.

"No, no," they cried, rolling with laughter on the icy floor. More seriously, being the oldest, Tim said, "He's like, well, he isn't like anyone we know."

"Is he like Mr. MacDonald?" Mr. MacDonald was the house painter.

"No, no," they shouted, still louder. "But," said John, "he has the same color eyes."

"He does not," Tim said. "Daddy has *blue* eyes."

"So does Mr. MacDonald," said Lucy.

The door opened. "What are you children doing up so early?" Their mother stood in the door, her bathrobe, bought by their father at Jaeger's, clutched around her, her eyes half-closed, her hair mussed.

"We are talking about Daddy."

"Children, it's dawn! You will all freeze to death! It's much too early to get up!" But she was touched by them so they all went and climbed in bed with her and she told them the legend of their father.

How long their mother was away, when she went to meet him! Several days. In the middle of each night Lucy called for her mother, and waking thoroughly, went down the lit hall to find the door open, and the bed made and empty. The boys, being older, woke at dawn, and raced to their doors to look down the hall.

"He didn't come last night," Tim said at breakfast, making islands in his cream of wheat.

"Perhaps he will come tonight," John made islands like Tim's.

When that night Lucy woke and called, and waking thoroughly went down the hall, the door was shut, so, oh, he was behind that door, and she flung it open.

"What the hell is that?" shouted her father, starting up in the blaze of light. In London then light meant bombs, it meant, if you did something secret, someone to take your papers. "What the hell is that?" he shouted.

"Nothing, nothing, darling," said her mother, and he, exhausted, went back to sleep, while she comforted the child, put her back to bed.

SOME CONVICTIONS ABOUT WRITING

BENJAMIN C. NANGLE
Yale University

I pose a question for your consideration without presuming to answer it. The question is whether a case can be made for the inclusion in your curriculum of some practice and training in nonexpository writing. The answer I would be indeed presumptuous to suggest. In fact, ever since the moment when I lightheartedly agreed to write on this topic, I have become increasingly aware of my temerity in doing so.

I am a voice of untrained experience. I have never taught in a secondary school and am unfamiliar with your problems. My only qualification is that I do try to teach courses in writing and in literature to graduates of your schools. And I have done so for some time. To bolster my flimsy credentials, I must insist on pointing out that I took Yale's course in "Daily Themes" in 1920, and have taught it continuously since 1923. During those years I have read, at a rough estimate, some 58,000 daily themes and 6000 short stories written by Yale seniors who had been trained in the discipline of the secondary schools. From this ordeal I have derived certain convictions which I can submit to you for consideration.

Now, we must first agree that a problem exists—that we can improve upon our present methods of teaching our children to write. This we may well question when we read in the *New York Times* of "the best class ever," see the schools congratulated on the superb job they are doing in preparing young people for college, and hear the testimony of college after college that they have abolished as no longer needed their courses in remedial English.

And yet, concerning this matter of writing, some doubts seem to linger. Addressing an earlier meeting of this conference my colleague Richard Sewall—one of the gentlest of men—cried out in anguish, "Quite frankly, the student writing that I see . . . strikes me as little short of appalling. It is dull and lifeless, stultifying to the imagination and blighting to the spirit." Recently, 4000 delegates of the National Association of Secondary School Principals received the report of a committee recommending return to more emphasis on basic reading, writing, and spelling. Their executive secretary summed up the report in a sentence, which is perhaps its own best argument: "What we are calling for is a return to firmer emphasis on the basic skills of the English language."

These remarks should not disturb us; spoken by teachers to teachers they serve rather to reassure us that all is normal in the academic world. Our profession is incurably addicted to self-castigation, to a restless feeling that while our present methods are criminally ineffective we may find in the next experimental program the magic formula of perfect teaching. For over two and a half centuries the faculty of Yale College has sat on this campus debating the same question—What is education?—and never coming up twice with the same answer.

More alarming is the evidence which comes to me from the world outside academic walls. In a recent letter to me the chief of the Washington bureau of the *New York Times* wrote, "Send me any student who can write. Writing is a vanishing art in the great Republic." Commenting on a novel published last month by a former student of mine, Warren Miller said, "He writes with wit and style, those two qualities so rare these days we sometimes think they have been lost forever." Recently the representative of General Mills, in New Haven to interview applicants for jobs, sought me out because he saw in the catalog that I taught courses in writing. He was hoping against hope that I could help him to find some young men sufficiently articulate to communicate ideas to their colleagues. And a partner in one of the great corporation law firms in New York made to me what sticks in my mind as the most terrifying comment I have heard on the state of American education. Concluding a glowing laudation of one of their young associates, he looked at me thoughtfully and said, "And you know, the best thing of all is—*he's literate*." If their firm, secure on the pinnacle of the legal world, is thanking God that they have discovered one young man who is literate, what must conditions be in the lower levels of this and the other professions?

Such comments as these, from the worlds of journalism, belles lettres, business, and the professions may justify the concern which has brought us together in this conference. Where does the truth lie—with the optimistic interpreters of academic records or with the disenchanted teachers and employers of the students who bear these records as credentials?

My own conviction is that General Mills is right—that our academic scores have tended increasingly to indicate how much a man knows, without guaranteeing that he can transmit or interpret that knowledge to other people. We have all become the victims of those two darlings of the educational theorists—rapid reading and the objective test. The machine reads the answers to the multiple-choice questions and assures us that our present freshman class has achieved the highest scores in history. But the highest possible score on our present entrance examinations does not, unfortunately, indicate that the candidate can write a literate sentence or read intelligently a simple paragraph.

I have made it clear, I believe, that you can get your students into college without teaching them how to write. If you still wish to make the effort, what form should that effort take? *The Advanced Placement Program Syllabus* has its answer in one sentence: "The writing in an advanced placement course should be primarily analytical, expository, and argumentative." I take it that I am expected to challenge the validity of that dogma and to suggest that we might find it rewarding to offer more than their allowable "occasional opportunities for writing of a more creative sort."

This brings us back to the fundamental—I suppose I should say "basic"—problem. What *is* education? Can we without heresy ignore the dictate of the *Advanced Placement Program Syllabus?* Must we maintain its doctrine that the purpose of education is to discipline the mind, and that, so far as composition is concerned, the mind can be disciplined only by analytical, expository, and argumentative writing? Can we put our faith in machine-read tests of "verbal aptitude" and "composition achievement?" Should I, a teacher, be startled when my own son, a successful young corporation lawyer, tells me that the two courses which he finds helping him most, day by day in his work, are courses in the English literature of the seventeenth century and of the Augustan Age? I am interested, but not startled, when he explains that he has learned that the all-important virtue is to say precisely, not approximately, what you wish to say. This he feels he learned in two ways: first, from the rigorous discipline of the instructor in the seventeenth century, who required weekly papers and challenged every imprecise word or sentence; second, from observing in the poetry of Pope and the prose of Swift a perfect object lesson in the use of words with precision of meaning.

All this is to say that if we know what we want to teach we can utilize diverse materials and methods to teach it. Specifically, then, can we by the use of "creative writing" teach what we are now attempting to teach by having our children write analytical, expository, and argumentative paragraphs and essays? Forced to look at my own course from this point of view, I must say that all through the years my ultimate objectives have been, I think, identical with those of the teacher of exposition. I too have been trying to enforce the primary virtues of unity, coherence, and emphasis. I have been trying to insist that effective writing in fiction, drama, or poetry requires a discipline analogous to, but even more rigorous than that required for analysis, exposition, or argument.

At this point I believe I have reached the crux of our problem. As teachers we are charged with the twofold responsibility of teaching our children how to write and how to read. If I may revert to the *Advanced Placement Program Syllabus,* we are told that "time and attention should be divided about equally between composition and literature." We are told by the same authority that the time spent on composition should be devoted to *substance, organization,* and above all *logic.* But the time spent on literature should be devoted to developing a sensitive appreciation of poetry, drama, and fiction. Here at last I come to my question. Is this a defensible program? Does it employ our efforts to teach the principles of writing in such a way that they will help us in our other effort of attempting to develop intelligent readers of literature? Am I not asked to devote half my time to teaching my child to write editorials and sermons, and the other half to teaching him to perceive what is involved in the creation of a poem, a drama, or a novel? Clearly it is not the substance, organization, or logic which he has been taught to strive for in his own compositions. Does this allocation of our efforts in teaching writing and reading perhaps explain why to the average freshman the teacher of English literature is a person who discovers "hidden meanings" in the apparently unsubstantive, unorganized, and illogical sequence of words presented to him in a poem or a story?

By the time the student graduates from secondary school he should realize, I think, that the meaning of the poet or novelist is hidden only from those readers who have been schooled to look only for *facts*. He should realize that the poem or the novel, to be effective, must be just as firmly based as the editorial or the sermon upon unity, coherence, and emphasis—that there is a unity of *impression* as valid as the unity of *fact*. If we can make him realize this, we shall have made easier our task as teachers of literature. He will approach the study of creative literature with greater sympathy and understanding if he has himself sought to identify, confront, and solve the problems confronting its author.

Thus far my remarks have been theoretical, giving you little idea of what the daily struggle is like in English 77a—"Daily Themes." This was my first mandate—to discuss why, if at all, we can urge the inclusion of some practice of "creative" writing in the curriculum of the secondary schools. Having attempted to answer the *why* I should devote my remaining moments to the *how*. Here I find myself somewhat embarrassed by Sewall's earlier speech to this conference, which was in effect a day-by-day syllabus of the course which I teach. Many of you must have heard it; the rest of you may read it in our published transactions. Let me therefore simply present a few rules which I think should guide the teacher in such a course.

1. The themes should be short. The student should be impressed with the fact that he has only 300 words with which to achieve his effect, and that therefore every word must count. Let me quote you the opening two sentences of a theme written by a Yale senior during the first week of the course. (The themes of the first week will be like this; those of the second week must not be!) "A young, rather attractive girl stood on the street corner." Young? How young? Two, five, twelve, eighteen, twenty-six? Attractive? What constitutes attraction? Color of hair, beauty

of face or figure, mode of attire? Attractive to what instinct—the maternal, the sexual, the esthetic, or some other? Can you see her? "She wore a very pretty dress of the latest design." Again, can you see her? What, in the author's eyes, makes a dress pretty? What is the latest design?

Three hundred words like these will only leave the reader with an image of his own designing; he must create his own girl, since the author has not presented his. And the author must begin to contemplate Conrad's dictum, as applicable to this small problem of detail as it is in the much larger context of Conrad's full meaning: "My task . . . is, by the power of the written word, to make you hear, to make you feel—it is, before all, to make you see. That—and no more, and it is everything."

2. There should be no assigned topics and no models of style to imitate. The author's subjects should come from his own observation or experience, and be expressed in his own words. After his attempt, and not before, he may profitably contemplate the treatment of his theme by another author. Let him first write his account of the very sophisticated young man meeting a socially ingenuous girl at a dance, and then suggest that he read Jane Austen's version of that scene as Henry Tilney first meets Catherine Morland in the Assembly room at Bath. He will see the difference and learn from the comparison. Or let him, as one of my students did last week, confront his nun, teaching in a parochial school, with the problem of dealing with two of her small students who solemnly tell her that they have seen a vision of the Virgin. Then suggest that his problem is essentially that confronting the author in certain scenes of *The Devil's Advocate,* a novel once a best seller.

Always let everything in the course start from the students' own writing; always if possible use for illustrative material quotations from their own themes of the week rather than from the works of famous authors. Always try to suggest ways in which they can improve their own writing, rather than give them an excuse to play the sedulous ape and produce pale, painful, imitations of the style of some master. If you read to the class, or allow them to read as an example, a scene from Hemingway, their deduction will be immediate and sure: "He wants us to write like Hemingway." You, the reader, will regret your folly.

3. There should be constant insistence on unity of impression, on the combination of details to show their relationship

and establish coherence, on the arrangement of details to produce the desired emphasis in the theme. The student must be reminded again and again that instead of selecting a few facts out of many and relating them to support the generalization expressed in his topic sentence he is now selecting a few details out of the thousands present in his scene, selecting them because it is his best perception that they were the ones responsible for producing the impression which the scene made on him, and presenting them *without the generalization* in the hope that he can transmit that impression to the reader. At times I feel that I could almost get through the course with these few comments—What is the unity? What is the focus? What are you saying? Or, in the face of a completely discursive and rambling assembly of utterly unrelated details, the most damning question of all—So what?

4. If you catch them young enough, you may be able to stamp out the generalization, the author's statement, the summarizing topic sentence. By the time they reach senior year in college, it's too late. They have been trained for too long to assemble facts and build them toward the statement of the topic sentence. If every detail in the scene has been chosen to produce disgust, the theme will end, "I turned away in disgust." Choke this hard; force them to take one scene, one situation, and strive to make it alive, dramatic, intense. Don't allow them to ruminate about it, reminisce about it, tell about it, or state it. Insist that, to use another of Conrad's words, they *present* it. "You tell it" or "you state it" is all that need be said in condemnation of a theme.

5. The short theme dramatizes the importance of the individual word. Make the most of this opportunity. As teachers of literature we are perhaps the chief victims of the cult of rapid reading. We teach our children to ignore the individual word and send the slow reader to the psychiatrists for remedial treatment. Having thus disqualified him as a reader of anything but modern textbook prose (written for his generation) we then ask him to read, study, and discuss the greatest literature, in which every word has been selected with care.

Here, in the short theme of his own composition, we can show him the damaging effect of a single ill-chosen word. Let me give you two actual and shocking examples, shocking even to the authors when I suggested that they have recourse to a dictionary. First a word used to describe the frenzied screaming crowd of

spectators in the closing seconds of a sudden-death period at a
hockey game—"conclave." Second, one word which collapses the
whole carefully established romantic mood. A beautiful golden-
haired girl is riding on horseback through the woods of spring,
a picture all green and gold romance, like Tennyson's Guinevere
—*until* the sunlight, filtering through the trees, strikes upon her
"shiny blonde pate." Realization of the ruin he has wrought with
one word can have a sobering effect upon even the most confident
young rapid reader turned writer!

6. The themes may deal with description, narration, or por-
trayal of character. When students ask, as seniors in college
should not but do, "Do you want description?" they must be
reminded that the most perfect objective description of, say, the
chapel tower, is the blueprint in the architect's office—a description so perfect that the contractor built the tower from it, but
of very little interest to you or me as readers. The author's description of the tower comes into being because, seen in the swirl-
ing fog of a November night or against a full moon during the
last week of senior year it has provoked in him an emotional
response which he would like to transmit to the reader. What
details created that response?

Or he may have to be told that he cannot simply write a
narrative theme about an encounter with the shine boy outside
the college postoffice—that there are a dozen different possible
themes about that boy. The theme is about the dominant emotional effect of that encounter—pity, irritation, amusement, physical disgust. The detail which is fine for physical disgust—licking
the dripping snot off his lip with his tongue, for instance—is not
so effective for inspiring pity for his underprivileged status.

When he comes to portraying character the beginner will
write anecdotes, under the mistaken impression that the situation
itself—the fact that his character was placed in this situation—
accomplishes his purpose. He must be convinced (and this is the
hardest task of all) that the situation is significant only because
it places his character in a position where he is under pressure,
and must make some response. It is not the situation, but the
response to the situation, that reveals to us what the author
wishes us to understand about the character. If he can be made
to understand this, the student will stop complaining that he
can't think of subjects, because he will now realize that, given

one situation, he has as many themes as he has friends whom he thinks he understands. Of course, in this situation, Tom would do this—but what would Dick do, or George, or Harry?

If you can get your student to this point the worst is over, and he will begin to get really excited about his writing. Scenes like the following will begin to take place every evening in the dormitories and will produce some of the best criticism in the course:

"Finished your theme yet?"

"Yes, twice. McMillin didn't like it the first time. Want to hear the second?"

"O. K. shoot."

I read my second effort. Charley looked at a magazine on the table. I finished and looked up hopefully.

"What was that last? I didn't hear it, something about laces!"

"When he untied his shoes he fumbled a little with the laces. It's a wonder you heard any of it."

"Fumbled—oh, I see, a little dizzy."

"No his eyes were full of tears."

"I didn't get tears. That's dime-novel stuff—cut a class for dear old Eli."

"No, he got cut from the *squad*."

"Well, I'll bet Olly didn't get it."

"Get what?" Olly's nose appeared out of a book.

"Tears in that theme."

"No, I don't see what he feels bad about."

"Well what do you want me to write? "He felt like hell because he was cut off the hockey squad"—period—theme?"

They looked at each other suddenly, then at me searchingly.

"Say Johnny," said Charley, more gently, "You weren't cut today were you?"

I looked at him sourly. My body ached with fatigue and stiff muscles. My elbow was badly bruised.

"Hell no," I said.

Well—the question has been posed to us, and in the light of all our experience we must answer it. Can we justify this kind of writing in the curriculum of the secondary schools? Can we by means of it teach certain disciplines which we regard as essential? If we can by this means produce better writers I am certain that we shall at the same time produce more thoughtful and intelligent readers.

This is, at any rate, the hope which I hold out each September as I greet a new generation of Daily Themers. The phrasing varies from year to year, but this is what they are told as they start the course:

> This course is fundamentally one in the practice of writing, in *learning how to write* by writing, which is the only way.
>
> But by practicing the art of writing yourself, by becoming, however humbly, a fellow craftsman in the art, you are developing, in the best way possible, your appreciation of the work of others. To appreciate achievement fully, you must have tried to do the same thing yourself. *The course is likewise, then, one in literary appreciation.*
>
> More than this, in studying the works of others creatively, and particularly in the light of your own struggles in the same direction—in hunting out the principles on which the great artists wrought, in facing, in rationalizing, the difficulties by which they (and you) were confronted, and learning how they overcame the particular obstacle—you are practicing the art of literary criticism from the best possible point of vantage.

This I believe.

Part
TWO

Literature

Introduction

The second section of this book is on the teaching of literature. The consideration here is; How do we read literature? The answer grows out of the idea that good reading is the ability to ask the right questions of the work under consideration. How well a person reads is limited by the extent and quality of the questions he asks.

W. K. Wimsatt, Jr., describes the kinds of questions one must ask of a poem to read it well. Marie Borroff discusses the language of poetry, poetic diction. She insists that words cannot be discussed separately from the context in which they appear in the poem. John Hollander, a poet himself, examines the sound of poetry, its various metrical patterns, the connection between sound and meaning.

The structure of the novel is the problem set by Martin Price. How does an author create a world and its characters?

The next three essays deal with literary works that are often taught: Alvin Kernan, "*Romeo and Juliet*," R. W. B. Lewis "Reading Walt Whitman," and Richard B. Sewall, "Reading Emily Dickinson."

The final two essays show how a teacher, by comparing works that have some points of similarity, can help a student arrive at more valid general statements about literature. Charles Feidelson, Jr., compares *The Scarlet Letter, Walden,* and *The Red Badge of Courage* under the heading "Three Views of the Human Person." Armour Craig compares three poems on a single theme.

WHAT TO SAY
ABOUT A
POEM

W. K. WIMSATT JR.
Yale University

What to say about a poem. How to say something special
about a poem, different from what is said by the ordinary reader,
by the *New York Times Book Review,* by the publisher's blurb—
different quite likely from what would be said by the poet himself. Why should anybody wish to say anything so out of the way
about a poem? Our professional preoccupation as teachers, scholars, critics, sometimes conceals from us the fact that our kind of
interest in poems is after all a very special thing—a vocational or
shop interest, somewhat strained perhaps at moments, even somewhat uncouth. Poems, a cultivated person might suppose, are
made to be read and enjoyed. If I read a poem and enjoy it,
why should I then proceed to dwell on it as an object about
which something deliberate and elaborate has to be *said*—unless
in a surreptitious effort to borrow or emulate some of the self-
expression enjoyed by the poet? What a teacher does with a
poem is not, certainly, the main thing the poem is intended for
or fit for. The poem is not the special property of teachers. What
the teacher does with the poem is at any rate different from what
most other people do with it. What he does in any deeper sense,
what his purpose and methods are, we had better not try to say
too quickly. It is the problem of this lecture.

What to *say* about a poem. I have been stressing the word
say—and I mean that no matter what the rationale of the teacher's
saying is—no matter what his purpose and his methods so far as
he is aware of them—the inescapable commitment of the teacher
is that he is to *say* things about the poem. For this he has a pre-
rogative, a more or less captive audience, and a heavy responsibility—five times a week or fifteen times a week, for one hour

or for two hours at a stretch. No matter how deep his devotion to the literature which he professes, no matter how sound his ideas, how fertile his invention, how spontaneous and genuine his utterance, it must occasionally have come home to any professor, in the course of a thirty- or forty-year career, that the fundamental, the invariable and inexorable demand of his profession is actually just that he be ready to say things about poems. This must be his unswerving loyalty.

II

Many centuries of literary theory have equipped us with a large array of now more or less standard topics, handles or labels, for the analysis of poems. We are disciplined to speak of the *theme* (the most abstractive and assertive kind of meaning which the poem has), and we wish to distinguish this from its realization or more concrete definition in various expressive features conceived as denser, more real, than theme, and yet translucent with meaning. We speak of *diction, imagery, metaphor, symbol* (above all *symbol*); we sometimes resurrect such older terms as *personification, allegory, fable.* And in our most ambitious, or in our vaguer and more portentous, moments, we sum up such terms and magnify them into the name of *myth.* At the same time, we speak of the movement of the poem in time, its *rhythm,* and more precisely its *meter,* its *lines, stanzas, rhymes, alliteration,* and *assonance,* its echoes, *turns,* agnominations, and puns, and also the more directly imitative qualities of its sound, the *onomatopoeia,* representative meter, and sound symbolism, the *orchestration,* and all that. Sound tangles with meaning. A whole poem has a *pattern,* both of meaning and of sound, interacting. It is an act of speech and hence a *dramatization* of a meaning; it is a set in a landscape or a decor, an *atmosphere,* a *world,* a place full of flora and fauna, constellations, furniture, accoutrements, all "symbolic" of course. It is spoken by some person, fictitious, or fictive, if we rightly conceive him, a *persona,* a mask, a mouthpiece, and hence it has a point of view and a variety of emotive endowments, an *attitude* toward its materials, and toward the speaker himself, a self-consciousness, and a *tone* of voice toward you and me the readers or *audience.* And often we too, if we rightly conceive ourselves, are a part of the fiction of the poem. Or at least we read

only over the shoulder of some person or group that is the immediate and fictive audience. The poem is furthermore (especially
if we are historical critics) a poem of a certain type or *genre*
(tragic, comic, epic, elegiac, satiric, or the like), and this conception implies certain *rules,* a tradition, a decorum, convention,
or expectancy. The genre and its aspects are in truth a part of
the language of the sophisticated poet, a backdrop for his gestures,
a sounding board against which he plays off his effects. Often
enough, or perhaps always, the exquisite poem presents a sort of
finely blended or dramatically structured opposition of attitudes
and of the meanings which lie behind them—their *objective cor-
relatives*. Hence the poem has *tension* (stress and distress), it lives
in conflict; its materials are warped, its diction strained, dislocated. *Catachresis* is only normal. That is to say, the poem is
metaphoric. The metaphoric quality of the meaning turns out
to be the inevitable counterpart of the mixed feelings. Sometimes
this situation is so far developed as to merit the name of *paradoxical, ambiguous, ironic*. The poem is subtle, elusive, tough,
witty. Always it is an indirect stratagem of its finest or deepest
meaning.

I have been running over some of the main terms of our inherited grammar of criticism and attempting just a hint at some
of their relationships—the pattern, if not of the poem, at least of
criticism itself. I hope it is evident that I am in no sense un-
friendly to this grammar of criticism or to any one of the terms
of which it is composed. I am all in favor of a grammar of criticism and of our making it as sober, tight, accurate, and technically useful as may be possible. The grammar, for instance,
must be especially firm in the areas of syntax and prosody, where
the poet himself has, at various times in various languages and
poetic traditions, been compelled to be, or has allowed himself
to be, most tight and technical. It is important, for instance, to
know that *Paradise Lost* is written in iambic pentameter, and if
we let ourselves be pushed around at the whim of random musical or linguistic theory into finding three, four, or seven or eight
metrical beats in a Miltonic line of blank verse, we are making
sad nonsense of literary history and of what this particular poet
did and said. An analogous difficulty would be the enterprise of
talking about the poet John Donne without the use of any such
terms at all as paradox, metaphysical wit, irony.

On the other hand, grammar is grammar. And I will confess to a decided opinion that the kind of technical and quasitechnical matters which I have been naming ought to be discussed mainly at the level of generalization—they ought to be taken mainly as the preliminaries, the tuning-up exercises, the calisthenics of criticism. An essay on the theme of metaphor, of symbol, of lyrical dramatics, of irony, of meter, of rhyme or pun, is one sort of thing—it is likely to be extremely interesting and useful. But an interpretation or appreciation of a specific poem by the means mainly of an appeal to categories expressed by such terms is another sort of thing—this is likely in my opinion to be somewhat less interesting.

The purpose of any poem cannot be simply to be a work of art, to be artificial, or to embody devices of art. A critic or appreciator of a poem ought scarcely to be conceived as a person who has a commitment to go into the poem and bring out trophies under any of the grammatical heads, or to locate and award credits for such technicalities—for symbols, for ironies, for meter. These and similar terms will likely enough be useful in the course of the critic's going into and coming out of a given poem. But that is a different thing. To draw a crude analogy: It would be an awkward procedure to introduce one human being to another (one of our friends to another) with allusions to commonplaces of his anatomy, or labels of his race, creed, or type of neurosis. The analogy, as I have said, is crude. Poems are not persons. Still there may be a resemblance here sufficient to give us ground for reflection.

I am supposing that the specific thing we are met here to talk about today is what a teacher is to say about a given poem —rather than how he might survey poetry in general in order to write a grammar of poetry. In trying to help a class or himself to read a poem, perhaps the teacher ought to be, at least to start with, more relaxed and uncommitted than in his fully grammatical moments. Not the most precisely definable and graded features of poems in general, the accepted grammar, but something in a sense even more generic, the basic activity of our own minds by which we examine a given individual poem—this is what I now wish to talk for a while about. This activity of our own in examining a poem, let me add immediately and firmly, does suppose that an object, with definable features, is there, independent of us, for us to examine.

III

Let us, for one thing, remember, and observe in passing, that as teachers we are likely to put ourselves in a Socratic relation to our pupils—setting them exercises, asking them questions. So that our own first question, what to *say* about a poem, is likely enough to assume the shape: What to *ask* about a poem. This I think is a very special, intrinsic and difficult aspect of our professional problem. (The book reviewer knows nothing of this.) If we assume that we do know, roughly, the correct things to say about a poem, how can these be transposed into good questions? Sometimes the very attempt will reveal the emptiness of what we thought we had to say. This question about questions is obviously a matter of art and tact, our own personality and that of our pupils, and I believe that nobody ought to presume to write any manuals about it. But let me stay long enough to suggest that a good question about a poem should have at least two qualities— it should stand in a middle ground between two kinds of fault. That is, in the first place, it should have in mind an answer that is better than arbitrary or prescriptive. It should not mean in effect merely: "Guess what I am thinking about," or, "tell me what I ought to be thinking about." "How does the imagery, or the meter, in this poem accomplish its purpose?" We may look on such a question, if we like, as setting an exercise, a way of eliciting or demanding an overnight paper. It is scarcely a part of a Socratic discussion. But then in the second place, the question ought not to be so good that it betrays or implies its own answer or the terms of its answer. "Is the imagery of the dead trees in this poem well suited to express the idea of mortality?" The answer that is being angled for ought to be more than simply Yes or No—unless perhaps as a mere preliminary to some further and more real question. Sometimes, oddly enough, the two faults of question making turn out to be the same thing—or at least some of our more careless questions will invite being taken in either of two ways, both empty. Rather accurate parodies of the world of discourse we teachers are capable of creating appear sometimes in the jokes, gags, or riddles (learned I suppose mostly over breakfast radio) which become the favorites of our youngest pupils. "What is large and red and eats rocks?" A certain father tried to be the ingenious pupil and answered, "A large poem by William Blake." But that, of course, was wrong. The answer was:

"A large red rock-eater." A good question should have a definite answer—different from the question and yet entailed by it. Some questions the teacher will ask mainly for the sake of giving himself the occasion for reciting the answer. (I do not say that is always bad.) A good question about a poem will be less like the example I have already given than like this other from the same source—though not exactly like this either. "What is the difference between a lead pipe and an infatuated Dutchman?" The father, though a teacher of poetry, gave up. The answer, of course, is that one is a hollow cylinder, the other is a silly Hollander.

IV

At the outset what can we be sure of? Mainly that a poem says or means something, or ought to mean something (or ought to if we as teachers have any business with it—perhaps that is the safe minimum). The meaning of the poem may be quite obscure and difficult (rough, opaque, and resistant to first glance), or it may be smooth and easy, perhaps deceptively smooth and easy, a nice surface and seemingly transparent. For either kind of poem, the simplest, but not the least important, kind of observation we can make, the simplest question we can ask, is the kind which relates to the dictionary. What does a certain word or phrase mean? We are lucky enough, I am assuming, to have a poem which contains some archaic, technical, or esoteric expression, which the class, without previous research, will not understand. If we are even luckier, the word has another, a modern, an easy and plausible meaning, which conceals the more difficult meaning. (Ambiguity, double or simultaneous meaning, our grammar instructs us, is a normal situation in poems.) In any case, we can put our question in two stages: "Are there any difficulties or questions with this stanza?" "Well, in that case, Miss Proudfit, what does the word *braw* mean?" "What does *kirkward* mean?" "When six braw gentlemen kirkward shall carry ye." We are lucky, I say, not simply that we have a chance to teach the class something—to earn our salary in a clear and measurable way. But of course because we hereby succeed in turning the attention of the class to the poem, to the surface, and then through the surface. They may begin to suspect the whole of this surface. They may ask a few questions of their own. This is success. A person who has been a teacher for a number of years masters the problem of knowing his lesson only to experience the more difficult problem of trying to remember what it is like not to know it.

V

The answers to the kind of questions we have just noticed lie in a clean, dictionary region of meaning. This kind of meaning is definitely, definably, and provably there—some of our pupils just did not happen to be aware of it. Let us call this *explicit* meaning. I believe it is important to give this kind of meaning a name and to keep it fixed. The act of expounding this meaning also needs a name. Let us call it *explanation—explanation* of the *explicit*.

Obviously, our talking about the poem will not go far at this level—not much farther than our translation of Caesar or Virgil in a Latin reading class.

And so we proceed, or most often we do, to another level of commentary on the poem—not necessarily second *in order* for every teacher or for every poem, but at least early and fundamental, or in part so. This level of commentary may usefully be called *description* of a poem—not *explanation,* just *description.* There is no way of describing the weather report, except to repeat what it says—describing the weather. A poem, on the other hand, not only says something, but *is* something. "A poem," we know, "should not mean but be." And so the poem itself especially *invites* description.

The meter of a poem, for instance, is of a certain kind, with certain kinds of variations and certain relations to the syntax; one kind of word rhymes with another kind (*Aristotle* with *bottle,* in Byron; *Adam* with *madam,* in Yeats); some conspicuous repetition or refrain in a poem shows partial variations ("On the Ecchoing Green. . . . On the darkening Green." "Could frame thy fearful symmetry. . . . Dare frame thy fearful symmetry"). Some unusual word is repeated several times in a short poem, or a word appears in some curious position. Some image (or "symbol") or cluster of images recurs in a tragedy or is played against some other image or cluster. Shakespeare's *Hamlet,* for instance, may be described as a dramatic poem which concerns the murder of a father and a son's burden of exacting revenge. At the same time it is a work which exhibits a remarkable number and variety of images relating to the expressive arts and to the criticism of the arts—music, poetry, the theater. "That's an ill phrase, a vile phrase; 'beautified' is a vile phrase." "Speak the speech, I pray you . . . trippingly on the tongue." "Govern these ventages with your finger and thumb . . . it will discourse most eloquent music."

Description in the most direct sense moves inside the poem, accenting the parts and showing their relations. It may also, however, look outside the poem. *Internal* and *external* are complementary. The external includes all the kinds of history in which the poem has its setting. A specially important kind of history, for example, is the literary tradition itself. The small neat squared-off quatrains of Andrew Marvell's *Horatian Ode* upon Oliver Cromwell go in a very exact way with the title and with the main statement of the poem. Both in ostensible theme and in prosody the poem is a kind of echo of Horatian alcaics in honor of Caesar Augustus. The blank verse of Milton's *Paradise Lost* and the couplets of Dryden's translation of the *Aeneid* are both attempts to find an equivalent for, or a vehicle of reference to, the hexameters of Greek and Latin epic poetry. A poem in William Blake's *Songs of Innocence* is written in simple quatrains, four rising feet or three to a line, with perhaps alternate rhymes. These are something like the stanzas of a folk ballad, but they are more like something else. A more immediate antecedent both of Blake's metric and of his vocabulary of childlike piety, virtues and vices, hopes and fears, is the popular religious poetry of the eighteenth century, the hymns sung at the evangelical chapels, written for children by authors like Isaac Watts or Christopher Smart.

VI

We can insist, then, on *description* of poems, both *internal* and *external,* as a moment of critical discourse which has its own identity and may be usefully recognized and defined. Let us hasten to add, however, that in making the effort to define this moment we are mainly concerned with setting up a platform for the accurate construction of something further.

The truth is that description of a poetic structure is never simply a report on appearances (as it might be, for instance, if the object were a painted wooden box). Description of a poetic structure is inevitably also an engagement with *meanings* which inhere in that structure. It is a necessary first part of the engagement with certain kinds of meaning. (*Certain kinds*—in the long run we shall want to lay some emphasis on that qualification. But for the moment the point is that there *is meaning*.) In the critic's discourse "pure description" will always have a hard time taking the "place of sense."

Perhaps we shall feel guilty of stretching the meaning of the word meaning slightly, but unless we are willing to leave many kinds of intimation out of our account of poetry, we shall have to say, for example, that Byron meant that criticism had fallen on evil days—and that it didn't matter very much. "Longinus o'er a bottle, Or, Every Poet his *own* Aristotle." We shall have to say, surely we shall wish to say, that Milton in the opening of his *Paradise Lost* means, "This is the language and style of epic, the greatest kind of poetry; and this is the one theme that surpasses those of the greatest epics of antiquity." ("This"—in a sense—"is an epic to end all epics." As it did.) Alexander Pope in his "Epistle to Augustus" means, "This is a poem to the King of England which sounds curiously like the Epistle of Horace to the Emperor Augustus. Let anybody who cares or dares notice how curious it sounds." Shakespeare means that the action of *Hamlet* takes place on a stage, in a world, where relations between appearance and reality are manifold and some of them oddly warped.

Through description of poems, then, we move back to meaning—though scarcely to the same kind of meaning as that with which we were engaged in our initial and simple explanation of words. Through description, we arrive at a kind of meaning which ought to have its own special name. We can safely and usefully, I think, give it the simple name of the *implicit*. What we are doing with it had better too be given a special name. Perhaps *explication* is the best, though the harsher word *explicitation* may seem invited. The realms of the *explicit* and the *implicit* do not, of course, constitute sealed-off separate compartments. Still there will be some meanings which we can say are clearly explicit, and some which are clearly but implicit.

I believe that we ought to keep ourselves keenly aware of, and on occasion ought to make as clear as we can to our pupils, two things concerning the nature of *implicit* meaning. One of these is the strongly directive and selective power of such meaning—the power of the *pattern,* of the main formally controlling purpose in the well-written poem (in terms of Gestalt psychology, the principle of "closure"). It is this which is the altogether sufficient and compelling reason in many of our decisions about details of meaning which we proceed, during our discussion of the poem, to make quite explicit—though the dictionary cannot instruct us. In the third stanza of Marvell's "Garden": "No white or red was ever seen/ So am'rous as this lovely green." How do we know that the words *white* and *red* refer to the complexions of the British ladies?—and not, for instance, to white and red roses? The word *am'rous* gives a clue. The whole implicit pattern of meaning in the poem proves it. In these lines of this poem the words can mean nothing else. In Marvell's "Ode on Cromwell": ". . . now the *Irish* are asham'd to see themselves in one Year tam'd. . . . They can affirm his Praises best, And have, though overcome, confest How good he is, how just, And fit for highest Trust." How do we show that these words do not express simply a complacent English report, for the year 1650, on the ruthless efficiency of Cromwell in Ireland? Only by appealing to the delicately managed intimations of the whole poem. The cruder reading, which might be unavoidable in some other context, will here reveal (in the interest of a supposedly stolid historical accuracy) a strange critical indifference to the extraordinary finesse of Marvell's poetic achievement. "Proud Maisie is in the wood, Walking so early. . . . 'Tell me, thou bonny bird, When shall I marry me?'—'When six braw gentlemen Kirkward shall carry ye.' " How do we know, how do we prove to our freshman class, that the word *proud* does not mean in the first place—does not necessarily mean at all—conceited, unlikable, nasty, unlovable, that Maisie does not suffer a fate more or less well deserved (withered and grown old as a spinster—an example of poetic justice)? Only, I think, by appealing to the whole contour and intent of this tiny but exquisitely complete poem.

> "Who makes the bridal bed,
>   Birdie, say truly?"—
> "The gray-headed sexton
>   That delves the grave duly.

"The glow-worm o'er grave and stone
    Shall light thee steady.
The owl from the steeple sing,
    'Welcome, proud lady.' "

The second thing concerning *implicit* meaning which I think we ought to stress is exactly its character as *implicit*—and this in reaction against certain confused modes of talk which sometimes prevail. It was a hard fight for criticism, at one time not so long past, to gain recognition of the formal and implicit at all as a kind of meaning. But that fight being in part won, perhaps a careless habit developed of talking about all sorts and levels of meaning as if they all were meaning in the same direct and simple way. And this has brought anguished bursts of protest from more sober and literal scholars. The critic seems all too gracefully and readily to move beyond mere explanation (being a sophisticated man, he feels perhaps the need to do relatively little of this). He soars or plunges into descriptions of the colors and structures of the poem, with immense involvements of meaning, manifold ex-plicitations—yet all perhaps in one level tone of confident and precise insistence, which scarcely advertises or even admits what is actually going on. The trouble with this kind of criticism is that it knows too much. Students, who of course know too little, will sometimes render back and magnify this kind of weakness in weird parodies, innocent sabotage. "I am overtired/ Of the great harvest I myself desired," proclaims the man who lives on the farm with the orchard, the cellar bin, the drinking trough, and the woodchuck, in Robert Frost's "After Apple-Picking." "This man," says the student in his homework paper, "is tired of life. He wants to go to sleep and die." This we mark with a red pencil. Then we set to work, somehow, in class, to retrieve the "sym-bolism." This monodrama of a tired apple picker, with the feel of the ladder rungs in his instep, bears nearly the same relation to the end of a country fair, the end of a victorious football season, of a long vacation, or of a full lifetime, as a doughnut bears to a Christmas wreath, a ferris wheel, or the rings of Saturn. *Nearly* the same relation, let us say. A poem is a kind of shape, a cunning and precise shape of words and human experience, which has something of the indeterminacy of a simpler physical shape, round or square, but which at the same time invites and

justifies a very wide replication or reflection of itself in the field
of our awareness.

> Till the little ones, weary,
> No more can be merry;
> The sun does descend,
> And our sports have an end.
> Round the laps of their mothers
> Many sisters and brothers,
> Like birds in their nest,
> Are ready for rest,
> And sport no more seen
> On the darkening Green.
>
> [Blake, "The Ecchoing Green"]

What experience has any member of the class ever had, or what
experiences can he think of or imagine, that are parallel to or
concentric to that of the apple picker? of the Ecchoing Green?—
yet the words of the poem do not *mean* these other experiences
in the same way that they mean the apples, the ladder, the man,
the sport, and the green. The kind of student interpretation which
I have mentioned may be described as the fallacy of the literal
feedback. Proud Maisie translated into conceited Maisie may be
viewed as a miniature instance of the same. And this will illustrate
the close relation between the two errors of implicit reading in
which I have just been trying to describe. The uncontrolled reading is very often the overexplicit reading.

VII

Explanation, then—of the explicit and clearly ascertainable
but perhaps obscure or disguised meanings of words; *description*
—of the poem's structure and parts, its shape and colors, and its
historical relations; *explication*—the turning of such description
as far as possible into meaning. These I believe are the teacher-
critic's staple commitments—which we may sum up, if we wish,
in some such generic term as *elucidation* or *interpretation.*

It is difficult to illustrate these matters evenly from any single
short poem. Let me, nevertheless, make the effort. Not to show
the originality of my own critical judgment, but to keep within
the area of what is readily available and plausible, I choose the

four quatrains of William Blake's "London" in his *Songs of Experience.*

> I wander thro' each charter'd street
> Near where the charter'd Thames does flow,
> And mark in every face I meet
> Marks of weakness, marks of woe.
>
> In every cry of every Man,
> In every infant's cry of fear,
> In every voice, in every ban,
> The mind-forg'd manacles I hear.
>
> How the Chimney-sweeper's cry
> Every black'ning Church Appalls;
> And the hapless Soldier's sigh
> Runs in blood down Palace walls.
>
> But most thro' midnight streets I hear
> How the youthful Harlot's curse
> Blasts the new born Infant's tear,
> And blights with plagues the Marriage hearse.

Let me remark briefly that Blake engraved and printed and illuminated this poem as part of a pictorially designed page. But I believe that this poem (if perhaps not all of Blake's similarly illustrated poems) can be fully understood without any picture.

A further special remark is required by the fact that an early draft of this poem, which is available in Blake's notebook, the celebrated Rossetti manuscript, gives us several variant readings, even variants of key words in the poem. Such avenues of access to the poet's process of composition, a favorite kind of resort for the biographical detective, may also, I believe, be legitimately enough invoked by a teacher as an aid to exposition. Surely the variant reading, the fumbled and rejected inspiration, makes a convenient enough focus on the actual reading. We suppose that the poet did improve his composition, and usually he did. So if word A is worse, *why* is word B better, or best? Comparison opens inquiry, promotes realization. Sometimes the discovery of such an unravelled thread, in our learned edition of the poet, will save a classroom discussion which was otherwise moving toward vacuity. Nevertheless I choose here not to invoke the interesting variants to Blake's poem, because I believe the existence and the exhibition of such genetic vestiges is not intrinsic to the confrontation of our minds with the poem. Not that to invoke the variants would be unfair—it is simply unnecessary. If we really need inferior variants, we can make up some of our own. And perhaps we ought to.

Perhaps there is no single word in this poem which calls for the simple dictionary work which I have defined as the level of mere *explanation*. But the word *charter'd,* used twice in the first two lines, is nearly such a word. At any rate, its emphatic and reiterated assertion, its somewhat curious ring in its context, as well as its position at the start of the poem, make it a likely word to begin with. How is a street chartered? How is the Thames chartered? A charter is a written document, delivered by a governmental authority and granting privileges, recognizing rights, or creating corporate entities, boroughs, universities, trading companies, utilities. It is privilege, immunity, publicly conceded right. The Great Charter (Magna Charta) is a glorious instance of the concept in the history of men who speak English. I have been following, where it led me, the article under the word *charter* in the *Oxford English Dictionary on Historical Principles.* But surely the great dictionary is mistaken when under meaning 3.2 *figurative.* "Privileged, licensed," it quotes Shakespeare's *Henry the Fifth,* "When he speakes, The Ayre, a Charter'd Libertine, is still," and shortly after that, Blake, *Songs of Experience,* "Near where the charter'd Thames does flow." Surely the eminent Victorian person who compiled that entry was little given to the modern critical sin of looking for ironies in poetry. The force of that reiterated word in the first two lines of Blake's poem must have something to do with a tendency of the word, in the right context (and Blake's poem is that context), to mean nearly the opposite of those meanings of advantage listed in the dictionary. For chartered privilege is a legalistic thing, which sounds less good when we call it vested interest, and which entails an inevitable obverse, that is, restriction or restraint. How indeed could the street or the river be chartered in any of the liberating senses listed in the dictionary? It is the traffic on them or the right to build houses along them that is chartered in the sense of being conceded—to somebody. And this inevitably means that for somebody else—probably for you and me—the privilege is the restriction. Thus the strange twisted aptness, the happy catachresis, of the wanderer's calling so mobile and natural a force as the river chartered at all. The fact is that this meaning of the word *chartered* is not listed in the *Oxford Dictionary.*

We began with the dictionary, but we have had to go beyond it, to correct it in a specific point, and even to reverse its general drift. Examples of dictionary explanations of words in poems almost always turn out to be not quite pure.

To turn away from the attempt at such explanation, then— what opportunities do we find for simply *describing* this poem— and first, with regard to its immediate historical contexts? Perhaps some note on the chimney sweeper will be needed for our twentieth-century American pupils. We can look a little to one side and see Blake's angry poem "The Chimney Sweeper" in the *Songs of Experience:* "A little black thing among the snow, Crying 'weep!' 'weep!' in notes of woe!" We can look back and see the companion "Chimney Sweeper," tenderly comical, poignant, in the *Songs of Innocence.* ". . . I said 'Hush, Tom! never mind it, for when your head's bare You Know that the soot cannot spoil your white hair!" An Act of Parliament of 1788 had attempted to prohibit the employment of chimney sweeps until they were eight years old. In winter they began work at 7 a.m., in summer at 5. Their heads were shaved to reduce the risk of their hair catching fire from pockets of smouldering soot. An essay on the eighteenth-century London practice of chimney sweeping would of course be an explication, *in extenso,* of the third stanza of this poem. We could add notes too for this stanza on the wars and armies of the period, on the condition of the London churches (the blackening of Portland limestone outside—suppositions about the failure of the ministry inside, priestly symbols of oppression in other lyrics by Blake), or for the fourth stanza we could investigate harlots in eighteenth-century London. But I believe it is part of the power of this particular poem that it scarcely requires any very elaborate descriptive explications of this sort. "We can do pretty well with the poem," says one commentator, "in contexts of our own manufacture or out of our own experience."

Another external point of reference, a part of Blake's immediate literary and religious tradition, has already been named —that is, when we alluded some minutes ago to the simple metrics and the innocent language of the eighteenth-century evangelical hymns. Blake's *Songs of Innocence and of Experience,* says one critic, are "almost a parody" of such popular earlier collections as the *Divine Songs Attempted in Easy Language for the Use of Children* by the nonconformist minister and logician Isaac Watts. Blake knew that collection well. And thus, a certain *Song* entitled "Praise for Mercies Spiritual and Temporal:"

> Whene'er I take my walks abroad,
>   How many poor I see;
> What shall I render to my God
>   For all his gifts to me.
>
> . . . .
>
> How many children in the street,
>   Half naked I behold!
> While I am cloth'd from head to feet,
>   And cover'd from the cold.

The echoes of such socially innocent hymnology in the minds and ears of Blake and his generation make, as I have suggested, a part of the meaning of his vocabulary and rhythm, part of a historic London sounding board, against which we too can enjoy a more resonant reading of the bitterness and irony of the wanderer in the chartered streets.

But to turn back to the words of our poem, the poem itself, and to inquire whether any *internal* features of it deserves descriptive notice: For one thing, I should want a class to notice how the simple hymnlike stanzas of this poem are fortified or specialized in a remarkable way by a kind of phonemic tune, or prominent and stark, almost harsh, succession of similar emphatic syllables. This tune is announced in the opening verb *wander,* then immediately picked up and reiterated, doubly and triply:— *chartered* street, *chartered* Thames, "And *mark* in every face . . . *Marks* of Weakness, *marks* of woe." The word *mark* indeed, the inner mental act, the outer graven sign, is the very motif of this marking repetition. It was more than a semantic or dictionary triumph when Blake, revising his poem, hit on the word *chartered* —rejecting the other quite different-sounding word which we need not mention, which appears in the Rossetti manuscript.

The student of the poem will easily pick out the modulations of the theme through the rest of the poem: the rhyme words *man* and *ban,* the emphatic syllable of *manacles,* the *black'*ning Church, the *hap*less sigh, the *Pa*lace *walls . . . Harlot, Blasts,* and *Mar*riage. But what is the meaning of this phonetic pattern? A certain meaning, not in the sense necessarily of what Blake fully intended or would have confessed or defined if we had asked him, but in the sense of something which is actually conveyed if we will let it be conveyed, has been pretty much implied in the very description of the pattern. According to our temperaments and our experiences, and as our imagination is more auditory, eidetic, or kinesthetic, we will realize the force of this phonetic marking in images of insistently wandering, tramping feet, in a savage motion of the arms and head, in a bitter chanting, a dark repetition of indictments. Any one of these images, as I attempt to verbalize it, is perhaps excessive; no one is specifically necessary. But all of these and others are relevant.

We have said that the word *chartered* when applied to the street and even more when applied to the river is an anomaly. A close inspection of this poem will reveal a good many curiosities in its diction. Notice, for example, the word *cry,* which occurs three times in the course of stanzas two and three. Why do men cry in the streets of London? In addition to various random cries of confusion, hurry, and violence (which we are surely entitled to include in the meaning of the word), there is the more special and more continuous London street *cry,* the "proclamation," as the Dictionary has it, of wares or of services. If we had plenty of time for history we could read Addison's *Spectator* on "Street Cries." A more immediately critical interest is served when we notice that the steadily clamorous background of the London scene of charter and barter merges by a kind of metaphoric glide, in the next two lines, into a medley of other vocal sounds, "cries," in another sense, of fear, "voices," "bans"—that is to say, legal or official yells, proclamations, summonses, prohibitions, curses. Are the kinds of cries really separate, or are all much the same? In the next line the infant cry of fear merges literally with the cry of service—"sweep, sweep," or "weep, weep," as we learn the pronunciation from Blake's two "Chimney Sweeper" songs. The whole poem proceeds not only by pregnant repetitions but by a series of extraordinary conjunctions and compressions, by a pervasive emergence of metaphoric intimation from the literal details of the Hogarthian scene. Consider, for instance, how to *appall* is to dismay or terrify, and etymologically perhaps to make *pale*. Doubtless the syntax says here in the first place that the unconsciously accusing cry of the infant sweep strikes dismay, even a kind of pallor, into these irrelevant, mouldering, and darkening fabrics. At the same time the syntax does not forbid a hint of the complementary sense that the walls throw back the infant cry in ineffectual and appalled echoes. The strange assault of pitiful sounds upon the very color of the walls, which is managed in these first two lines by verbal intimation, erupts in the next two beyond verbalism into the bold, surrealistically asserted vision of the *sigh* which attaches itself as blood to palace walls.

> But most thro' midnight streets I hear
> How the youthful Harlot's curse
> Blasts the new born Infant's tear,
> And blights with plagues the Marriage hearse.

The devotee of Blake may, by consulting the Rossetti manuscript, discover that the poet took extraordinary pains with this last stanza of the poem (which was an afterthought): he wrote it and rewrote it, deleting words and squeezing alternatives onto his already used-up page. Clearly he intended that a lot of meaning should inhere in this densely contrived stanza—the climax, the *most* appalling instance, of the assault of the city sounds upon the citadels, the institutions, the persons of the chartered privilege. The new role of the infant in this stanza, lying between the harlot and the major target of her curse, and the impatient energy, the crowding of sense, from the harlot and her curse, through the blight, the plague, to the ghastly paradox of that final union of words—the marriage hearse—perhaps we had better leave this to a paper by our students rather than attempt to exhaust the meaning in class.

I have perhaps already said too much about this one short poem. Yet I have certainly not said all that might be said. Relentless criticism of a poem, the technique of the lemon squeezer, is not to my mind an ideal pedagogic procedure. It is not even a possibility. A descriptive explication of a poem is both more and less than a multiple and exhaustive précis. Our aim I think should be to say certain selected, intelligible things about a poem, enough to establish the main lines of its technical achievement, of its symbolic shape. When we have done that much, we understand the poem—even if there are grace notes and overtones which have escaped our conscious notice.

VIII

Let me back off then from the poem by William Blake and return once more, briefly, to my main argument. *Explanation, description,* and *explication:* we can recognize three phases of our interpretation of the poem, though they prove to be more closely entangled and merged with one another than we might have realized at the beginning. But are they all? Is there not another activity which has been going on in our minds, almost inevitably, all this while? The activity of *appreciation.* All this time, while reading the poem so carefully, have we not also been liking it or disliking it? Admiring it or despising it? Presumably we have. And presumably we ought now to ask ourselves this further question: Is there any connection between the things we have managed so far to say about the poem and the kind of response we experience toward it? Our liking it or our disliking it? Are we inclined to try to explain why we like the poem? Do we know how to do this? More precisely: Would a statement of our liking for the poem, an act of praise or appreciation, be something different from (even though perhaps dependent upon) the things we have already been saying? Or has the appreciation already been sufficiently implied or entailed by what we have been saying?

At the first level, that of simple dictionary *explanation,* very little, we will probably say, has been implied. And very little, we will most likely say, in many of our motions at the second level, the simply *descriptive.* It is not a merit in a poem, or surely not much of a merit, that it should contain any given vocabulary, say of striking or unusual words, or even that it should have metaphors, or that it should have meter or any certain kind of meter, or rhymes, as any of these entities may be purely conceived.

But that—as we have been seeing—is to put these matters of simple *explanation* and simple *description* more simply and more abstractly than they are really susceptible of being put. We pass imperceptibly and quickly beyond these matters. We are inevitably and soon caught up in the demands of *explication—*

the realization of the vastly more rich and interesting implicit kinds of meaning. We are engaged with features of a poem which —given always other features too of the whole context—do tend to assert themselves as reasons for our pleasure in the poem and our admiration for it. We begin to talk about patterns of meaning; we encounter structures or forms which are radiant or resonant with meaning. Patterns and structures involve coherence (unity, coherence, and emphasis), and coherence is an aspect of truth and significance. I do not think that our evaluative intimations will often, if ever, advance to the firmness and completeness of a demonstration. Perhaps it is hardly conceivable that they should. But our discourse upon the poem will almost inevitably be charged with implications of its value. It will be more difficult to keep out these intimations than to let them in. Critics who have announced the most resolute programs of neutrality have found this out. Take care of the weight, the color, the shape of the poem, be fair to the explanation and description, the indisputable parts of the formal explication—the appreciation will be there, and it will be difficult to avoid having expressed it.

Explicatory criticism (or explicatory evaluation) is an account of a poem which exhibits the relation between its form and its meaning. Only poems which are worth something are susceptible of this kind of account. It is something like a definition of poetry to say that whereas rhetoric—in the sense of mere persuasion or sophistic—is a kind of discourse the power of which diminishes in proportion as the artifice of it is understood or seen through— poetry, on the other hand, is a kind of discourse the power of which—or the satisfaction which we derive from it—is actually increased by an increase in our understanding of the artifice. In poetry the artifice is art. This comes close I think to the center of the esthetic fact.

IX

One of the attempts at a standard of poetic value most often reiterated in past ages has been the doctrinal—the explicitly didactic. The aim of poetry, says the ancient Roman poet, is double, both to give pleasure and to teach some useful doctrine. You might get by with only one or the other, but it is much sounder to do both. Or, the aim of poetry is to teach some doctrine—and to do this convincingly and persuasively, by *means* of vividness and pleasure—as in effect the Elizabethan courtier and the eighteenth-century essayist would say. But in what does the pleasure consist? Why is the discourse pleasurable? Well, the aim of poetry is really to please us by means of or through the act of teaching us. The pleasure is a dramatized *moral* pleasure. Thus in effect some theories of drama in France during the seventeenth century. Or, the pleasure of poetry is a pleasure simply of tender and morally good feelings. Thus in effect the philosophers of the age of reason in England and France. And at length the date 1790 and Immanuel Kant's *Critique of Judgment:* which asserts that the end or effect of art is not teaching certainly, and not pleasure in anything like a simple sensuous way—rather it is something apart, a feeling, but precisely its own kind of feeling, the esthetic. Art is autonomous—though related symbolically to the realm of moral values. Speaking from this nondidactic point of view, a critic ought to say, I should think, that the esthetic merit of Blake's *London* does not come about because of the fact that London in that age witnessed evils which cried to Heaven for remedy, or because Blake was a Prophet Against Empire, or a Visionary Politician, or because at some time, perhaps a few years after he had written the poem, he may have come to view it as one article or moment in the development of an esoteric philosophy of imagination, a fearful symmetry of vision, expanded gradually in allegorical glimpses during several phases of his life, into a quasi-religious revelation or privilege which in some sense, at moments, he believed in. Blake's "London" is an achievement in words, a contained expression, a victory which resulted from some hours, or days, of artistic struggle, recorded by his pen on a page of the Rossetti manuscript.

Between the time of Immanuel Kant, however, and our own, some complications in the purity of the esthetic view have developed. Through the romantic period and after, the poetic mind advanced pretty steadily in its own autonomous way, toward a claim to be in itself the creator of higher values—to be perhaps the only creator. Today there is nothing that the literary theorist —at least in the British- and American-speaking world—will be more eager to repudiate than any hint of moral or religious didacticism, any least intimation that the poem is to measure its meaning or get its sanction from any kind of authority more abstract or more overtly legislative than itself. But on the other hand there has probably never been a generation of teachers of literature less willing to admit any lack of high seriousness, of implicit and embodied ethical content, even of normative vision in the object of their study. Despite our reiterated denials of didacticism, we live in an age, we help to make an age, of momentous claims for poetry—claims the most momentous conceivable, as they advance more and more under the sanction of an absolutely creative and autonomous visionary imagination. The visionary imagination perforce repudiates all but the tautological commitment to itself. And thus, especially when it assumes (as now it begins to do) the form of what is called the "tragic vision" (not "the vision of tragedy"), it is the newest version of the *everlasting no*. Vision *per se* is the vision of itself. "Tragic vision" is the nearly identical vision of "absurdity." (War-weariness and war-horror, the developing mind and studies of a generation that came out of the Second World War and has been living in expectation of the third may go far to explain the phenomenon, but will not justify it.) Antidoctrine is of course no less a didactic energy than doctrine itself. It is the reverse of doctrine. No more than doctrine itself can it be located or even approached by a discussion of the relation between poetic form and poetic meaning. Antidoctrine is actually asserted by the poems of several English romantic poets, and notably, it would appear, though it is difficult to be sure, by the "prophecies" of William Blake. The idea of it may be hence a part of these poems, though never their achieved result or expression. Any more than an acceptable statement of Christian doctrine is Milton's achieved expression in *Paradise Lost,* or a statement of Aristotelian ethics is the real business of Spenser's *Faerie Queene.* Today I believe no prizes are being given for even the best doctrinal interpretation of poems. (The homiletic or parabolic interpretation of Shakespeare, for example, has hard going with the reviewer.) On the other hand, if you are willing to take a hand in the exploitation of the neuroses, the misgivings, the anxieties, the infidelities of the age—if you have talents for the attitudes of Titanism, the graces needed by an impresario of the nuptials of Heaven and Hell, you are likely to find yourself in some sense rewarded. It is obvious I hope that I myself do not believe the reward will consist in the achievement of a valid account of the relation between poetic form and poetic meaning.

LANGUAGE
AND THE
POEM

MARIE BORROFF
Yale University

My essay is prompted by the following question: How is it possible to talk about the language of the poem, isolating it as a part within the whole and going on to describe its contribution to the whole? The problem is anything but simple, for there is a sense in which the language of the poem *is* the poem. All the power of the poem, all it expresses, everything we know about it, comes from the language, just as everything we know about a painting comes from the paint. Take away the paint and the frame is empty; take away the language and there is nothing on the page.

To continue the analogy to painting, I suggest that we begin by setting up a small gallery of poems or passages, choosing poems in which perceptibly, even startlingly, different effects are produced by what I shall call their language, without as yet having given that term a definition. Among poems of the twentieth century on the ancient and wordy theme of love, none can match the simplicity of Yeats's "A Drinking Song":

> Wine comes in at the mouth
> And love comes in at the eye;
> That's all we shall know for truth
> Before we grow old and die.
> I lift the glass to my mouth,
> I look at you, and I sigh.[1]

---

1 Reprinted with the permission of Mrs. W. B. Yeats and The Macmillan Company from *Collected Poems* by W. B. Yeats. Copyright 1912 by The Macmillan Company. Renewed 1940 by Bertha Georgie Yeats. All subsequent quotations by W. B. Yeats in this paper are from this edition.

At the opposite extreme, there is John Crowe Ransom's "The Equilibrists," which brilliantly portrays the struggle between illicit passion and honor. At the end of Ransom's poem, the speaker imagines the alternatives for the lovers after death: a heaven without passion, a hell without honor. He then proceeds to entomb them and write their epitaph:

> In Heaven you have heard no marriage is,
> No white flesh tinder to your lecheries,
> Your male and female tissue sweetly shaped.
> Sublimed away, and furious blood escaped.
>
> Great lovers lie in Hell, the stubborn ones
> Infatuate of the flesh upon the bones;
> Stuprate, they rend each other when they kiss,
> The pieces kiss again, no end to this.
>
> But still I watched them spinning, orbited nice.
> Their flames were not more radiant than their ice.
> I dug in the quiet earth and wrought the tomb
> And made these lines to memorize their doom:—
>
> *Epitaph*
>
> *Equilibrists lie here; stranger, tread light;*
> *Close, but untouching in each other's sight;*
> *Mouldered the lips and ashy the tall skull.*
> *Let them lie perilous and beautiful.*[2]

Different from both Ransom's poem and Yeats's is a haunting lyric of W. H. Auden's which deserves to be better known. It is sung, to a tune entitled "The Case Is Closed" played on a jukebox in a bar, by Rosetta in *The Age of Anxiety,* Auden's narrative poem in alliterative verse. Rosetta's song begins:

> Deep in my dark the dream shines
> Yes, of you, you dear always;
> My cause to cry, cold but my
> Story still, still my music,

and it ends:

---

2 Reprinted with the permission of the publisher from *Selected Poems*, Rev. Ed., by John Crowe Ransom (New York: Alfred A. Knopf, Inc., 1945). All subsequent quotations from John Crowe Ransom in this paper are from this edition.

> You touched, you took. Tears fall. O
> Fair my far, when far ago
> Like waterwheels wishes spun
> Radiant robes: but the robes tore.[3]

And finally, there is George Starbuck, who won the Yale Series of Younger Poets prize in 1960. One of Starbuck's poems about love ends with these lines:

> Lady, in a word,
> this fabled headlong bird
> Love is a strange coot.[4]

But I like even better his sonnet, "On First Looking In on Blodgett's *Keats's 'Chapman's Homer'* (Sum ½C. M9–11)." Here the setting is a beach on the Pacific Ocean. The poem begins:

> Mellifluous as bees, these brittle men
> droning of Honeyed Homer give me hives.
> I scratch, yawn like a bear, my arm arrives
> at yours—oh, Honey, and we're back again,
> me the Balboa, you the Darien,
> lording the loud Pacific sands, our lives
> as hazarded as when a petrel dives
> to yank the dull sea's coverlet . . . .

Here, surely, is material enough for our purpose. Let me raise again, applying it to these examples, the question with which I began: How can we talk about language in isolation as a part of the poem? One way, certainly, would be to find descriptive categories and terms that apply to language as language, based on facts about words that are subject to verification rather than impressions from which there is no appeal to facts. All those who have taught poetry are familiar with the impressionistic pitfalls into which students leap, and from which it is often virtually impossible to pull them out. If we ask for a description of the words in Rosetta's song, for instance, we will probably be

---

3 Reprinted with the permission of Random House and Faber & Faber, Ltd., London, from *The Age of Anxiety* by W. H. Auden (New York: Random House, Inc., 1947). All subsequent quotations from W. H. Auden in this paper are from this edition.

4 Reprinted with the permission of the publisher from *Bone Thoughts* by George Starbuck (New Haven, Conn.: Yale University Press, 1960). All subsequent quotations from George Starbuck in this paper are from this edition.

told that the words are sad. If we ask what it is about the words that is sad, we are all too likely to hear that in such a line as "Deep in my dark the dream shines," the consonant *d*, which is a heavy, sad sound, is repeated in *deep, dark,* and *dream.* Or, the explanation may be that the poet uses "sad words," such as *dark, cry, cold,* and *tears.*

What we should like the student to do in such a case is to start with an effect—a feeling of sadness that he gets from the words of the poem—and to try to locate the causes of this effect. He tells us that cause A—the sound of a certain letter, or the presence of certain words—is, in and of itself, sufficient to produce or enhance effect B—a feeling of sadness—regardless of other conditions prevailing. The only way I know to refute such errors convincingly is to produce a sample of A that obviously does not cause B. For instance, when I am told that alliteration in poetry makes the words move slowly, I always recite "Peter Piper picked a peck of pickled peppers; a peck of pickled peppers Peter Piper picked." In discussing Rosetta's song, one might make up a line like "Dance with me, darling, dip and sway," which has as many d's as "Deep in my dark the dream shines," but is not sad. Or, one might point out that the words *dark, cry, cold,* and *tears* are not sad in *darkroom, cry-baby, cold cuts,* and *tears of joy.* Or, one might discover examples in the same stanzas of "happy" words which ought to cancel out the sad ones, specifically *shines, yes, dear, fair, waterwheels,* and *radiant.*

What the student has done, of course, is what I am trying to find an alternative for: he has identified the poem with its language. If he continues to think about the problem, he will hopefully come to see that what is sad cannot be Rosetta's words; it can only be Rosetta herself. Words are neither sad nor glad: who has ever seen a word laugh or cry? Terms describing emotions do not fit the specification I made above because they do not apply to language as language. There are in fact no words whose emotional force is constant, which cannot arouse different, indeed opposite, responses in different contexts of use. What word, offhand, could seem more agonizing than *agony?* But in Starbuck's sonnet, the lover on the beach speaks of "the sand that's rink / And record of our weekend boning up / On *The Romantic Agony*"—referring to the well-known book by Mario Praz in which Professor Blodgett has presumably made an assignment.

We smile at this kind of agony. And then there is the "agony" of the long moment preceding—an enormous sneeze. *Desolate* may seem inevitably to express a profound sadness, but what of such a remark as "I'm desolate—the decorator can't get any more of that lovely slipcover fabric." And quite apart from all these examples, there is irony, in which meaning becomes its opposite. One says, to a friend who has just told us about his latest piece of bad luck, "Oh, *fine*—that's just *delightful*," or, on an opposite occasion, "That's really *sad*—I weep for you."

How, then, can the effect of the language be isolated from the effect of the poem? There is a simple method of accomplishing this, though it has limitations I shall come to later. Take the words from a given passage and list them in alphabetical order, drawing an equal number of words from each of the poems to be studied. The list need not include every word in the passage; it will save time to omit such colorless words as the definite article *the,* the indefinite article *a* or *an,* the demonstratives *this* and *that, these* and *those,* the prepositions, the conjunctions, the personal pronouns and possessives, and so on. All poets have to use these words, so that comparing them does not reveal differences in their choice of language. What remain to be listed are the nouns, verbs, descriptive adjectives and adverbs—the "optional" words for which the language usually provides the poet with alternatives. Ransom could have said *dangerous* instead of *perilous;* Yeats could have said *enters* instead of *comes in;* Auden could have said *garments* instead of *robes;* Starbuck could have said *fragile* instead of *brittle.*

If we compare a list of words drawn from Ransom's poem with a list of equal length from Auden's poem, we will find that many of the words Ransom uses resemble those Auden uses: Ransom's *again, away, blood, bones, dug, each, earth, end, great,* and *heard* resemble Auden's *ago, alone, always, ball, believed, black, blossom, cause, cold,* and *cry.* What is the resemblance? All these words are "simple"; almost all of them are literally "words of one syllable." To say this is to describe language as language—in this sense, *sad* and *glad, cold* and *hot, laugh* and *cry* are alike as words although they express opposite meanings. But though there is a good deal of overlap in the two lists, there are also words in Ransom's list which differ from those in Auden's list, specifically *infatuate, lecheries, orbited, rend, sublimed, tis-*

sue, wrought, and especially *stuprate.* The only comparable word
in Auden's poem is *radiant,* which, as it happens, is also used by
Ransom. How do *infatuate, sublimed,* and *stuprate* differ from
again, ago, alone, and so on? They are "difficult" words, or we
could call them "learned" words; most of them have two or
more syllables and one, *infatuate,* has four. In this sense, *sad* and
lachrymose, cold and *gelid, laughter* and *cachinnation* are different as words though they express similar meanings. (Looking
parenthetically at Yeats's "Drinking Song," I might point out
that it is entirely composed of words of one syllable, the total
list being *all, comes, die, eye, glass, grow, in, know, lift, look,
love, mouth, old, sigh, truth,* and *wine.*)

When we call a word like *cold* simple and a word like *gelid*
difficult or learned, we are of course basing our judgments on
impressions. But our impressions here presuppose facts which
may not have been verified but presumably could be. These facts
can best be explained comparatively. A word like *cold* is simple
in comparison to a word like *gelid* because it is known to, and
used by, a far greater number of people. This in turn is because
it is learned at an early stage of education which is reached by a
large proportion of adults, whereas *gelid* is learned at a late stage
which is reached by a comparatively small group. A student's
impression of simplicity and difficulty in individual words is
likely to be valid because he will have known the simple words
for some time but will have made the acquaintance of the difficult
words recently or perhaps not at all.

Another way of expressing the difference between simple and
difficult or learned words in factual terms is to say that simple
words are used more often than difficult words. If we could count
up, day by day, the number of times the words *cold* and *gelid* are
used, counting both speaking and writing as "uses," the total of
occurrences for *gelid* would clearly be smaller than that for *cold.*
This is partly because fewer people know the word *gelid* But it
is also because *gelid* is more restricted than *cold* as to the kind of
context in which it appears. I said that uses in writing were to be
counted, together with uses in speech, to make up the total. If it
were possible to examine all the occasions on, say, April 4, 1963,
on which the word *gelid* was used, it would turn out that most of
them belonged to the written language. Even those speakers who
know the word do not generally use it in conversation; one would

not say "It's gelid out this morning" or "The radio says we can expect some gelid weather for the next few days." Difficult or learned words may be called literary words, since we use them primarily as writers, and encounter them primarily in our reading.

Ransom's poem makes use of literary words and Auden's, with perhaps the one exception of *radiant,* does not. Within the group of literary words I identified in "The Equilibrists," there is a subgroup which calls for a special description. It is exemplified by *rend* in "They rend each other as they kiss" and *wrought* in "I dug in the quiet earth and wrought the tomb." These words resemble *gelid* in that we are not likely to use or hear them in conversation. But we are not likely to use or encounter them in all kinds of writing, either. In an article about the American automobile industry for *U. S. News and World Report,* I might say that a certain number of passenger cars were *manufactured* in 1963, or were *made* in 1963, but I would not say that a certain number of passenger cars were *wrought* in 1963. In writing an advertisement for a particular fabric, I might say that it does not *tear* easily, but I would not say that it does not *rend* easily. In these contexts *wrought* and *rend* sound slightly ludicrous, out of place. This is because they are associated primarily with literary works of the past—poetry, Shakespeare, the Bible—which are regarded with reverence. Such words are used today chiefly in writings where the effect aimed at is one of solemnity and elevation, or where the past is in some way to be alluded to, or its aura evoked, in the present. Because they essentially belong to the past, these words may be called literary archaisms. They constitute a special group within the more general group of literary words.

So far, I have been talking about simple words and literary words, including literary archaisms. By a literary word I mean one that appears chiefly in written contexts such as an article, a poem, this lecture. As the word list taken from Ransom's poem demonstrates, it takes only a sprinkling of literary words to give a distinctly literary flavor to a passage. In "Great lovers lie in Hell, the stubborn ones / Infatuate of the flesh upon the bones," the one word *infatuate* colors the style of the whole couplet.

A comparison of a list of words from Auden's poem with one from Starbuck's shows that Starbuck uses more literary words than Auden. Examples are *hazarded, mellifluous,* and *romantic,* mixed in with such simple words as *again, arm, back, bear, bees,* and *honey.* But there is one word on the list that does not belong to either of the groups I have described so far. This word is *yank,* in "a petrel dives / To yank the dull sea's coverlet." It means "to pull sharply," and it is certainly not a literary word—it is known to speakers having little education. But it is a different sort of word from *pull,* as can be demonstrated by trying it out in an elevated literary context. Compare "Then mighty Agamemnon laid hold of the spear and pulled it sharply from the lifeless body of Adrestes" with "Then mighty Agamemnon laid hold of the spear and yanked it from the lifeless body of Adrestes." A student sensitive to the uses of language will see that *yank* sounds a bit ludicrous in this context just as *wrought* sounds ludicrous in "So-and-so many cars were wrought in Detroit in 1963," but for the opposite reason. Literary words like *gelid* and literary archaisms like *wrought* are more at home in writing than in everyday speech, but a word like *yank* is more at home in speech than in writing. The difference between *pull* and *yank* is of the same sort as the difference between *sad* and *blue,* or *very much pleased* and *tickled pink.* In saying that *yank, blue,* and *tickled pink* are not at home in written contexts, I must of course make an exception of writing that imitates speech, as in the dialogue of short stories and novels, or in poems whose speaker seems to be talking directly to us rather than declaiming or loftily meditating. Robert Frost uses *blue* instead of *sad,* and other similar words, in his description of the bluebird in "Two Tramps in Mud-Time":

> It is snowing a flake: and he half knew
> Winter was only playing possum.
> Except in color he isn't blue,
> But he wouldn't advise a thing to blossom.[5]

Words that have the flavor of talk about them are distinctively colloquial words. Perhaps you feel that a student's judgment will not be as reliable in identifying the distinctively colloquial words as it is in identifying the literary words. Fortunately, the diction-

---

5 From *Complete Poems of Robert Frost.* Copyright 1936 by Robert Frost. Copyright renewed © 1964 by Lesley Frost Ballantine. Reprinted with the permission of Holt, Rinehart and Winston, Inc.

ary is of some help in labeling certain words *colloquial* (one can only pray that when a new collegiate dictionary is based on the unabridged Webster's Third, such labels will not be discarded). It also happens that a distinctively colloquial word will in general have fewer meanings than its noncolloquial synonym, so that a comparison of number of definitions given can help in verifying one's impression. *Pull,* for instance, has sixteen meanings in all in the present Webster's Collegiate, whereas *yank,* which is labeled *colloquial,* has only one.

Words that are neither distinctively literary nor distinctively colloquial are called common, so that we have now arrived at a threefold classification, with literary archaisms as a special subgroup. The common words are common in two senses. First, they are used more often—more commonly—than either the literary words or the colloquial ones. And this is because, second, they are common to language of all levels, from casual speech to a polished essay. The criterion of number of definitions works two ways: a large number of definitions is a *sign* that a word is common, and it is also a *result:* the more a given word is used, over a wide range of contexts, the more meanings it tends to acquire.

I have suggested a procedure whereby words are lifted out of the context of the poem in which they appear, arranged artificially, and examined, with a view to discovering whether an author uses simple words only, or mixes in a certain proportion of literary or colloquial words or both. It is a sensible procedure as far as it goes, but it is based on the assumption that we can tell whether a word is literary, common, or colloquial by looking at it. Unfortunately, this is not true. Consider the word *honey,* which appears on Starbuck's list along with *again, arm, back, bear, bees,* and so on. It looks like a common word, neither literary nor colloquial. But suppose we put it back into its context: "I yawn, scratch like a bear, my arm arrives / At yours—oh, Honey, and we're back again." *Honey* may be a common word, suitable equally for use in literature and in conversation, when we speak of a product or a substance sweet to the taste, but when used as a term of endearment in direct address, it is colloquial. It thus should be added to *yank* as another example of the mixture of colloquial with common and literary words characteristic of Starbuck's poem.

On the opposite side, consider the word *nice,* which occurs on Ransom's list. In such a sentence as "He was always nice to his associates," it seems to be a common word; in "This is a nice mess!" it seems to be colloquial. But what the speaker of Ransom's poem says is this: "And so I watched them spinning, orbited nice." Here we must send our students, and possibly go ourselves, to the dictionary to discover the exact meaning of the word. This meaning, as given in Webster's Collegiate Dictionary, is "Susceptible to fine distinctions . . . hence, of instruments, methods, etc., minutely accurate." In this meaning, *nice* is no common word; it should thus be added to *infatuate, orbited, stuprate,* and so on, as another example of the admixture of literary words characteristic of Ransom's poem. And so also with *fair,* in Rosetta's song. Rosetta calls her lover "O / Fair my far"; the meaning of the word here must be "pleasing to the sight." But if in conversation someone were to ask whether we thought Miss Smith was fair, we would assume he wanted to know whether she was just or impartial. *Fair,* in the meaning "pleasing to sight, beautiful," has strong associations with the literature of the past —one thinks of "fair damsels" and lines of poetry like "Fair is my love, and cruel as she is fair." In this meaning, then, *fair* is a literary archaism, and Auden's use of it in this meaning adds an element to his language which has not been noted previously.

I have led myself into a paradox. My purpose was to isolate the language from the poem and describe it as language: to consider the building materials apart from the building. In order to do this, I removed the words of the poem from their contexts and set up categories into which they could be classified. But it has now become apparent that the building materials cannot be fully identified apart from their use in the building. They can be identified in part: *mellifluous,* for instance, is a literary word no matter in what meaning it is used. But in many cases the kind of word cannot be known unless the meaning is known, and the meaning can be known only from the context. Does it follow that the method of listing words out of context is of little or no value? Not at all. A poet's use of long and obviously literary words is an important part of his style, one which ought to be considered, and similarly with his use only of simple-looking monosyllables. But the study of words out of context should be

supplemented by noting meanings where these have an effect on
stylistic value. And it is, in any case, only a first step, a step in the
direction of the poem as a whole.

If we cannot fully know the qualities of the individual words
apart from the poem, we can know still less about the qualities
of the words in sequence. Here is the first part of a word list
compiled from a poem built entirely of simple, common words:
*any, anyone, autumn, all, bells, bird, both, cared, children,
cryings, danced, did, down.* Here are the first three stanzas of the
poem, which is by e. e. cummings:

> Anyone lived in a pretty how town
> (with up so floating many bells down)
> spring summer autumn winter
> he sang his didn't he danced his did.
>
> Women and men (both little and small)
> cared for anyone not at all
> they sowed their isn't they reaped their same
> sun moon stars rain
>
> children guessed (but only a few
> and down they forgot as up they grew
> autumn winter spring summer)
> that noone loved him more by more[6]

The verbal difficulties here are acute. (I remember being asked
once in a seminar whether cummings meant by "a pretty how
town" that the town was both pretty and how, or that it was
only *pretty* how, not *very* how.) Part of the trouble, obviously,
is that the words of the poem are frequently transformed from
their normal parts of speech into different ones—"they sowed
their isn't they reaped their same"—and that syntax and sentence structure are scrambled or nonexistent—"(with up so floating many bells down) / spring summer autumn winter." I have
neither the temerity nor the time to attempt to explain the
meaning of anyone's love affair with noone, or to trace the
stages of its story. I simply wish to make the point that if one

---

6 From *Fifty Poems* by e. e. cummings (New York: Duell, Sloan & Pearce, Inc.,
1940). Reprinted with the permission of the publisher.

were to discuss the language of a poem fully, one would have to talk not only about individual words but also about syntax, word order, and sentence structure. Though I can do no more than mention these other aspects of language—not to speak of meter and sound—on this occasion, I am aware that they exist and are important.

Everything I have said so far is summed up in the statement that the expressive powers of language cannot be predicted from words out of their contexts. They must be studied in the poem. I want now to examine in some detail a passage from each of the four poems I have taken as my major examples.

This problem too can be considered fruitfully in terms of causes and effects. Suppose we begin by assuming that the language of a poem, or of several lines of that poem, has power. This power is obviously not in any individual word but in a certain combination of words. The poet has the ability to put words together in such a way that they rouse our interest and stir our emotions. His words are striking and stirring, and so they tend to linger on in our minds—it was not for nothing that the ancient Greeks called the Muses the daughters of Memory. Our ordinary language does not have—or at least rarely has—these qualities. One way, then, of getting at the sources of the expressive power of a poetic passage would be to translate it into ordinary language, language such as you and I, who are not poets, would use to say somewhat the same thing. The same technique can be applied more narrowly: take any word in a passage that seems particularly striking or memorable and try substituting for it other words of similar meaning. In either case, compare the result with the words the poet himself used.

Rosetta's song begins, "Deep in my dark the dream shines / Yes, of you, you dear always." In ordinary speech, this might be "I dream of you all the time," or, as the popular song has it, "All I do the whole day through is dream of you." In the first phrase, the word *dark* stands out. I would not say "deep in my dark"; I would say either "deep in my *heart*," or "in *the* dark." But Rosetta's dark is not *the* dark—the literal absence of light—nor in fact is it anything that can be found in the dictionary. The noun *dark* is defined in Webster's Collegiate only as "nightfall," "dark color," and "the condition of being secret or obscure." Yet the reader knows immediately what Rosetta's dark is. He transfers to the noun the meaning of the adjective *dark* in such familiar expressions as "the future is dark." And this interpretation is unconsciously reinforced by such familiar expressions as "The bad news cast a shadow over the group" or "things look pretty black." The adjectives *dark, sombre,* and *gloomy* are all defined in the dictionary in terms both of color or light and of emotion. Rosetta's next phrase, "the dream shines," is similarly easy to interpret, though again the relevant definition of *shines* is not in the dictionary. We speak of a face as "shining with joy," of "the one bright spot in the situation," of "a sunny smile." And the same thing happens when we hear Rosetta call her lover her "story" and her "music." Of an event having a pattern that seems to dominate our experience we say "that's the story of my life"; news that brings us happiness is "music to our ears."

When words are made to take on meanings which cannot be found in the dictionary they become metaphors. But metaphors that are used often enough become established in the language, and once they are established, the dictionaries will include them. When Rosetta calls her lover "cold," she is using the word in a long-established metaphorical meaning, "lacking emotion," found in Webster's Collegiate. We use words all the time in metaphorical meanings so old that we have forgotten they are metaphorical. *Deep,* in "deep in my heart," is a metaphor, like *high* in "high in my estimation," or *low* in "a low rating," or *tall* in "a tall order." Perhaps you would like to have metaphors that are not in the dictionary distinguished from those that are, calling the former "original" or "true" metaphor and the latter "dead" metaphors. But this distinction, as you recognize, is not always easy to make. It is not a matter of black and white—if I may use yet another metaphor—but a matter of degree.

It is now possible to say a little more about Rosetta's language. Her words in themselves are simple; as she uses them, they are frequently metaphorical. Some of her metaphors are dead metaphors, like *cold* for "lacking emotion." But even her true metaphors—those that cannot be found in the dictionary—are obvious ones, having close affiliations with the language of everyday speech and such unliterary forms of poetry as the popular song. This is because they express simple resemblances between states of mind and physical conditions or sensations which tend to be universally felt. *Profundus,* in Latin, and *tief,* in German, have the same metaphorical meaning with reference to emotions that *deep* has in English; *frigidus* in Latin and *kalt* in German have the same metaphorical meaning as *cold* in English, and *tenebrae* in Latin and *Finsternis* in German have the same metaphorical meaning as Rosetta's *dark*. Such metaphors as these are quite different from the obscure and complicated metaphors modern poets often use. Dylan Thomas calls a plant stem a "fuse" in his line "The force that through the green fuse drives the flower." Sylvia Plath says of the wind blowing from the sea that it "flaps its phantom laundry in my face." There is little likelihood that *fuse* will become a common expression for stem, or "flapping of phantom laundry" for sea breeze.

Rosetta uses simple language which includes a number of simple and universal metaphors. You may ask, if her metaphorical language is so closely related to the language of everyday speech how then does it exhibit the poet's extraordinary power over language—why is it more memorable and stirring than the things we ourselves would say? The answer lies partly in the concentration of metaphors in a line like "Deep in my dark the dream shines." Any of us, in ordinary speech, might use a darkness metaphor and a brightness metaphor, but we would be unlikely to use both within a compass of seven words. In addition, the two metaphors are related in such a way that each reinforces the other, and their relationship of fruitful opposition is further reinforced by later images in the poem. We in ordinary speech tend to combine metaphors that are unrelated, or even to mix them in some ludicrous way, as in saying "he brightened up and pulled himself together," or "when I finally saw the light, the situation looked pretty black."

This description of what Rosetta's language is makes it possible to say what Yeats's language, in "A Drinking Song," is not. The language of that poem is almost entirely devoid of metaphors. The only example is "Love comes in at the eye": what literally comes in is the set of visual sensations making up the image of the woman. The rest of the poem is composed entirely of literal, as well as simple, language:

> That's all we shall know for truth
> Before we grow old and die.
> I lift the glass to my mouth,
> I look at you, and I sigh.

Another kind of contrast with the language of Rosetta's song is to be found in George Starbuck's sonnet. Let me remind you of the title—"On First Looking In on Blodgett's *Keats's 'Chapman's Homer'* (Sum. ½C. M9–11)"—and of the opening lines:

> Mellifluous as bees, these brittle men
> droning of Honeyed Homer give me hives.
> I scratch, yawn like a bear, my arm arrives
> at yours—oh, Honey, and we're back again, . . .

A passage like this is ideal for teaching purposes. It suggests an obvious program of homework: check on the definitions *and* the etymologies of all important words, watching particularly for connections among them. If he does this, the student should discover, first, that *mellifluous* literally means "flowing like honey," its first two syllables being derived from Latin *mel, mellis* 'honey.' It also has the metaphorical meaning "flowing smoothly" in application to the human voice. There is thus a connection between the honey in *mellifluous* and the bees of the simile, and a further connection with "Honeyed Homer" in the second line. The information on *droning* is similarly revealing. *Drone* is both a noun and a verb. The definition of the noun in Webster's Collegiate is "the male of bees, especially of the honeybee. It has no sting and gathers no honey." The definition of the verb is "To make a low, dull, monotonous, murmuring sound; hence, to speak monotonously." Here there is a relationship of opposition: men whose voices are said to be flowing with honey, like bees, are also said to resemble a kind of bee that does *not* gather honey.

According to the dictionary, there are two kinds of hives—beehives and eruptions on the skin. If the student perseveres and also looks up *urticaria,* the word used in the second definition, he will discover that hives involve itching, and sometimes result from eating shellfish or strawberries. This ought, at least nowadays, to suggest an allergy: it comes as no surprise that the next line of the poem begins "I scratch." The speaker is allergic to the "brittle men" who talk on monotonously in their books about Homer—Keats's Homer. His distaste and restlessness are expressed by a metaphor—"They give me hives"—which has affiliations with such common expressions as "itching to get away" and the vulgar term *antsy.* His description of the droning authors as "brittle men" implies, among other things, that their words are dry. *Mellifluous*—sweetly flowing—now appears clearly as ironic. The words of the "brittle men" do indeed flow, but so far as the speaker is concerned, they are anything but sweet.

The emphasis on bees, honey, and hives gives point to the speaker's description of himself as scratching and yawning "like a bear." The bear is a great honey-lover and raider of hives, and in this case his foraging is successful: "My arm arrives / at yours —oh, Honey, and we're back again."

This study leads to a more complete description of Starbuck's language. It is a language composed of several different sorts of words, including literary and colloquial words as well as common ones. But as he uses it, it is also a complicated language in which two or more meanings of a word are often significant at once. *Mellifluous,* as applied to the words of the "brittle men" whose books the speaker is studying on the beach, ostensibly means "sweetly flowing." We are also supposed to realize that it originally meant "flowing like honey." *Droning* means "speaking monotonously"; a drone is also a kind of bee, one disassociated from honey. Homer is metaphorically called "Honeyed Homer" because of the sweetness of his style; we are also supposed to associate the literal meaning of *honeyed* with both *mellifluous* and the bees that have previously been mentioned. To appreciate the connection between *mellifluous* and "Honeyed Homer" fully, we must also know—though we cannot find this out from the dictionary—that Homer himself was once called *Homerus mellifluus oris:* "Homer of the honey-flowing mouth." In addition, we must understand the two senses of *hive,* and we must know that bears like to rob hives of their honey. Our wits are taxed by the language, much as they are in riddling jokes. "When is a lover like a bear?" "When he reaches for his honey." "Why is a beekeeper like a man with an allergy?" "Because he has hives." Starbuck's plays on words in his sonnet resemble puns in that they require us to be conscious of more than one meaning at a time; his language may be called witty or playful. The wit is sometimes learned, as in the play on the original meaning of *mellifluous,* and sometimes fairly broad, as in the double sense of *hives*—in the latter, Starbuck may fairly be said to be clowning with language. The learned wit is in keeping with the learned words he uses, the broad wit with the colloquial words.

I have already pointed out that the language of Ransom's "The Equilibrists" includes both literary words and literary archaisms. One of Ransom's literary words, *stuprate*, is further removed from the level of learning of the ordinary man than any of the other literary words I have cited. In fact, it does not even exist in English as an adjective, though a verb *stuprate* occurs rarely. The adjective *stuprate* could have been coined only by a man familiar with the Latin language: it is taken over directly from Latin *stupratus*, debauched. Two important words in the last stanzas of the poem, in addition to *nice*, which I have already mentioned, have archaic literary meanings. *Memorize*, in "[I] made these lines to memorize their doom," means not "commit to memory," but "commemorate in writing." The Elizabethan poet Spenser, in "The Ruins of Time," urges mighty lords to cherish the poets, who may "their names forever memorize." And *tall*, in "the tall skull," is used by Shakespeare and other Elizabethan writers in meanings quite different from its most common meaning today, meanings such as "quick," "handsome," and "brave, good at fighting." Caesar, in *Antony and Cleopatra*, urges Pompey to put away his sword and return to Sicily with "much tall youth / That else must perish here." To find out exactly what Ransom means by calling the skulls of the dead lovers *tall*, it will be necessary to look at the adjective in the context of the concluding epitaph, and the epitaph in the context of the whole poem.

> *Equilibrists lie here; stranger, tread light;*
> *Close, but untouching in each other's sight;*
> *Mouldered the lips and ashy the tall skull.*
> *Let them lie perilous and beautiful.*

In all but the first of these lines, pairings of ideas occur: "close, but untouching"; "mouldered lips and ashy skull"; "perilous and beautiful." I have already quoted from the poem a similar pairing, the two four-line descriptions of love in heaven and love in hell. In heaven there is honor without passion; in hell, passion without honor. The two motives of passion and honor are not merely set in opposition to each other throughout the poem, they are precisely or "nicely" balanced, given scrupulously equal space by the speaker, line for line and stanza for stanza. *Lips* and *skulls* are elements of this pattern. In the opening of the poem, the lover is shown traveling far from his beloved haunted by mem-

ories of their passion and her dismissal of him, which was
prompted by honor:

> Mouth he remembered: the quaint orifice
> From which came heat that flamed upon the kiss,
> Till cold words came down spiral from the head.
> Grey doves from the officious tower illsped.

The kiss and the cold words are given a couplet apiece; one is
associated with the passionate mouth, the other with the head,
which is symbolically portrayed as a tower. This tower, in the
stanza that follows, is described as looming over the lily-white
"field" of the woman's body like a menacing fortress. In the
epitaph, then, the "mouldered lips" stand for the lovers' passion;
the "tall skull"—tall like a tower and tall in the warlike fierceness
with which it guards the body—stands for their sense of honor.

Balance is equilibrium, and Ransom's poem is called "The
Equilibrists." The lovers are equilibrists in that they are held in
an unchanging relationship by opposed and equally balanced
forces.

> At length I saw these lovers fully were come
> Into their torture of equilibrium;
> Dreadfully had forsworn each other, and yet
> They were bound each to each, and they did not forget.
>
> And rigid as two painful stars, and twirled
> About the clustered night their prison world,
> They burned with fierce love always to come near,
> But honor beat them back and kept them clear.

The very form of the poem—its four-line stanzas divided into
two couplets—expresses the exact balance which is its theme. The
speaker sees the two lovers, in a brilliant and difficult analogy, as
binary stars, those paired stars which circle endlessly around
each other in a dual orbit, the mutual attraction of their masses
exactly counter-balancing the onward momentum which would
send them veering out into space. It is this equilibrium, I think,
more than the lovers themselves, which the speaker sees as
"perilous and beautiful" at the end of the epitaph—an equilibrium both perilous and beautiful in the delicacy of the adjust-
ment of forces on which it depends. The passerby is warned to
"tread light" in order not to disturb it.

The language of "The Equilibrists" is the most difficult of the four poems. Not only are the words difficult in themselves, but simple-looking words turn out to have unfamiliar meanings, and choices among possible meanings depend on an interpretation of the theme of the poem, which is expressed in difficult metaphors and symbols. The theme is also expressed symbolically by the deliberate and consistent patterning of the poem's language. Throughout the poem we find paired words, phrases, lines, and stanzas of parallel form set side by side.

I have considered the words of the four poems, of passages from them, first in themselves, and then as they are used. In both kinds of analysis I have suggested certain classifications. Words may be literary, common, or colloquial, either in all uses or in a particular meaning. They may be used metaphorically or literally, and as metaphors they may be simple and universal or complicated and personal. They may be used simply, or wittily, in more than one meaning at once, and the resultant word play may be learned and subtle or obvious and broad. They may or may not be put into conspicuous patterns, such as pairs of parallel units. All these are possible characteristics of the language of a poem. By calling them characteristics I mean that they are consistently present. We should expect to find other simple metaphors in other lines of Rosetta's song, other witticisms in other lines of Starbuck's sonnet, other difficult words and meanings in other lines of Ransom's poem. These devices are characteristic—they are there. But we have yet to ask why they are there, what part they play in relation to each poem as a whole.

One answer to these questions can be ruled out immediately. The poems I have been discussing are all concerned with love, passionate love between men and women. The kind of language used cannot, therefore, be dictated by subject matter in any obvious sense. We cannot conclude that passionate love is best expressed in simple, literal language, or simple, metaphorical language, or witty language, or learned and complicated language. In fact there is no one kind of language that is best for poetry. Each of the kinds of language I have analyzed in the four poems seems right in the poem in which it appears.

If a certain kind of language is not right in itself, it must be right in relation to something else, some basic principle of the poem in terms of which it can be explained and justified. What is this principle? I suggested the answer when I said, in

talking about the words of Rosetta's song, that what was sad
could not be the words; it could only be Rosetta herself. What
we really mean by sad words is words used to express sadness. The
two terms, *expression* and *use,* must be emphasized. First, it is
necessary to distinguish what words express from what they mean,
as something broader and far more important. I have already
spoken of irony. If we call a fat person "Tiny," or a tall fellow
"Little John," our words mean one thing but express the opposite. The translation from meaning to expression can only be
made in the context of use—we see "Tiny" or "Little John" and
judge the intention of the words accordingly. The situation, or
context of use, is as important in poetry, where it is fictional, as
in life, where it is real. I have talked a good deal about Rosetta's
"Deep in my dark the dream shines" and what it means, but
nothing I have said so far indicates what emotion it expresses.
The answer to this question depends on Rosetta's situation, on
whether she is dreaming of a bright future which will surely
come or a bright past which is irrevocably lost. From the rest of
the poem we learn that the second alternative is the correct one.
Rosetta's words are thus profoundly sad; her dark is not a tempo-
rary state of deprivation, but a permanent one with no expectation of change.

Words express ideas and things, attributes and actions—in
general, they express subject matter. But more importantly, they
express the speaker who uses them. This part of their expressive
value is derived from their significance as action, from the act or
fact of using words rather than the meanings of words used. I
have talked about learned or literary words, which are part of
the vocabulary of the highly educated few. But just as no one
has ever seen a word laugh or cry, no one has ever seen an educated word. The education belongs to the person using the word
and is implied by his correct use of it. The speakers of Starbuck's
and Ransom's poems are men of intellectual sophistication, and
the poems are not so much about passionate love as about such a
man's experience with regard to passionate love.

A particular series of words, used on a certain occasion, is
not only a statement or thought but an act. It is the act of
speech as much as the content of speech that is of the essence,
both in life and in poetry. The basic principle of the poem in
terms of which its language can be explained and justified is the

speaker: his character and his actions. By actions I do not necessarily mean something overt, an embrace or a farewell slam of
the door. Thinking too is an act; it is something we do on a
certain occasion, and its form depends on what we are as well as
the circumstances in which we find ourselves. To meditate, to
exclaim, to tell a joke—all these are verbal acts, and the language used in performing them expresses the person using it as
much as the meaning and subject matter it communicates.

I maintain that poems should be studied with the purpose of
finding out, not so much what the speaker is saying, but what sort
of person he is and what he is doing. To explain fully how these
questions might be answered for each of the four poems I have
been considering would require a second lecture. What I shall
do instead is to divide the four poems into two pairs, putting
Yeats's "A Drinking Song" with Rosetta's song and Ransom's
"The Equilibrists" with Starbuck's sonnet, and contrast the two
poems in each pair briefly, without arguing in detail for my
interpretations.

"Rosetta's Song" is a reverie. The words are those of a
woman sunk in a melancholy daydream, and they have something
of the universal poetry of the dream. Rosetta's sorrow is deep,
but it is also childlike, as the imagery of the poem's ending
shows:

> You touched, you took. Tears fall. O
> Fair my far, when far ago
> Like waterwheels wishes spun
> Radiant robes: but the robes tore.

The shining water that streams from the waterwheel suggests a
child's pleasure in bright moving things; the insubstantial robes
spun from it, and the wishes that do the spinning, suggest the
world of the fairy-tale. The robes tear and become rags as the
radiant garments worn by Cinderella at the ball became rags at
the stroke of midnight. When we first meet Rosetta in *The Age
of Anxiety,* we learn that she is a department store buyer. Aided
by the protective surroundings of the bar, a few drinks, and the
music of the jukebox, she escapes from her prosaic world into
the poetry that lies deep in all of us.

The simple language of Yeats's poem does not, like that of
Rosetta's song, express an intellectually unsophisticated speaker.

The key to this poem lies in the pronoun "I" in the final lines, "I lift the glass to my mouth, / I look at you, and I sigh." This will become clear if the ending is altered as follows:

> Wine comes in at the mouth
> And love comes in at the eye;
> That's all we shall know for truth
> Before we grow old and die;
> We lift the glass to our mouth,
> We gaze at our loves, and sigh.

What we now have is a series of generalizations, which is what the original poem might at first have seemed to be. But in comparison with this altered version, Yeats's poem is revealed as the expression of a state of mind the speaker has deliberately adopted and pursued. The comparison between wine and love implies the familiar idea that love is a kind of physical intoxication—but the point is that it resembles intoxication in that the speaker deliberately brings it upon himself. He affirms that love and wine are all-important *as* he drinks and *as* he falls in love—this is why the poem is called "A Drinking Song." He not only feels this, he wants to go on feeling it, to disregard the contradictory aspects of experience, to continue in this mode of action and exclude all other preoccupations. As he speaks, he lifts the glass to drink again, and looks again at the woman with whom he is falling, and wishes to fall, in love. His language in its simplicity expresses this deliberate limitation of consciousness; it is significant that such simplicity is not generally characteristic of the language of Yeats's poems. Indeed the assertion that "That's all we shall know for truth / Before we grow old and die" is what Kenneth Burke would call a "counter-statement." The speaker has heard many other truths. But he rejects them in favor of the one truth that possesses him here and now.

If the language of "A Drinking Song" expresses the deliberate exclusion from consciousness of all except the simple experience of the present moment, that of "The Equilibrists" expresses an exactly opposite state. The consciousness of this speaker is saturated, both in general and at this moment, with the literary past. I have already pointed out a number of his literary archaisms, words associated in now obsolete meanings with Shakespeare and other Elizabethan poets. What I consider the central literary allusion of the poem evokes a still earlier period in the history of English poetry. Seeing the suffering brought upon the lovers by the conflict between passion and honor, the speaker becomes angry on their behalf. He says,

> With puddled brow
> Devising for those gibbeted and brave
> Came I descanting: Man, what would you have?

Devising and *descanting* are both used in archaic literary meanings. The speaker *devises*, or considers, on behalf of the lovers, and *descants*, or comments, on their situation. His question, "Man, what would you have?" echoes the question put by Chaucer into the mouth of the dying Arcite in that greatest of the *Canterbury Tales*, "The Knight's Tale":

> What is this world? what asketh men to have?
> Now with his love, now in his colde grave
> Allone, withouten any compaignye?

And his vision of the fate reserved for great lovers in hell, though so far as I know original in its details, is reminiscent of Dante's *Divine Comedy*. The speaker of the poem deliberately assumes the mantle of the poet, and his final act of the poem is the act of a poet: he composes an epitaph for the lovers which in its phrasing is reminiscent of the verse epitaphs of Greek and Roman antiquity. His claim that this epitaph will "memorize" or commemorate the lovers' doom is equally traditional. The central experience of the poem is not the suffering of the lovers; it is the pride of the poet, whose creative intellect can give a form to this suffering through which it becomes beautiful.

In contrast, the speaker of Starbuck's sonnet is, as his language implies, a man torn amusingly between literature and life. At the end of the poem he seems to reject literature entirely. His girl breaks away from him and runs down to the water's edge, and he watches with approval as she throws the collected poems of Keats into the Pacific, "plump / In the sun's wake." But this rejection is not as simple as it seems. We must not overlook the fact that the poem is not only a sonnet but is written in the very rhyme scheme, out of all possible rhyme schemes of the sonnet, that Keats himself used in the sonnet "On First Looking into Chapman's Homer," which is the subject of the fictitious summer session literature course of the title. What has given the speaker hives is not Keats's poetry but the droning of the scholars. When the girl in the poem tosses the book into the sea, the "parched pages" are said to drink the waves. Keats himself was a passionate man, a man thirsty for the youthful joys of the senses, who expressed in one of his most famous poems his longing for a cool "draught of vintage," that he might drink and escape the realm of aging and pain. When his parched pages drink the sea, it is as if they are rescued in this way from the intolerable dryness of the scholarship which all too often takes away their life.

I said earlier that the poet puts words together in such a way that they linger on in our minds, and that one way of making this power visible is to translate his words into our own less memorable language. You or I might call the ocean the ocean, or the Pacific, or the bounding main, but we could never have called it, as Starbuck does, a "great whale's blanket party." Earlier in the poem a petrel has dived "to yank the dull sea's coverlet." Beneath that dull coverlet the speaker now imagines life in all its brute energy: the lovemaking of whales. I should like to take what happens at the end of Starbuck's poem, "On First Looking In on Blodgett's *Keats's 'Chapman's Homer'* (Sum ½C. M9–11)," as symbolic of the immersion of language in life which it is the duty of both the critic and the teacher of poetry to maintain. And I can think of no better way to end these remarks than to quote the description of that moment, when,

> breaking from me across the sand that's rink
> and record of our weekend boning up
> on *The Romantic Agony,* you sink
> John Keats a good surf-fisher's cast out—plump
> in the sun's wake—and the parched pages drink
> that great whales' blanket party hump and hump.

THE
TEACHING OF
METRICS

JOHN HOLLANDER
Yale University

I take for my subject some of the problems involved in the teaching of poetic meter and versification. I am sure that you all have a grim and immediate knowledge of these problems. Even specially selected groups of college freshman, with some vague idea of the existence in English verse of something called "iambic pentameter," will write learnedly and convincedly of how Donne's intricate stanza forms are in blank verse. Others, even more anxious to please, will inform one in their papers that "the 'K' sounds in this line set up the feeling of clicking noises that one associates with very hot metal." Some of them will even have read a little Virgil, patiently scanning feet in their Latin classes, and, if anything, they will be more confused about why we call the meter of *Hiawatha* "trochaic tetrameter."

Meter appears to be as self-contained and as systematized a body of subject matter as grammar, say, or as keyboard harmony as it is classically taught. But in practice, we are always confronted with the difficulties that emerge from trying to communicate to students on the one hand the actual verbal music of any poem itself, and, on the other, the systematic regularities of verbal and sound patterning that have become conventional in English verse since Chaucer.

To these difficulties are added others. First, having taught students that the iambic pentameter is common to many lines of English verse, we are confronted with an attentive and energetic pupil who will point out most of the good "regular" lines we show him deviate from the norm that we have been trying to insist that they embody.

Second, the actual terminology that we have inherited from misapplications of classical prosody by Renaissance theorists is usually confusing and often completely inadequate. The concept of the foot originates in a musical measure, such as our modern one wherein, by convention, a half note equals two quarters. A foot, that is, governs the durations or length or, as it is called, the "quality" of syllables in classical verse. But English is, of course, organized around a beat, not an equivalent length of time, and to call an alternating sequence of accented and unaccented syllables a "foot" is fundamentally misleading. And yet again, it is conventional in literary studies to do so. When it comes to such additional questions of what might be called pathological meters, such as Whitman's, some of Blake's, Gerard Manley Hopkins', the free verse of Pound, William Carlos Williams, and other recent poets, the use of syllabics by some of these, and so forth, we are in even greater difficulty.

Finally, there is the problem of how to get a student not so much to hear as *to notice that he is hearing* the "sound effects" even in such spectacular cases as Tennyson's celebrated lines "The moan of doves in immemorial elms / And the murmur of innumerable bees," and after that, to give an account or description of what is happening "musically" in a line that will be less tautological than merely "well, it sounds like murmuring."

But these are relatively technical difficulties that depend for their solution upon our own schematic interpretative system and upon the clearing away of centuries of vain polemics among students of metrics and poets themselves. There is another more perplexing kind of problem that I am sure you have all experienced in one form or another. Let us suppose that one or two of the same attentive and energetic students mentioned earlier do in fact learn to come to terms with both what they hear in poetry and with the awkward and ill-fitting language by which we ask them to describe these metrical phenomena. But after having thoroughly understood what it means to say that *Paradise Lost* is in blank verse, for example, that despite irregular or ambiguous lines like the famous "Rocks, caves, lakes, fens, bogs, dens, and shades of Death," where important words are variously stressed or unstressed almost at whim, certain regularities do unquestionably control Milton's prosody, one of these bright students may ask a perplexing question. Having learned our rituals of scansion, he may very simply ask us, "So what?" An even rarer student might mutter in addition something about "murdering to dissect," and, especially if he has responded to the poetry at all, dismiss the whole question of metrical analysis as poisonous casuistry.

In the case of Milton, it would be our pleasant duty to go into some of the conditions and pressures that underlay the choice of blank verse for Milton's English version of what he calls "heroic verse." The desire to adapt classical hexameters rather than elegiac couplets, of course, militated against the couplets that later became the Augustan Age's choice for just such an analogue. Italian precedents were also influential. Finally, the great corpus of Elizabethan and Jacobean tragedy had forged an authentic, monumental style in its use of blank verse and made it the tone of the language's own most serious voice. *Paradise Lost* is, among other things, a revenge tragedy with Satan as hero-villain. His doomed kingdom of hell becomes the hell within him in the course of the poem, just as the Jacobean revenger's machinations drive him to feign, and to be overpowered by madness. Here is a case, of course, where the *conventional* aspect of meter may be shown very clearly. The answer to the mythical student's "So what?" thrusts us right into the heart of the poem.

There are thus two ends always to be kept in view in the teaching of meter. I should like to expound them in a little more detail and to suggest some ways in which the more usual difficulties in attaining them may be handled. I shall tentatively distinguish between the *expressive* and the *conventional* dimensions of any poem's metrical patternings. The expressive power of meter consists, of course, in what we traditionally and sometimes misleadingly refer to as "the music of poetry," the ways in which a poem's sound patterns act to reinforce its meaning at various points, and to set a continuous underlying basis for its tone. The conventional or traditional aspect of meter consists of the way in which a poem's metrical pattern engages, suggests, modifies, evokes, or even affronts or flatly refutes the metrical procedures of other poems written in its own or other languages at various times. Our ability to make measurements, as it were, along these two dimensions in any poem reminds us of the pair of axes along which T. S. Eliot suggested that all poems are generated, in his influential essay "Tradition and the Individual Talent." In meter also, the poet's voice, raised on a particular occasion, is dialectically involved with the whole history of such raisings of voice in all of the literature preceding him of which he may be aware.

Before going any further in my discussion of these two aspects of meter and of ways in which we may represent them more clearly to students, I should like to set up and define a few metrical terms that I intend to use. With a couple of exceptions, these will not be unfamiliar. They have often been misconstrued, however, and students of meter have often debated about their meaning. This is particularly true where the terms denote sound elements of spoken languages that *may be employed* in the meters of poems written in those or other languages. I shall use these terms as follows:

Stress accent is that contrast between syllables so important to the phonemic system of English and, incidentally, of Russian. The difference between the words "cóntent" and "contént" in English is a matter of stress. Where, as in English and Russian, the contrast of stress is as fundamental a sound unit as the difference between "p" and "b" (like '*con*tent" and "con*tent,*" "pet" and "bet" are distinguished with reference to it), then we say that the language has *phonemic stress.* In languages like Italian and Spanish, where the stress tends so usually to occur on the penultimate syllable that exceptions are marked by an accent sign, the stress is certainly audible and may be used in organizing the meter but it is not essentially structural. In French, where the stress is called *configurational,* operating on whole phrases rather than on syllables, stress accent is not employed in the meter of poetry. I shall indicate stressed syllables in poetry by ! unstressed by . .

Quantity or duration-accent is a characteristic of certain other languages. It is *not* the same as the difference between so-called "short" "i" in "bit" and "long" "i" in "bite." The latter is a diphthong based on an utterly different vowel. We may truly say that different syllables, such as the English indefinite article and the word "lunch," differ in the absolute length of time required to enunciate them. But this does not represent a case of the structurally essential long and short vowels of Greek and Latin. Quantitative verse is framed in terms of groups of lengths, much like our musical rhythmic notation, in which a quarter note equals two eights. So, despite differences in absolute length, the long and short syllables of classical verse are arbitrarily cast in the ratio of two to one.

Syllabic verse or *syllabics* is a metrical system that organizes not the number of strong stress accents in a line, as in *accentual* verse, nor the groups of longs and shorts in *quantitative* verse. Instead the absolute number of syllables per line determines the meter, and often, as in the case of French poetry, the caesura, or breaks between words, is very important and much more audibly prominent than in accentual verse. French verse, somewhat influenced by the placing of caesuras in classical meters, often prescribes the place in the line, between which syllables, these are to occur. We get the wrong idea of a caesura, incidentally, by thinking of it in terms of the textbook definition of a "pause" which might be syntactic, rhetorical, or expressive. A caesura can occur in the middle of any phrase.

Finally, I should like to distinguish in my own words between a metrical *system* and a metrical *style*. In various phases of the literary history of any language, one or another basic set of metrical devices will constitute the basis of most poetry. In English, for example, the so-called *accentual-syllabic* system rules rather uninterruptedly from Chaucer through Tennyson. Exceptions like Whitman, Christopher Smart, and Hopkins are few and far between. The accentual-syllabic system provides for lines of varying length, rhymed or unrhymed, governed by the principle of alternation of stressed and unstressed syllables. The line length is determined by both the total number of syllables and the total number of stresses, although variation in the former is more frequent than in the latter. Nevertheless, Pope, Yeats, Keats, and Milton write in startlingly different ways, metrically speaking. We might say that their particular styles are characterized by the ways they utilize *degrees of freedom* not covered by the strictures of the system. Pope's careful regularity, and his use of syntactical and rhetorical balance and antithesis, Keats's richnesses of alliteration and tonal manipulation of vowel sounds, for example, are all elements of individual style. To say that all of these poets write iambic pentameter is to say of them only that they are all operating within one system. We may also speak, incidentally, of the "style" of a particular poem, either as an example of, or a divergence from, the poet's metrical style in general.

With these terms established, then, let me return to our two dimensions of metrical analysis. It is obvious that the expressive aspect of meter will tend to be concerned with questions of style and its relation to system, in any poet's work, with a view to anatomizing the style and showing how it operates in that quasi-musical way in any particular poem. The conventional study of meter will turn its attention upon the history of styles and indeed of systems. More specifically, when we examine a poem with respect to its metrical conventions, we are always asking what other styles within or even outside of the metrical system the poet can have been making implicit reference to.

The most immediate problems in teaching meter arise in relation to the simple process of scanning verse and analyzing its expressive effects. First, it is clear, I think, that one cannot abandon completely the traditional terminology of iambs, trochees, pentameters, and the like, leaving a student to the mercy of conventional usage, armed only with the *ad hoc* ways of scanning poems one has taught him. It must be pointed out to him, however, that these terms used in connection with verse written within the accentual-syllabic system were borrowed from an utterly different system, and used only analogically. For example, a 4/4 measure in Greek verse, containing a half-note and two quarters, and stressed normally (on the first half-note syllable) is called a "dactyl." It becomes in its applied sense, simply a group of three syllables, the first stressed, the other two weak. See Example 1 at the end of this paper. Example 1 is thus scanned: ! . . ! . . ! . . ! . . ! . . !. This is a "dactyllic hexameter" in English, the meter of *Evangeline,* a seventeen-syllable line with six stresses. In the Greek musical measure, a half-note may be substituted at certain points for two quarters, thus the Greek hexameter line has no fixed number of syllables. But Renaissance critics, in an effort to make English poetry as respectable as that of classical antiquity, lost no chance to insist on analogies, even when they were equivocal. Their legacy was the confusion that besets us when we are forced to consider pairs of syllables in English poetry, that tend to alternate with respect to stress accent, as mysterious things called "feet." They aren't. They have nevertheless always been called so. Additional confusions come from the fact that the alliterative verse system that governs early English poetry before Chaucer provides in itself for no fixed number of syllables per line, instead there is only a fixed number of *stressed* syllables (namely, four, with three of them alliterating). See Example 2. This line sounds as if it had been written in the English version of dactyls, and to read a line that might follow it which had fewer syllables might lead one to make the mistake of assuming that the last word of our line, "cadence," ought really to be scanned $-\smile$ in the notation that classicists use to indicate that the last syllable (half-note) of a dactyllic hexameter is counted as a long even when it would otherwise be short, to fill out the measure. Even the traditional scanning marks for English, by which what I have notated . ! . ! . ! . ! . !, is written as $\smile / \smile / \smile / \smile /$ are an uneasy blend of the mark for a short syllable or quarter note and the acute accent by which many languages indicate a stressed syllable.

At all events, a student must learn to recognize normative English five-beat verse and to learn to call it iambic pentameter. More trivial debates among metrists, such as whether a blank-verse line with its first two syllables inverted ought to be spoken of as starting with a trochee, will, we hope, eventually appear to him to be as ridiculous as they actually are.

When one has worked out to some degree a method for confronting the problems engendered by misleading inherited terminology, there still remains the question of dealing with individual metrical styles and their most effective moments, musically speaking.

For example, I made reference earlier this evening to two lines of Tennyson's, "The moan of doves in immemorial elms/ And the murmur of innumerable bees," and to the sort of comment which we don't want to elicit about it. But questions of onomatopoeia are always tricky, and we tend often to think in fictions ourselves about this whole matter. The question whether or not there are any minimal sound units and clusters in English which of themselves seem to evoke certain meanings has concerned linguists for some time. On the surface, it would seem that words like "slide," "slip," "slick," "slim," "slink," "slop," "slope," and others all seem to be associated, through their initial cluster, with a general idea of smoothness. But such cases are too rare to allow us to assume that onomatopoeia operates in any other way than to associate words already given us with others having common sounds. Assonance, alliteration, and even rhyme do some of the work of metaphor by associating words through their sounds alone and by thus juxtaposing them with some of the same strength as an actual image. Thus, in the lines from Tennyson, the alliterating words are "moan," "imme-morial," "elms," "murmur," and "innumerable," with "bees" being related to the last syllable of "innumerable" and the phrase "of doves" being linked by a rhyme. Clearly the *core word* for these alliterations is "murmur," and we associate with it all the connected words. But it is flatly misleading to tell a student that the "m" sounds have any meaning or evocative power, apart from words they connect. I realize that such assertions are frequent, and some appreciators of poetry like Dame Edith Sitwell carry this method to an idiotic extreme. Clearly Tennyson's lines have a suggestive musical richness. But just as clearly, this is a music of words, not of extrapolated sounds.

As a case of a problem more particularly metrical, we might take some lines from Keats's "Ode to Autumn." The personified "Season of mists and mellow fruitfulness" is invoked in the second stanza in images of harvests, and after proceeding through references to indolent play, winnowing and reaping Keats says of her the lines given in Example 3. A very fine critic, Dr. F. R. Leavis, has remarked of these lines that they actually imitate or embody the action that they describe. Certainly the so-called *enjambment,* the line break between "keep" and "steady" is a remarkable one, all the more since the rest of the poem consists of end-stopped lines. The *enjambment* does operate here to give us a feeling of a heavy bale of grain balanced upon autumn's head as she picks her way through the waters of a stream or across steppingstones. But there need be no mystery in explaining the way that Keats's metrical device works for him. In ordinary speech the English phrase "keep steady" is accented . ! .. That is, the first monosyllable abandoning principle stress to the first syllable of the second word. But here the word "keep" is in a stressed position in the first line, as if it were to be followed by something like the lines in Example 4. Here, the phrase "Keep/A bale of grain" is stressed, as in ordinary speech, ! . ! . ! . But the next line as it appears in Keats's poem makes us realize that a phrase has been cut in between the words—indeed, "Keep steady" must almost be considered a verb in itself. And thus we read, !/! . , "Keep/Steady," giving it the stress pattern that in ordinary speech would be used only in urging someone balancing something not to drop it, as if the phrase, in short, were an imperative. Just as we almost *feel* someone's predicament when he is balancing something and may even add what bowlers like to call "body-English" to our verbal help, so do we *feel* the balancing problem here. But it is by the reversal of normal stress-patterns (which Keats seldom violates elsewhere) that we are made to feel it.

A wonderful collection of such "imitative" metrical effects, all working within the tight style of perfect couplets, is to be found in lines 337–373 of Part II of Pope's "Essay on Criticism." In a brilliant attack on the cult of pure sound in poetry dislocated from all meaning, Pope manages to commit all sorts of offenses against effective metrical rhythm in the very lines in which he designates them. Here, too, no mystique is needed to explain the success of the effects. A careful glance at the use of consonantal clusters well spaced out with vowels or bunched together to slow down the absolute time of enunciation will suffice to show the workings of this most skillful way of making the sound seem, in Pope's own words, "an echo to the sense." The entire passage is quoted in Example 5.

In short, we might paraphrase Goethe's famous remark about epic style, that it does our thinking and poetizing for us, by saying that the expressive metric of lyric poems does our feeling for us, by forcing us to go through certain rhythmic verbal motions that make us respond to the content of the line in appropriate ways. Other examples of this abound, and time permits me to mention only a few. Shakespeare's Sonnet 116, quoted in Example 6, is one. An insufficient comment would be that we seem to hear the sound of the blade cutting down the grass to which the scriptural text likens all flesh. The effect depends upon several things. In the first place, as William Empson has observed, "bending" means both "bent" and "causing to bend." Second, the core word "sickle" suggests words like "click," "flick," "nick," and so on. And the alliterating words "compass" and "come" naturally suggest "cut." The reiteration of the hard "c" sound repeats the effect of "sickle" and suggests the repeated blows that we know a reaping blade to give. Also, one is reminded of Andrew Marvell's famous refrain in his "The Mower's Song," quoted in Example 7. Marvell makes use of the very fact that an alexandrine, a hexameter or six-beat line in English, tends to fragment into two three-beat lines. We almost "hear" the gentle, swaying, reciprocating movement of the scythe. The meter and the arrangement of syntax over the lines cause us to await the return of the fractured portion of the main clause—actually this is a type of clausal *enjambment*.

"Imitative movement" of words can, of course, really only imitate the sounds of other words or sounds. Some of the finest examples of it occur when a semantic relation is reinforced by a rhythmic parallel between words or phrases, and when we are almost tempted to say that the designatum of the phrase is being represented by that movement rather than the phrase itself. Thus in Florizel's great speech to Perdita in *The Winter's Tale* (Example 8) the description of the girl's imitative dance doesn't "sound like the sea" but rather follows the rhythm of the phrase "a wave o' the sea." Also, in Yeats's "Sailing to Byzantium," the "Monuments of unaging intellect" at the end of stanza 1 are betrayed and made mockery of by institutions like universities, scholarly practices, and the like, devoted to studying them. These are only narcissistic, as it were, and involuted, and Yeats demonstrates this in the second stanza by referring to the singing schools that all study "Monuments of their own magnificence." Here again, the repetition of the word "monuments" is reinforced by the symmetrical alliterating rhythm of the final word in the line: the whole line, so to speak, looks into a mirror and gazes at itself.

If I have devoted most of my time to a discussion of how to interpret the expressive effects of meter, it is largely because the teaching of its traditional dimension is demanded only by the requirements of a more advanced study of literary history. But I should like to refer to a few more cases like that of *Paradise Lost,* mentioned earlier, where the poet's choice of meter will obviously involve some of his basic intentions, his fundamental literary commitment to one convention or another.

This dimension is most easy to perceive, of course, in two extreme kinds of case. The first is that of the poem written in a literary age where one or another canonical metrical style seems to govern all practice. The emergence of blank verse as the medium for English drama during a sixty-year period ending in 1642, for example, provides us with a tradition within which we may examine the varying styles of poets as different as Marlowe and Ben Jonson, Webster and Dekker. To ask why a particular Jacobean tragedy is in blank verse is to question a tautology. The Augustan Age, also, employed the couplet for satire, pastoral, heroic verse, epigram, and speculative poem alike; no one would have thought in 1720 of writing a meditative poem in blank verse, or a speculative ode like Wordsworth's "Immortality Ode." In strict neoclassical terms, the ancient correspondence of genre, content, occasion, and style was resurrected. The fact that the English heroic couplet was as old, and as surely unclassical as Chaucer, made no difference—the Augustans saw in it the English analogue of classical elegiacs and made it their own.

On the other hand, an experimental or avant-garde meter is also easy to trace in its conventional perspective. Christopher Smart's use of structural features of Biblical Hebrew verse in his monumental *Jubilate Agno,* for example; the almost emblematic shock value of the dropping of initial capital letters by modernist poets of the 20s; Whitman's adaptation of both the translated psalmody of the King James Bible and some of the cadences of Emersonian prose; the adoption of syllabic verse structure by contemporary poets like W. H. Auden and Marianne Moore—all of these more or less pathological styles result from a clear desire on the part of a poet to invoke some part of some literary tradition in his own or in other languages. When he is successful, his use of the same tradition will have expressive value as well. Edward Arlington Robinson used, in some of his best shorter poems, the resources of Victorian light-verse writers like Gilbert and Calverley, but in *Eros Turannos* and others he used their ironic possibilities to collapse Jamesian novels into a miniature form. The short, flat, ironic fourth line of each stanza in *Minivercheevy* does the work of debunking the illusions in the previous three, but its traditional source is the conventional nineteenth-century form translation of Horace's Odes in sapphic meter, although Robinson's lines are always end-stopped and the syntax never moves on in rambling Latinate fashion over all the stanzas.

Even larger poetic forms extend themselves through the conventional dimension of meter. A pocket history of the English sonnet would show its development from a strictly Petrarchan ideal love poem, usually as part of a sequence, through the isolated love lyric as set by Elizabethan composers, through its use by metaphysical poets as a tight, short form, embodying almost any sort of content. Then the sonnet passes into oblivion after Milton's almost unique use of the form in English, only to be resurrected half-heartedly by later eighteenth-century poets for short preromantic meditations derived from Milton's use of the Italianate form of the poem. In Wordsworth the sonnet again comes into its own, for Wordsworth made a programmatic effort to revive its use, and even allegorized its formal strictness in his "Nuns fret not at their convent's narrow room" as the task that the imagination must set itself in order to realize its freedom.

It is really only with the twentieth century that metrical convention separates itself so sharply from the general question of genre. Postsymbolist demands for novelty, organic unity, an inherently "poetic" rather than merely a logical or even a cognitive coherence, have led twentieth-century poets writing in many languages to abandon the metrical traditions of the generations preceding theirs in favor of new styles. But these new styles are themselves not without traditional affiliations. Yeats moved from *fin-de-siècle* post-Swinburnian meters to a renewed contact with both Shakespeare and folk song. T. S. Eliot absorbed metrical as well as rhetorical material from French poets like Gautier, Laforgue, and Corbière and from the Jacobean tragedians as well. Pound turned away from his romantic versions of troubadour lyrics to Japanese influences, and even tried, metrically, to come to terms with Whitman. Wallace Stevens evolved a magnificent personal blank verse style from what Wordsworth had made of it. Hart Crane, after dabblings with the French symbolists, rarely came to terms with Whitman and Melville as writers, but with a finally unabashed use of romantic prosody as well as rhetoric.

But time grows short, and such examples must be limited to a few. Suffice it to say that even the most polemical of modern poets' remarks on meter, such as those of Pound and William Carlos Williams, have their analogues in other periods in literary history. Pound's demands that poetry be "as well-written as prose," for example, and Williams' request for a true American idiom are only recent outbreaks in a long tradition of metrical controversy that includes the demands of Thomas Campion and other Elizabethans that the only truly classical (and hence authentic) poetry in English abandon "barbarous" rhyme and stressed scansion and return to quantitative verse. This could be done, Campion felt, by assigning to every English written vowel (no matter how pronounced) the length value that it had in Greek and Latin, with subsequent adoption of other classical rules of scansion. The result, of course, was little more than a written code. And yet, because of the fact that in the meter of written poetry audible and purely graphic elements enter into the verse structure at the same level, an accustomed reader of verse will often confuse what he sees with what he thinks he hears.

This is always a problem in the interpretation of the significance of poetic form. Even the most sophisticated critics have stumbled over it, even poets themselves. But if students are to be taught anything of meter at all, they might as well be taught it in a way that will both avoid these confusions and enable them to account for the hitherto almost mystical effect that the so-called music of poetry has upon them. To understand even the deepest of experiences is by no means, romantic ideology to the contrary, to do any more than intensify them.

EXAMPLES

Example 1:

> Please, never make the mistake of confusing these
> two kinds of dactyls

Example 2:

> Bumpily beating in *Beowulf's* cadence
> (! .. ! .. ! . . ! .)

Example 3:

> Who hath not seen thee oft amid thy store?
> Sometimes whoever seeks abroad may find
> Thee sitting careless on a granary floor,
> Thy hair-soft-lifted by the winnowing wind;
> Or on a half-reaped furrow sound asleep,
> Drowsed with the fume of poppies, while thy hook
> Spares the next swath and all its twinèd flowers:
> *And sometimes like a gleaner thou dost keep*
> *Steady thy laden head across a brook;*
> Or by a cider-press, with patient look,
> Thou watchest the last oozings hours by hours.

Example 4:

> And sometimes like a gleaner thou dost keep
> A bale of grain against the winter's blast

Example 5:

> But most by Numbers judge a Poet's song;
> And smooth or rough, with them, is right or wrong:
> In the bright Muse tho' thousand charms conspire,
> Her Voice is all these tuneful fools admire;
> Who haunt Parnassus but to please their ear,
> Not mend their minds; as some to Church repair,
> Not for the doctrine, but the music there.
> These equal syllables alone require,
> Tho' oft the ear the open vowels tire;
> While expletives their feeble aid do join;
> And ten low words oft creep in one dull line:
> While they ring round the same unvary'd chimes,
> With sure returns of still expected rhymes.
> Where-e'er you find "the cooling western breeze,"
> In the next line, it "whispers thro' the trees;"
> If crystal streams "with pleasing murmurs creep,"
> The reader's threaten'd (not in vain) with "sleep."
> Then, at the last and only couplet fraught
> With some unmeaning thing they call a thought,
> A needless Alexandrine ends the song,
> That, like a wounded snake, drags its slow length
>   along.
> Leave such to tune their own dull rhymes, and know
> What's roundly smooth, or languishingly slow;
> And praise the easy vigour of a line,
> Where Denham's strength, and Waller's sweetness
>   join.
> True ease in writing comes from art, not chance,
> As those move easiest who have learn'd to dance.
> 'Tis not enough no harshness gives offence,
> The sound must seem an Echo to the sense:
> Soft is the strain when Zephyr gently blows,
> And the smooth stream in smoother numbers flows;
> But when loud surges lash the sounding shore,
> The hoarse, rough verse should like the torrent roar:
> When Ajax strives some rock's vast weight to throw,

> The line too labours, and the words move slow;
> Not so, when swift Camilla scours the plain,
> Flies o'er th' unbending corn, and skims along the
>   main.

Example 6:

> Love's not Time's fool, though rosy lips and cheeks
> Within his bending sickle's compass come

Example 7:

> For Juliana comes, and she
> What I do to the grass, does to my thoughts and me.

Example 8:

> When you speak, sweet,
> I'd have you do it ever. When you sing,
> I'd have you buy and sell so, so give alms,
> Pray so, and, for the ordering your affairs,
> To sing them too. *When you do dance, I wish you*
> *A wave o' the sea, that you might ever do*
> *Nothing but that. . . .*

SELECTED READINGS

T. S. ELIOT, "The Music of Poetry" in *On Poetry and Poets* (New York, 1957).

I. A. RICHARDS, *Principles of Literary Criticism,* notably Chapters XVII and XX (paperback edition, New York, 1961).

ELIZABETH DREW, *The Enjoyment of Poetry* (paperback edition, New York, 1959).

CLEANTH BROOKS AND R. P. WARREN, *Understanding Poetry,* Rev. ed., Section III (New York, 1960).

NORTHROP FRYE, ED., *Sound and Poetry* (New York, 1957).

JOHN HOLLANDER, "The Music of Poetry" in *Journal of Aesthetics and Art Criticism* XV (December 1956), 232–244.

THE
PATTERN
OF THE
NOVEL

MARTIN PRICE
Yale University

I

Of all the novels I was taught in high school, the one I came to like most was *A Tale of Two Cities*. We had a very young teacher. He was probably a student-teacher. We weren't sure of his status, but we were sure that it was low. And he was full of "methods." He would draw the window blinds until there was just enough light for him to read Gray's *Elegy* aloud, in as close an approximation as one can get to twilight at Stoke Poges in midmorning Manhattan. He had us act out Sheridan's *Rivals* with our books in our hands. He had us recall and write down our counting rhymes and riddles and revealed to us that they might be interesting to adults. When we read *The Deserted Village*, he sent us out into our city streets to look for visual images of the Depression. When we came to *A Tale of Two Cities* he sent us to interview three people who had read the book more than five years before and to ask them which scene they could remember best. We were very competitive boys, and each of the twenty of us searched out his own treasure. I remember the awe with which I discovered that my Latin teacher had not read *A Tale of Two Cities* in twenty-seven years. And he was suitably vague about that woman who knitted while the heads were chopped off. Twenty-seven years! He seemed so remarkably rare and old that I recorded his words exactly; some of the other nineteen would reach him, but I would have had the first run of that so-long untapped memory. It was an exciting task. When I scurried to my last year's English teacher—the one who had made *Silas Marner* so appallingly dull—he explained that he had read too many critical discussions of Dickens to give an unprejudiced answer. It was my first direct experience of academic humbug, and I had enough satiric awareness to record his refusal along with the more candid answers.

Our young teacher was somewhat foolish, I suppose, and quite wise. He gave us the feeling that we were contributing to his education, and in our own dim way we were well aware of it and gratefully eager. But he did not make us complacent. He had us read *A Tale of Two Cities* through on our own and he gave us a factual test on the book before we discussed it in class. It was the first time that I'd been made to see how badly I'd been reading, how large were the patches of fog in what I took to be a familiar landscape. Even more, he used those answers we brought back from our bustling interviews to ask us why people remembered the scenes they did and what made them memorable. And with the whole book before us, read and by now with some chagrin reread, we could see it as a novel should be seen.

II

I want to talk primarily about the pattern of the novel; but it is important to recognize that only the rare high school student is ready to see the novel as a formal problem. I don't think we should want this otherwise. The novel is a source of vicarious experience, first of all. It records how strange people behave, it describes their work and their surroundings; as a character in one of Iris Murdoch's novels puts it, "nothing is more educational, in the end, than the mode of being of other people." Bad novels give this as often as good, and the line between fiction on the one hand, and history or sociology or geography on the other, is scarcely maintained in many of our current children's books. It is in those kinds of vicarious experiences that affect the moral imagination that the difference between good novels and bad becomes most telling. And it is precisely there that I think we must make distinctions between the novel as information and the novel as pattern.

A student who reads novels in order to find an accurate image of a world he has not yet entered will feel cheated as soon as he has entered that world even a little way. We all know of the countless heroes and heroines of fiction—Jane Austen's, Stendhal's, George Eliot's, Flaubert's—who have come to ask of

life what only fiction can give them. It is in fact one of the
great and perennial themes of the novel that it *is* a fiction: something made sharper, clearer, more limited and more intense
than life can be. There have been many ways of saying this since
Aristotle first made his distinction between poetry and history.
André Gide has said, "I arrange facts in such a way as to make
them conform to truth more closely than they do in real life."
This is striking enough so long as we take the word truth for
what it is: the statement of a problem rather than the solution
of it.

Students of high school age have a strong appetite for truth,
and many of them become convinced that they have tasted very
little so far. The novel should, as it well can, feed this appetite;
it is about the choice and decisions, the commitments and re-
nunciations, that they recognize as important. But it cannot be
offered as a simple picture of life. One does not need much reading in any author to see a Hemingway world or a Faulkner
world, a Dickens world or a Hardy world. And these worlds are
not simply geographically distinct. Each world has its own kind
of landscape, its own kind of people, its own kind of events and
even of causality. And all of these worlds in turn coexist in us,
whether we are in New Haven or in London. Without accepting
this fact, insisting upon it, and building upon it, we offer the
novel as too little or too much—as a kind of recreational playground with bright new swings and ladders, or as a false image
of a possible life.

There are exercises by which one can make a student familiar
with the peculiar status of the novel. Choose an hour that you
walked along the street, one might suggest, and record it in the
way Dickens would have done. Take a conversation you had at
lunch, and see what Jane Austen might have made of it. The
chances are that a first try will reveal how little of Dickens or
Jane Austen a student sees; but the second try will be better. And
a few of these read aloud will raise the question of what kind of
characters one must create to produce the kind of talk Jane Austen
does. How much of what was actually said must be left out? What
range of feeling can be admitted? And how directly can it be
expressed? What happens to a neon sign if one sees it as Dickens
might have, and just how lonely or frightened must one be to see
it that way? Trying to see what Dickens has Pip see at Newgate
makes us imagine more sharply what Pip must feel. And if a

teacher finds himself transformed into Jaggers, he may at least be sure that Jaggers is no longer simply a fictional lawyer of mid-nineteenth century London, of that time and place so frequently believed to exist only in "novels for young people." Nor will the student be long, one hopes, in seeing how much less consistent and less intense, how much less definable and perhaps less interesting, is an actual teacher than a fictional Jaggers. One has only to consider the number of gestures Jaggers makes, the settings in which he is seen, the amount of himself that he reveals, and—even more—the fact that he exists in a limited world which also contains a Wemmick and a Joe Gargery—in order to see how much Jaggers is made by the novelist and made for one novel called *Great Expectations*.

III

The problem of character provides the most immediate approach to the novel; students are interested most of all in their possible selves. And, as I have tried to suggest in the case of Jaggers and the teacher, one of the ways of coming at the novel is to see the difference between encountering someone we address in the second person and encountering someone we think of in the third. The second person confronts us with a force we must meet, answer, or resist; the third person with a character we can see at a distance, with understanding, with a free play of our own minds. And that freedom is given us by the pattern of the novel: the character is part of a design we can see as a whole. The characters of a novel do not so much exist as coexist; as Pope says of man when he pictures him within the design of the universe, he gains his strength from the embrace he gives. Jaggers could not be Jaggers if Joe were not Joe, any more than Desdemona could be Desdemona if Iago were not Iago. We can speak of polar characters, of symmetrical characters, of a spectrum of characters. In a novel like *Tom Jones,* Tom and Blifil are polar; somewhere in the spectrum that lies between them are various sets of symmetrical characters. Tom has his Partridge, Sophia her maid, Honour. Thwackum needs Square, Squire Western needs his citified sister Mrs. Western at some points, his neighbor Squire Allworthy at others, to give him stability and definition. In the same way Falstaff needs Hotspur in the first part of *Henry IV;* he needs both Shallow and the dying king in the second part. We are all familiar with those novels which give us paired heroines: Becky Sharp and Amelia Sedley, the sisters of *The Old Wives' Tale,* Elinor and Marianne in *Sense and Sensibility.* Even more interesting are those novels of multiple plot, like *Middlemarch* or *Anna Karenina, Bleak House* or *Ulysses,* where the whole curve of a single plot is defined by the plots that coexist with it in the same novel. Anna Karenina's descent into boredom and jealousy gains force from—and gives force to—Constantin Levin's faltering search for a meaningful life; her suicide is defined by the birth of Levin's son. Even in a novel like *Middlemarch,* where the conception of Dorothea Brooke came to George Eliot before the conception of Dorothea as part of the "home epic" of *Middlemarch,* we can recognize the pleasure the author must have found in seeing a necessary relationship between her stories.

Clearly, in actual life, we are Lydgates without Dorotheas, or Dorotheas without Lydgates. We may be able to recognize a counterpart or an opposite in other persons, but we do not live out our lives in constant juxtaposition to theirs. We may provide entertaining or telling designs to others who can see us from enough distance, and much gossip is a kind of primitive—not always primitive—art work. We shake our heads over a strange and tragic fatality in the life of a friend, or we smile complacently over the comic pattern of our neighbors' marriage. This may be an exercise of our best or worst feelings, but it is an exercise, too, of our desire for meaningfulness, for a pattern that makes sense of experience. And it is often the very lack of that sense in our immediate experience that makes us all the more eager to find it in others'. Some novelists sacrifice the fullness of experience for the sake of its pattern; one thinks at once of Fielding and Jane Austen, perhaps of Dickens and Hardy. Others, like George Eliot, delight in pointing out how life refuses to accommodate any of those purer patterns we see in epic or tragedy. Their interest is in the interplay between the glimpse of a pattern and the imperfect, untidy realizations that our lives allow it.

> The pencil is conscious of a delightful facility in drawing a griffin—the larger the claws, and the larger the wings, the better; but that marvellous facility which we mistook for genius is apt to forsake us when we want to draw a real unexaggerated lion. . . . It is for this rare precious quality of truthfulness that I delight in many Dutch paintings, which lofty-minded people despise. I

find a source of delicious sympathy in these faithful pictures of a monotonous homely existence, which has been the fate of so many more among my fellow-mortals than a life of pomp or of absolute indigence, of tragic suffering or of world-stirring actions.

[*Adam Bede*, Ch. 17]

"We are, most of us," Trollope writes, "apt to love Raphael's madonnas better than Rembrandt's matrons. But, though we do so, we know that Rembrandt's matrons existed; but we have a strong belief that no such woman as Raphael painted ever did exist." The realistic nineteenth-century novel recurs again and again to the example of Dutch painting, to the interest of a scene composed of low elements with rich texture, composed with difficulty out of unlikely materials instead of out of those heroic forms and lucid gestures that we see in the painting of the high Renaissance. This kind of analogy may be imperfect and misleading if taken too far, but it did have meaning for the novelists themselves and it might again for a student. For one can see before one at once the two kinds of painting, see the kinds of clarity each painting seeks and the kinds of detail it chooses to present.

This in turn can lead to those novels which, like *Madame Bovary* or Conrad's *Nostromo,* present a surface of realistic detail —the full detail that seems as inexhaustible and therefore as baffling as our familiar experience—but make of every element at once something actual and something meaningful. A novel like *Nostromo* calls attention at every moment to the fact that its setting is not just a neutral world. The shimmering white peak rising over the placid bay, the great mountain of silver—these are details that move toward pattern. They move rather heavily and loudly, and they can be seen and heard with ease. Conrad is good enough to reward study and obvious enough to ask for it, and he makes clear how certain kinds of character demand certain kinds of setting. Eustacia Vye needs Egdon Heath, Heathcliff and Catherine need Wuthering Heights, as much as Lear demands the heath and the cliff. So Charles Gould's tyrannical idealism, in *Nostromo,* demands a mine precisely of silver rather than copper; and the mixture of appetite and principle, of brutal energy and imperious doctrine, demands the political setting of the Latin American republic with its foreign exploiters, its cosmopolitan intellectuals, and its swaggering dictators. So, too, the guilt of a society that has turned its institutions into the denial of justice and charity needs the fog of *Bleak House* and the infection of Tom-All-Alone's, the slums held by Chancery; or it needs the Circumlocution Office of *Little Dorrit,* where statesmen learn How Not To Do It, and the Marshalsea Prison where debtors are forgotten and left to spend their lives in captivity. In E. M. Forster's *A Passage to India,* the landscape of India, and particularly of the Marabar hills and caves, is a monstrous assertion of that kind of world where the familiar virtues of European Christians find no purchase, no hold. It is a landscape of extreme cases, and it surrounds the preserve of the club where the pinko-grey Englishmen keep their culture intact.

This landscape of extreme cases will be familiar to many students in those "new maps of Hell" (to use Kingsley Amis's title) that we call science fiction. It is a landscape which obeys laws that make moral problems sharper and choices more dramatic. We might call it a satiric landscape, especially if we think of George Orwell's *1984,* where the possibilities of our present political tendencies are actualized in a nightmare of dehumanization. What Orwell projects into the future is the world he had previously simplified through the fable of *Animal Farm.* And the problem of distortion for the sake of truth is nicely raised by Aldous Huxley's *Brave New World* and the essays that make up *Brave New World Revisited.* It is just this kind of distortion that in some degree, for some reason, lies behind the pattern of all novels. To call it distortion is only to recognize that desire for vicarious experience I spoke of earlier, to recognize the claim of realism. But whatever we call it, distortion or pattern, the real need is to see how it works and what end it serves. Only by taking the novel for what it is can we take it seriously, and only by taking it seriously can we give it the appeal to intelligence that a student has a right to expect, whatever his resources for meeting it. Here again exercises are possible. It has always been an easy stimulant to have students cast a novel for the films; this can be an invitation to banality or an occasion for defining characters, for seeing how a character can be cut down to a type or how well it resists one choice of type or another. But more interesting is the problem of setting: the camera lingers over details, it has a pace of its own and a range of focus (I'm thinking here of a large screen, that still surviving area between television and Cinemascope). Any translation from fiction to film is a sacrifice, most of all a sacrifice of an author's voice and idiom. But the problem of what the camera shall see and which images it shall relate, as it cuts from one to another, is a way of interpreting the novel. And if it can lead away from the book, it can also lead back with new intensity. If it leads away as far as some of the great books on film technique, it can also lead into the differences between slickness and penetration, in both film and novel.

IV

It has been hard to talk about character without sliding into setting; it is hard to talk about setting without discussing incident. That is, of course, as it should be. I mentioned the Marabar Caves a moment ago. What Mrs. Moore finds in the caves is the echo "entirely devoid of distinction. Whatever is said, the same monotonous noise replies, and quivers up and down the walls until it is absorbed into the roof. . . . Hope, politeness, the blowing of a nose, the squeak of a boot, all produce 'boum.' " But the cave only provides the vertigo that characters approach at every point. Mrs. Moore cannot reach the Indians through "the echoing walls of their civility." When may she call? "All days are convenient." What about the time? "All hours." As Professor Godbole sings there is "the illusion of a Western melody." But the ear is soon baffled and wanders "in a maze of noises, none harsh or unpleasant, none intelligible." Or we have the discussion between the two devoted missionaries. Does our Father's house have mansions for all kinds of men? Surely. But for monkeys, for jackals? "And the wasps? . . . . And oranges, cactuses, crystals and mud? and the bacteria inside Mr. Sorley? No, no, this is going too far. We must exclude someone from our gathering, or we shall be left with nothing." The vertigo of Mrs. Moore in the caves is the vertigo of the undifferentiated. When we cannot find footing or direction, when all our efforts at measure and balance are frustrated, when the world defies all our categories, sheer inclusiveness becomes negation, the all becomes a void.

A Passage to India has its plot, of course, but it makes clear how the plot of a mature novel differs from those stories which are an end in themselves. Events do not drop out of sight as they are succeeded by new events; all exist in a simultaneous as well as a sequential order. We can speak of this as musicalization of form and talk of theme, of variation, and development; or we can speak of it as spatialization of form and talk of the copresence of all the elements of a painting or of a building. We may be able to see one at a time, but we can and must relate each part to every other. We move in time through a building, but the building is always open to us at any given time, to be walked through and around. The turning of pages or the passing of time do not close off earlier parts of a novel from the latter, and there is no better way of studying a novel than to circulate within it once one has explored it all. The opening chapter is itself an interesting problem; but it can be studied effectively only at the end of a novel. Even more, the student has to feel the way in which the themes of a novel move gradually to the surface—the way in which each movement forward is also a new stage of emergence of meaning.

Take, again, a speech by Maggie Tulliver near the close of *The Mill on the Floss*. Stephen has declared to her that their feeling for each other has the claim of a natural law. And Maggie replies, "if we judged in that way, there would be a warrant for all treachery and cruelty—we should justify breaking the most sacred ties that can ever be formed on earth. If the past is not to bind us, where can duty lie? We should have no law but the inclination of the moment." This is a critical incident in the novel, but its meaning is trivialized if we do not read its terms well. We must think back to the remarks much earlier in the book: "We could never have loved the earth so well if we had had no childhood in it." Or the passage on the way our affections twine around "old inferior things" and the "loves and sanctities of our life" have "deep immovable roots in memory." It is in remarks like these that we get George Eliot's vision of a life given depth by the memory of joy and terror, of places sanctified by the feelings we have known there, of duty as something not embodied in revealed law but in funded loyalties. The incident is the culmination of Maggie's character; but character in this novel is conceived in such a way that we must have a full account of childhood. Why we should need to begin with the child is an important question to ask about *The Mill on the Floss* or about *Great Expectations;* and we can—if we want—move back to Wordsworth, who was so great an influence on George Eliot, or forward to Proust, who was so great an admirer of her novels.

V

I have been trying to recover my own sense of what first made the novel seem important to me, and I have been suggesting various kinds of counterparts to the novel—painting, architecture, films, gossip—that might make its problems more familiar and compelling, as well as more obviously universal, to students. What remains to be stressed is the way in which the novel can open up to them some feeling for the connectedness and therefore the meaningfulness of their own experiences. There is a morbidity in trying to be a Maggie Tulliver, but there is real health in trying to be a George Eliot. The point at which the student's intelligence is engaged, as well as his sympathy or identification, is the point at which he can see the novel somewhat as the novelist does. Any work is the outward form of the art that has gone into it. That art is a supremely interesting human activity, and it is an activity that—diluted, imperfect, and often casual—enters into most other human affairs. We may recall Mrs. Ramsay in Virginia Woolf's *To the Lighthouse* creating her dinner party —the delicate casserole, the subtly elicited conversation, finally the achieved human warmth and the light of the candles against the gloom of the darkness outside. It is what Frost calls a poem— "a momentary stay against confusion." Mrs. Ramsay's party ends and she dies; her little friend, Lily Briscoe, lives on and completes her painting, a painting that includes Mrs. Ramsay, and exclaims, "I have had my vision." As one of Henry James's characters put it, "All art is one."

It is not so much with the view of every student his own novelist that I wish to close. But once the art of the novel is seen and understood and even consciously used by the student, in whatever form and to whatever degree, its "truth" can become more clear and more engaging. Once the novel is seen as a rich and sustained metaphor—although it need not be called that— its way of shaping experience can be taken for what it is and taken more seriously. This seems to me the best way of recovering for any art what has been called "the reek of the human."

ROMEO
AND
JULIET

ALVIN KERNAN
Yale University

I understand that *Romeo and Juliet* is not much taught in secondary schools today, though it was once a favorite in bowdlerized versions which eliminated such indelicate passages as Mercutio's explicit description of Rosaline's charms or the Nurse's crude reference to a childhood accident of Juliet's in which she stumbled and fell on her face, producing a large bump on her forehead. But times have changed, and I suspect that it is no longer the bawdy passages—most students won't understand them anyway—but rather the fine language, the supercharged poetry, which works against the teaching of the play. After all, the first and most necessary step in teaching literature, as we all know, is to close the gap between the experience of the reader and the events of the work, and the dense, pressurized poetry of *Romeo and Juliet* is apt to form a barrier to this identification for today's student. Any young idealist can share in a comment on the senseless feuds and strange behavior of his "practical" elders when it finds expression in an accent such as this in *Huckleberry Finn:*

> All of a sudden, bang! bang! bang! goes three or four guns—the men had slipped around through the woods and come in from behind without their horses! The boys jumped for the river—both of them hurt—and as they swum down the current the men run along the bank shooting at them and singing out, "Kill them, kill them!" It made me so sick I most fell out of the tree. I ain't a-going to tell *all* that happened—it would make me sick again if I was to do that. I wished I hadn't ever come ashore that night to see such things. I ain't ever going to get shut of them—lots of times I dream about them.

But it is not so easy to hear the same protest against the idiocy of adults in this voice reflecting on the shambles made of the square of Verona by the families of Capulet and Montague:

230

O me, what fray was here?
Yet tell me not, for I have heard it all.
Here's much to do with hate, but more with love.
Why then, o brawling love, o loving hate,
O any thing of nothing first create!
O heavy lightness, serious vanity,
Misshapen chaos of well-seeming forms,
Feather of lead, bright smoke, cold fire, sick health,
Still-waking sleep, that is not what it is!
[I, i, 180–188]

It seems likely that the best way of getting a student to see that Romeo is talking—in a much more complex and ultimately more interesting way than Huck Finn—about something of vital importance is not to approach this kind of verse head on. It should, I believe, be ignored for a time, treated as if it were prose rather than blank verse, as if soaring imagery were a part of ordinary speech, and as if oxymorons (bright smoke, cold fire) were as commonplace as blackberries. In the end, of course, the full meaning of the play is in the poetry, and any study of the play must come to at least some close examination of its language. But at the outset, interest and identification can be fostered by dealing with some of the larger and more immediately interesting elements of the play, by tracing out some of its more evident structural patterns; and then beginning, as if by chance, to look more closely at the verse to answer questions and verify judgments. Such an approach will not make all students into connoisseurs of Petrarchan love poetry, but it may avoid evoking their prejudices about poetry and blocking any possibility of their seeing what the play has to say to them about their lives and their natures.

The most obvious structural pattern in the play, and the one most certain to arouse interest in the classroom, involves a series of definitions of love. *Romeo and Juliet* may be regarded as an extended love debate, a running argument between a number of theories about the nature of love, in which each theory is given full and sympathetic expression. There is, first of all, the kind of fashionable love which we see in Romeo when he first appears, sleepless and disheveled, suffering the agonies of unrequited love for Rosaline. He groans, he sighs, he tosses in his bed, he moons about unaware of his surroundings, he seeks

out isolated places; but his pain is not so great that in the midst
of describing his miseries to Benvolio he cannot stop to inquire,
"Where shall we dine?" And the sight of Juliet is enough to make
him forget Rosaline forever. This kind of love is a game in
which the lover who "kisses by the book" is most in love with love
and appearing a lover.

For the witty Mercutio love is a game too, but a very realistic
game in which the prize, no matter what fancy words disguise it,
is sexual pleasure. The realities of love for this young cynic are
not the union of souls and the adoration of beauty, but such solid
facts as Rosaline's

> straight leg and quivring thigh,
> And the desmesnes that there adjacent lie.
> [II, i, 19–20]

It should not be difficult to find a partisan for this theory of love
in any class.

Then there is the Nurse who also takes a practical view of
love. For her it is simply a physical act natural to life—"Thou
wilt fall backward when thou hast more wit, wilt thou not, Jule
. . . and pretty fool, it stinted and said, 'Ay'." This view, attractive
enough in some contexts, has an unacceptable grossness in it,
however, when carried to the point toward which it tends. When
Juliet seeks advice from the Nurse on what to do about her
parents' demand that she marry Paris, when she is already married
to Romeo, the Nurse's practicality passes belief:

> Then since the case so stands as now it doth,
> I think it best you married with the County.
> O he's a lovely gentleman.
> Romeo's a dishclout to him; an eagle, madam,
> Hath not so green, so quick, so fair an eye
> As Paris hath. Beshrew my very heart,
> I think you are happy in this second match,
> For it excels your first; or if it did not,
> Your first is dead, or 'twere as good he were,
> As living here, and you no use of him.
> [III, v, 218–227]

"Use" is the key word here, the touchstone by which the
Nurse judges all questions of love; and her betters in the play
have the same standard, though they do not apply it so grossly.

Friar Lawrence cannot understand this strange, violent passion which so drives the young, but he can see that it can be harnessed and made to serve the good of the families, the church, and the state. When Romeo approaches him to announce his new love of Juliet, the Friar sees an opportunity by marrying them to end the long feud of Capulet and Montague.

> this alliance may so happy prove,
> To turn your households' rancor to pure love.
>   [II, iii, 91–92]

The elder Capulets' understanding of love is equally practical and equally attractive. Juliet is their last living child, and their concern, they believe, is only for her. She is for Capulet, "the hopeful lady of my earth." When first approached by Paris, old Capulet objects that his daughter is but thirteen and then tells Paris that he must first get Juliet's consent. But Paris is obviously the catch of the season—young, handsome, wealthy, a kinsman of the Prince, the kind of husband any careful father would dream of for his daughter—and obviously the idea is planted in Capulet's mind, for, despite his reluctance to give Juliet to Paris at once, we next see Lady Capulet breaking the subject with Juliet. The matter is delayed for a time, but when it is opened again the reason is once more Juliet's welfare. Romeo is banished and Tybalt dead, and thinking that Juliet is languishing because of Tybalt, Capulet decides to marry her to Paris, on Thursday next. When she refuses, Lady Capulet has to explain to her husband that the girl is obdurate, for Capulet cannot even conceive of so dreadful a thing.

> Soft, take me with you, take me with you wife.
> How! will she none? Doth she not give us thanks?
> Is she not proud? Doth she not count her blessed,
> Unworthy as she is, that we have wrought
> So worthy a gentleman to be her bridegroom?
>   [III, iv, 142–146]

For Capulet, love and a prosperous marriage are synonymous, and since young girls are inexperienced in the ways of the world they must allow a careful parent to select their husbands.

All of these views, different as they are, share a common quality: love is not an end in itself but a means to an end, fashion, pleasure, civic peace, being well provided for. Only in the love of

Romeo and Juliet do we see a love which attempts to be pure, which loves for the sake of loving, and which finds its complete fulfillment within love. To examine this love we shall have to move from a consideration of the play as a series of static ideas and fixed definitions of love to a consideration of it as drama, ideas in action seeking to realize themselves fully.

It is not unusual for Shakespeare to hold a type of judicial and critical inquest at the end of his tragedies. The survivors gather about the dead bodies and attempt to decide just what has happened and what its meaning is. This is, of course, the essential problem of the critic. At the end of *Romeo and Juliet* after the bodies of the two lovers, and that of Paris, have been discovered, there is considerable confusion among the survivors about just what did happen, and a formal inquisition is begun by the Chief Watchman's words:

> We see the ground whereon these woes do lie,
> But the true ground of all these piteous woes
> We cannot without circumstance descry.
>
> > [V, iii, 179–181]

The remainder of the *dramatis personae* enter, look at the fact of death, provide the circumstances which they know, and search in different ways for the true ground of all these piteous woes.

The kinds of answers given are of a nature extremely familiar to any teacher of English who has corrected very many student themes. To the direct question of the Prince as to what actually happened here, the Watchman is the first to reply:

> Sovereign, here lies the County Paris slain,
> And Romeo dead, and Juliet, dead before,
> Warm and new killed.
>
> > [V, iii, 195–197]

This is a very familiar type of paper indeed, and it obviously deserves a grade of F with the comment, "You didn't read the play." The Friar is the next to try his hand at an explanation, and he does a trifle better:

> Romeo, there dead, was husband to that Juliet,
> And she, there dead, that Romeo's faithful wife.
> I married them, and their stolen marriage day

Was Tybalt's doomsday, whose untimely death
Banished the new-made bridegroom from this city;
For whom, and not for Tybalt, Juliet pined.
You, to remove that siege of grief from her,
Betrothed and would have married her perforce
To County Paris. Then comes she to me,
And with wild looks bid me devise some mean
To rid her from this second marriage,
Or in my cell there would she kill herself.
Then gave I her, so tutored by my art,
A sleeping potion; which so took effect
As I intended, for it wrought on her
The form of death. Meantime I writ to Romeo,
That he should hither come on this dire night,
To help to take her from her borrowed grave,
Being the time the potion's force should cease.
But he which bore my letter, Friar John,
Was stayed by accident, and yesternight
Returned my letter back. Then all alone
At the prefixed hour of her waking,
Came I to take her from her kindred's vault,
Meaning to keep her closely at my cell,
Till I conveniently could send to Romeo.
But when I came, some minute ere the time
Of her awakening, here untimely lay
The noble Paris and true Romeo dead.
She wakes, and I entreated her come forth,
And bear this work of heaven with patience.
But then a noise did scare me from the tomb,
And she, too desperate, would not go with me,
But as it seems, did violence on herself.

[V, iii, 231–264]

This obviously deserves a slightly better grade, perhaps a "C," and the comment written on the paper should probably be, "You have read the story but you have gotten none of the meaning of it"—with perhaps the added remark, "Try to write more simply."

Next the Prince tries his hand. Pointing to the dead bodies, he says:

> Capulet, Montague,
> See what a scourge is laid upon your hate,
> That heaven finds means to kill your joys with love.
> Have lost a brace of kinsmen; all are punished.
>   [V, iii, 291–295]

This shows some improvement. The Prince has interpreted the facts to form a political and social moral: the deaths of the lovers show the necessity of men loving one another and the stern maintenance of civil order within the state. No doubt this explanation deserves a B, but somehow the political meaning that the Prince finds in the story seems a little thin for what actually has happened. Perhaps the only genuinely satisfactory answer about the meaning of the play is that which Romeo himself provides in the letter he leaves behind. It contains the briefest and, as is often the case, the best answer:

> I came to this vault, to die, and lie with Juliet.
>   [V, iii, 290]

I think that I would give this answer an A, despite its brevity and its obvious ambiguity, for it seems to mean several things at the same time. "To die and to lie" means first of all simply to be dead and to lie in the grave, but the word "lie" in this context suggests a consummation also, and this suggestion is supported by the lovers' final speeches in which they treat the gloomy vault of death as a place where they conquer rather than being conquered. Juliet's radiant beauty makes "the vault a feasting presence full of light." Death becomes her hateful lover whom Romeo vanquishes in his death, and the poison which Juliet kisses from Romeo's lips is transformed to a "restorative."

To the world, of course, the plain fact is that Romeo and Juliet are dead, the victims of fate, their own impetuous natures, and of the senseless feud of their families. For Arthur Brooke, the Puritan author of *The Tragical History of Romeus and Juliet*, Shakespeare's immediate source for his play, the cause of the lovers' death lay in their weak characters and moral failings, such as disobedience to parents, commerce with a wicked old nurse, and engaging in the wicked practice of "auricular confession." But Shakespeare's play leaves considerable doubt about whether the lovers' death is ultimately and conclusively either a defeat or a triumph, a punishment or a reward. The plain fact is, I believe, that our own feelings are a mixture of joy and sorrow at the conclusion, and most stage productions substantiate this emotional ambiguity. In one recent production, for example, the bodies of the lovers lying on the tomb were bathed in a radiant light while around them the remainder of the stage was dimly lit and filled with confused bustling and the bewildered voices of the living guessing at the meaning of the sight before them. This *liebestod* effect may be a trifle too strong, too weighted in the direction of triumph, but it does realize in stage terms a paradox which seems to be at the very center of the play.

To understand Romeo's paradox of "die and lie," we must go back through the play, trying to see how its action is summed up in this key phrase. From the very beginning of the play, the lovers are unrealistic to say the least. Shakespeare has emphasized this fact by providing them with a symbolic setting of a walled garden where the world is shut out, and by having them meet ordinarily in the night when the harsh outlines of reality have disappeared to be replaced by the forms which imagination creates. The language which they speak in this setting is the language of extreme idealism, the language of the Petrachan lover who makes a world in the image of his own desires. The beauty of the beloved becomes a sun, her eyes the stars, her cheeks a luminescence that makes the birds sing and think it is not night. A new religion of love replaces the more orthodox varieties, and the lover becomes a pilgrim and a martyr to beauty. The beloved becomes a saint and a god who can say,

> My bounty is as boundless as the sea,
> My love as deep; the more I give to thee
> The more I have, for both are infinite.
>   [II, ii, 133–135]

Even time is remade into lovers' time, and a few hours of separation become twenty years while a few moments of being together becomes forever.

But even as the lovers, using this language of creation, fashion their new lovers' world in the isolation of night and the walled garden, another world speaks to them in the voice of the Nurse who has entered Juliet's bedroom behind the balcony and calls insistently, "Madam, Madam." Juliet lingers over the edge of the balcony, leaves for an instant only to return; but in the end she cannot deny the voice that calls her to bed like the young child she, in one sense, is. The Nurse's voice has called and will call Juliet to many realities which force themselves on all men who live in that city which lies outside the garden walls. This voice has told Juliet, with great good humor, of the fate that lies in store for her because she is flesh and blood, "Thou wilt fall backward when thou hast more wit, Wilt thou not Jule?" And it tells her, more cynically, after Romeo has been banished from Verona, that though married to Romeo, she might as well marry Paris anyway, for one Paris in Verona is worth any number of Romeos in Mantua. This is the voice of practicality, vulgar but thoroughly human and understandable, and it speaks seemingly undeniable truths about all of us who live in nature, time, and society.

The voice speaks, in fact, for the city of Verona, with its hot, harsh sunlight which raises tempers to the boiling point; for the streets where yokels like Sampson and Gregory ape their masters and start riots merely because they like quarreling; for the hot-blooded young men who will quarrel with a man for coughing in the street and wakening one's "dog that had lain asleep in the sun." It speaks too for more homely truths such as the fact that men have to eat and servants like Antony and Potpan have to clean up afterwards; that time passes with such unbelievable swiftness that a man can discover that the son of a man whose wedding he danced at a few years ago is over thirty; that a messenger may by accident be locked up in a house of plague; and that careful parents seek to marry their daughters to rich handsome, well-born young men like the County Paris and are unable to understand why the ungrateful baggage refuses. The Nurse's voice speaks, finally, for all those ordinary facts of life which most of us accept as the only realities of human existence.

If the walled garden and the night are the symbolic settings Shakespeare supplies for the lovers, the counting house, the kitchen, the ballroom, the church, the town square, and at last the graveyard are the symbolic settings he supplies for natural and social man who must live out his life in terms of such hard practicalities as money, food, family, state, time, and death. To this world most of the characters of the play acquiesce—as most men do—and Shakespeare treats with understanding young cynics like Mercutio who have concluded that love is only a rather amusing pleasure, or ribald creatures like the Nurse who have learned that the substantial must be grasped when possible in a world where it passes so quickly, or like the Friar who knows that impetuosity does cause trouble and needs to be tempered with patience and wisdom, or parents like the Capulets who know that in this uncertain place in which we live a girl cannot be too well provided for. But for all the sympathy with which he treats these figures and their practical, realistic viewpoints, Shakespeare does not allow us to forget one crucial fact: for all their practicality, the world of these realists is a world of feud, civil violence, and bloodshed. No one knows, or at least no one bothers to mention, the origin of the Montague-Capulet feud. It is just a fact of life, an inherited and unquestioned manifestation of human quarrelsomeness and hatred—that quality in man of which Tybalt is the essential expression. No one, with the possible exception of Tybalt, even seems particularly interested in continuing the feud, but continue it does; and when it boils up old men who need crutches call for their long swords and neighbor thirsts for the blood of neighbor.

Against this world imposed on man by nature and custom, the lovers in the garden scene hurl a series of challenges. We all know the quality of these challenges even without looking at the text, for they are special versions of those defiant gestures against all that seems so solid and practical made by lovers in all ages and at all times. What lover worth his salt will not for his beloved climb the highest mountain, swim the deepest ocean, or fight the fiercest tiger? Romeo makes essentially these same idealistic brags, but in more elegant language than the writers of popular songs usually employ. Since the lovers are idealists, they are concerned with essences rather than with accidents. And what could be more accidental than a name, even if it happens to be a name hated by your family?

> 'Tis but thy name that is my enemy;
> Thou art thyself, though not a Montague.
> What's Montague? It is nor hand nor foot,
> Nor arm nor face, nor any other part
> Belonging to a man. O be some other name.
> What's in a name? That which we call a rose

> By any other word would smell as sweet;
> So Romeo would, were he not Romeo called,
> Retain that dear perfection which he owes
> Without that title. Romeo doff thy name,
> And for thy name which is no part of thee,
> Take all myself.
>
> [II, ii, 38–49]

To this idealistic challenge Romeo answers immediately and confidently, "Henceforth I never will be Romeo." A little later on when Juliet expresses adoring surprise at Romeo's daring at entering the Capulet garden, he replies in typical lover's fashion,

> With love's light wings did I o'er-perch these walls,
> For stony limits cannot hold love out,
> And what love can do, that dares love attempt.
>
> [II, ii, 66–68]

But perhaps the most daring brag of all comes shortly after this when Romeo brags of how far he would go and what he would endure for his Juliet:

> I am no pilot, yet wert thou as far
> As that vast shore washed with the farthest sea,
> I should adventure for such merchandise.
>
> [II, ii, 82–84]

Perhaps the cruelest joke that can be played on any idealist or any lover is to take him up on the unrealistic brags made in the heat of the moment, which ignore such realities as fear, flesh, and time. If the lover offers to fight the fiercest tiger, you simply produce a ravening, bloodthirsty beast and let him see what he can do with it. This is just the strategy Shakespeare uses to construct the remainder of his play. The man who had bragged in the garden that his name is only an accidental, not an essential, part of him, is shortly afterwards accosted in the public square by the fiery Tybalt, about as fierce a tiger as one could find. And this tiger insists that the figure before him is no essential spirit but Romeo, a Montague, and thus a villain. Armed with his new knowledge that "a rose by any other word would smell as sweet," and blissfully happy in his new marriage to Juliet, Romeo protests that he loves the name of Capulet as well as his own, and refuses to fight with Tybalt. Mercutio, a more practical man, is forced to take up his friend's quarrel and is subsequently killed when Romeo, still thinking there is nothing in a name, tries to come between the fighters. Romeo then discovers that such concepts as honor and friendship can override love and in a rage he kills the kinsman of the lady he has just married. Obviously in this public, practical world, names do have consequences and cannot be sloughed off as the lovers had bragged. But this is only the first disillusionment. The Prince as punishment for the duel banishes Romeo from the city, and the man who a few short scenes before had boasted so confidently that, "stony limits cannot hold love out" now learns that it is death for him to be found within Verona's walls. Though he knows "there is no world without Verona walls," he is forced to accept this banishment to Mantua. And the man who had boasted that he would adventure farthest seas for the prize of Juliet is forced to languish in a nearby city, unable to cover the few easy miles that separate him from his beloved; and the force which keeps him there is only the word of a mortal man, the Prince of Verona.

But the lovers' woes and disillusionments do not come from society alone. They are betrayed from within their own natures as well. Even at the instant of plighting their love in the purest, the most refined terms, the lovers who thrust aside all accidents and deal only with essences find themselves subject to passions and fears hitherto unsuspected. The lover who a moment before only wishes to be a glove upon his lady's hand or her pet bird finds something within him more selfish, more material, which forces him to call out, "O wilt thou leave me so unsatisfied?" The beloved whose bounty she proclaims to be as boundless as the sea, finds herself forced to wonder a few short lines afterwards, about the intentions of her lover: "If that thy bent of love be honorable, and thy purpose marriage, send me word tomorrow." But perhaps the most poignant moment in the garden scene comes when the lovers find themselves subject to the decay of feeling in time. Juliet and Romeo have declared their love, and Juliet has reassured Romeo that she is his absolutely. But even as she gives him this vow, she remarks sadly, "I would it were to give again." The supreme moment—that moment which is the subject of Keats's poetry—has passed, and from now on in the real world of self and time love can only be a shadow of that pure realization which it was for an instant in the garden.

It would seem from this evidence that Shakespeare has constructed a play about the disillusionment and betrayal of innocence, a play which suggests that we are all somehow "star crossed" in that we are born with high ideals of love and limitless aspirations which the flesh and the world will not allow us to maintain. And it is true that Romeo and Juliet seem for a time utterly helpless before the facts of existence. Romeo rolls on the floor of Friar Lawrence's cell and whines like a schoolboy; Juliet cowers before the awesome wrath of her father when he demands that she marry the County Paris. But a change comes over these two lovers as they toughen into the world. Their poetry in the garden is the richest love poetry in English, but it is a trifle too studded with extravagant metaphor and soaring hyperbole to stand the pressures of the workaday world where its genuineness must finally be tested. But this language is replaced with a newer, sparser kind of verse when the lovers come face to face with the full reality of their situations. At the exact point of recognition, the change is marked by a startling brevity of speech. When Juliet, seeking some escape from the bigamous marriage forced upon her with the County Paris, turns to her family and at last to the Nurse, she finds no comfort. She finds in fact only the words of the sensible world, of a world which has long ago given over its ideals and its aspirations in exchange for the harsh realities of existence. Her mother refuses to intervene with her father, and her Nurse gives her words about what a lovely gentleman Paris is and how happily he is here at hand. When Juliet has assured herself that these words are meant, her answer is extremely simple, "Amen." Having found a kind of death, she then gives herself over to the romantic scheme of the Friar, pretending to be dead. When Romeo hears the news of her supposed death, his change in style is equally marked: "Is it e'en so? Then I defy you, stars!" and he returns to Verona to make good his original boasts.

Here at the place of the final reality, the place where man comes really to know death, the crypt of the Capulet family, Romeo at last encounters the highest of stony walls and these ultimate seas which he has earlier said that he would adventure for his Juliet. And here indeed stony limits and perilous seas do not hold love out. Romeo pries aside the stone cover of the tomb and descends into the darkness. The world continues to dog them. A few moments difference in Juliet's awakening would have avoided the deaths, but despite this last stroke of fate the lovers with their language and their faith to one another turn the place of darkness into light and establish with their lives the validity of those ideals which they once took for granted. There is enormous waste here, but there is also magnificence. Where others gave in to the world and its sad realities, these proved that essences are what count and that the spirit can triumph.

If this were all, there would still be only limited grounds for accepting Romeo's interpretation of his act—"to die and lie with Juliet"—as a true marriage as well as a death. But there is more. None of the survivors, as we have seen, quite understands what has happened here, and Shakespeare drives this point home by allowing Montague to offer to erect statues of the lovers decked in pure gold. This is too ostentatious, too gaudy, for the lovers. Gold is the primal stuff of that material world which Romeo and Juliet have denied in the name of their ideals. It is, as Romeo has pointed out, the true poison of the world, while the so-called poison which he buys from the apothecary becomes for him a restorative. But the failure of the survivors to comprehend the nature of what has happened does not mean that certain triumphant events have not taken place. The long feud between the families of Capulet and Montague, which has disrupted the civic peace of Verona for so many years, and which the authorities tried so vainly to end by law and force, has at last been brought to a conclusion by the sacrifice of Romeo and Juliet. They are truly love's martyrs, the very spirits of love who, born "star-crossed" into a world of hate and of materialism, have maintained their belief in love through all the trials and reductions and diminutions which this belief has been subjected to in life. A world of age, tiredness, resignation, and death has been miraculously renewed by youth, by idealism, and by love, though the cost of the renewal has been so great as to make us question its value. The inability of the survivors to understand how they have been saved must necessarily make us skeptical about the future when hatred and feud will once more boil up in Verona and elsewhere. But the play comforts us in the midst of this loss

too. When he hears the soft steps of Juliet coming through the
cathedral on the way to her secret marriage, the Friar remarks
resignedly, "So light will ne'er wear out the everlasting flint."
And this, the play tells us, is true, but we are reminded also of
hard stone steps unmarked by the passing of any single foot but
gradually worn out by the unending movements of many generations over them.

READING
WALT
WHITMAN

R. W. B. LEWIS
Yale University

At the present moment, Whitman is the most blurred, as
well as the most mysterious, figure in the classical or midnine-
teenth-century period of American literature. Emerson and
Thoreau, Hawthorne and Melville: the psychological contours
of those men, the essential rhythms of their work, the crucial
attitudes and stresses in their account of human experience—all
these matters have been sufficiently well established; they compose, for us, a complex literary tradition with which we are
clearly enough related, and serious argument has to do with their
peripheries. But Whitman remains a mystery, and his work a
jumble. He is the most misrepresented of our major poets, and
the misrepresentation began with Whitman himself, in the latter
decades of his life. The problem can be formulated in a rather
simple paradox: namely, that Whitman, initially the most self-
assertive of poets, a writer for whom, indeed, the self—his particular and personal self—was the beginning and end of poetic

concern; that this poet became, in the course of time, deliberately and willfully self-concealing, asserting in all the ways available to him an entity, a being, that was radically other than the being that lay at the heart of his best poetry.

The principal mode of concealment and misrepresentation was not creative. Whitman, who died in 1892, wrote little of lasting value after the poem "Passage to India" in 1871. His main device was, rather, editorial; and it consisted in a steady reshuffling of the contents of *Leaves of Grass,* dispersing the poems out of their original and effective order, arranging them in new and fundamentally misleading groups, and even suppressing some of the more telling and suggestive of the items. What resulted was a nearly fatal shift of emphasis, whereby the authentic Whitman (the Whitman I want to discuss) got dismembered, and was replaced by what, adapting a phrase from the critic Randall Jarrell, we might call the only genuine Walt Whitman in captivity: the center of a nonliterary cult; an exhaustingly buoyant personality, patriotic and bombastic, the prophet and cheerleader of a nonexistent democracy, a man who sang songs of joy and of the open road, who saluted the pioneers and listened to America singing and chanted the square deific and worshipped the splendid silent sun, and wept over his captain lying cold and dead on the deck of the ship of State. This is the Whitman that was extravagantly admired in nonliterary circles and among persons equipped, in the slang phrase, with a tin ear; and the Whitman who was cordially and wrongheadedly detested in most literary circles—until very recently. Of late, as you probably know, there has been a concerted movement to re-establish Whitman as a *literary* power; but this movement threatens to rebuild, exactly the same old bombastic Whitman—the "cosmic" Whitman (Whitman liked to speak of himself as a cosmos, and his disciples referred portentously to his "cosmic consciousness"). All this needs to be said, for the career of Whitman's reputation is a critically important aspect of his work; and the first task of both teachers and students of Whitman is not so much to interpret him as to disentangle him, to separate the authentic from the spurious, to divide off the poet from the cosmos.

The poet is a very great figure indeed, incomparably the greatest of American poets; and not only that. He is also the seed and source of almost every significant poetic development and body of verse that have appeared since his own creative prime; the crucial ancestor not merely of neoromantic and "beat" writers, but to a considerable degree of *symboliste* poetry in France and imagist poetry in England and America; the chief, if of course by no means the only, American begetter of Wallace Stevens and Hart Crane, and also, surprisingly, but unmistakably of Ezra Pound (who acknowledged his Whitmanian parentage vehemently but in secret) and of T. S. Eliot.

To come to terms with this, the real Whitman, we must first of all put the poems back into their original and chronological order; and ideally, back into their original or at least their most successful versions; for Whitman not only reordered his poems to fulfill the public image of him as a bardic prophet—he also rewrote parts of them, sometimes, to be sure, by way of distinct improvement. If it is piously argued that we have no right to tamper with the poet's own judgment, that *Leaves of Grass* is his book and not ours and that we must take it as he left it on his deathbed, then we can answer in somewhat the way the lady of historic legend answered Philip of Macedon: appealing, if not from Whitman drunk to Whitman sober (though that is not an altogether inappropriate metaphor) at least from the Whitman of 1871 and 1881 and 1891 to the Whitman of 1855 and 1856 and 1860 and 1867. All the dates I have just named are the dates of the seven successive editions of *Leaves of Grass;* and the latter, the dates we appeal to, are those of the editions in which the real Whitman came into being.

The whole question can be focused by considering the two poems printed at the end of this essay, eventually for purposes of detailed analysis; and by glancing at the chronological list of what seem to me Whitman's most rewarding poems. The poem "There Was a Child Went Forth" was, originally, the tenth of twelve untitled entries in the first or 1855 *Leaves of Grass*—a volume, by the way, which was reprinted in nearly facsimile form a couple of years ago and published by the Viking Press, with an excellent introduction and helpful editorial commentary by Malcolm Cowley. The exceedingly beautiful poem "As I Ebb'd with the Ocean of Life," as you see, made its appearance in the 1860 *Leaves of Grass,* the last completely satisfactory version of the book, and a volume, which is (as I understand) to be reprinted in facsimile form by the Cornell University Press, with a

commentary by Professor Roy Harvey Pearce, that will discuss
many of the bibliographical puzzles that I am only alluding to
sketchily.

Now, although "As I Ebb'd" was thus written five years
after "There Was a Child Went Forth" and represents—as we
shall see—a most engrossing change both of psychological attitude
(of Whitman's attitude, that is, to himself) and of poetic technique, it invariably appears very much *earlier* than "There Was
a Child Went Forth" in all standard editions of *Leaves of Grass.*
For example, in the otherwise valuable Houghton Mifflin paperback of the *Complete Poetry and Selected Prose,* "As I Ebb'd"
(an 1860 poem) can be found on page 184; and "There Was a
Child" (an 1855 poem) turns up seventy-five pages *later.* This is
only a single instance of virtually countless similar reorderings
which resulted in the suppression of the real and the inflation of
the cosmic Whitman. What happens, as a consequence of such
reshuffling, is a multiple loss of very serious proportions.

The blurring of chronology leads, to begin with, to a loss
of any clear sense of the development of Whitman as a consciousness and a craftsman. This is an affair of far graver concern
with Whitman than with most other poets of his stature; for
the development of his consciousness is the very root and center
of his poetic subject matter. It is what his poems are about: the
thrust and withdrawal, the heightening and declining, the flowing
and ebbing of his psychic energy. And the shift from the forthgoing impulse of 1855 and "There Was a Child Went *Forth*" to
the ebbing movement of 1860 and "As I *Ebb'd* with the Ocean of
Life" is the most important event in the whole of Whitman's
spiritual and creative career. The loss of our perception of that
event leads, in turn, not only to a fuzzy understanding of the
poems in question but also to something still worse, perhaps: to
the general loss of any awareness at all of the sheer existence of
the ebbing and declining Whitman. The burgeoning, the morning and springtime mood of poems like "There Was a Child
Went Forth" become, through Whitman's old-age strategy of
placement, the only mood in which we recognize Whitman and
expect him to express himself. A poem like "As I Ebb'd" is therefore skipped over as an occasional and uncharacteristic aberra-
tion. But returned to its proper context, "As I Ebb'd" turns out
to be surrounded by a score of poems striking the same melan-

choly, almost desperate note: a note amounting in fact to a sense of impending annihilation.

Reading those poems within their proper, 1860, cluster we realize that there are in fact two Whitmans, not one. (There are several other Whitmans as well, but the essential Whitman is double.) There is the poet of morning and the poet of night, the poet of vitality and the poet of death, the poet of creation and the poet of annihilation. The alternation is evident at once in the four poems I have listed from the 1855 volume: "The Sleepers," as the title suggests, is a night-time poem (one of the first serious poems Whitman wrote, but one that in the standard edition is tucked far away in the latter pages of *Leaves of Grass*), a poem which presents the self in its opening stanza as "Wandering and confused, lost to myself, ill-assorted, contradictory." "Song of Myself," on the other hand, is Whitman's masterpiece of daytime poetry. "To Think of Time" is a poem about death: Whitman's own original title for it was "Burial Poem"; and "There Was a Child Went Forth" is, again, an invocation of the power of growth. There are two Whitmans, we realize, and it is even possible that we shall come to cherish the Whitman that got edited away, blurred or lost, the poet of death—or anyhow, that we shall come to cherish those poems in which both his voices can be heard, opposing each other in a vital tension.

It is unlikely, I suppose, that many of Whitman's night-time poems—his "desolation poems," as some unusually knowledgeable critic has called them—will find their way into the fashionable anthologies. A poem like "The Sleepers" or "As I Ebb'd with the Ocean of Life"; or "Scented Herbage of My Breast," in which he speaks of his poems as "Tomb-leaves, body-leaves, growing up above me above death"; or "Hours Continuing, Sore and Heavy-Hearted," a poem of 1860 that bespeaks a profound wretchedness due possibly to sexual guilt, but expressive in any case of the ineradicable tears of things; or "A Hand Mirror," also of 1860, and an extraordinary statement of self-loathing, also touched off perhaps by sexual guilt—"Outside fair costume, within ashes and filth . . . Blood circulating dark and poisonous streams. . . . Such a result so soon—and from such a beginning"; poems like those probably demand more human experience, a greater moral generosity, a more developed sense of verbal nuance than younger students can be reasonably expected to possess.

But we, as teachers, should examine those writings very carefully; and in addressing ourselves to Whitman in class, we have to be fully aware of this aspect, arguably the determining aspect, of Whitman the poet. In the same way, *Measure for Measure* is unlikely to be taught in most schools, or the sonnets of Shakespeare that reflect his feeling for the ravages of sexuality, but in discussing *The Merchant of Venice* or *Romeo and Juliet,* the understanding of them must, surely, be colored by an awareness of those darker and more psychologically tangled works. In the case of Whitman, such an awareness is a safeguard against a dangerously false identification of the poet and his poetry: an identification that, in its very falsehood, is untrue to American literature, in general, and hence to the very sense of experience which our literature has characteristically expressed.

Let me now attempt a truer identification, and a detailed illustration of some of these contentions, by looking at the two poems, considering each in itself, and then the two in their curious and suggestive relation. Read the first of the two poems that appear at the end of this essay.

It is probably wise to be as leisurely in the discussion and analysis of this poem as the poem is in its own process of evolution. Instead, that is, of plunging at once to the question of its ultimate "meaning" or "purpose," it might be better to begin with some obvious and yet easily overlooked notations. The author of this poem, the Whitman of 1855, was a far less meticulously self-conscious craftsman than, say, Robert Frost—or indeed than the Whitman of 1871 and "Passage to India." But contrary to legend, the Whitman of 1855 did not erupt all at once (within hours, say, of some sudden fit or vision) in a flood of beautifully artless, spontaneous, and purely "inspired" poetry. He had been serving his own private apprenticeship for at least six years, during which time he always carried a little notebook with him, in which he experimented in new techniques of meter and stanzaic structures, with phrase—and line jottings for future verses. So we are justified in looking at his technique, even at his handling of mechanical and syntactical resources (if we do not look too rigidly and joylessly), as the resources of a poet on the verge of becoming an original master of his craft.

It is worth, for example, arriving at the observation, via questioning, that each of the stanzas in this poem consists of a single grammatical sentence. It is worth noticing, too, that these sentence stanzas tend to grow increasingly longer, to contain a larger number of lines on the page. The exception, of course, is stanza four, which amounts to only three lines, after the eight-lined sentence stanza that precedes it and the eighteen-line one that follows and concludes the poem. That exception itself turns out to be illuminating—for, looking more closely, but still at the mechanical and syntactical aspect, we see not so much a steady and uninterrupted process of increasing size and length but rather a process of alternation in which, however, the impulse toward growth is dominant. This holds true, to some extent, even of the length of the individual lines, as well as of the stanzas. Thus, the constitution of the very first stanza is reflected, or repeated, in the constitution of the first four stanzas taken as a group: a rhythmic movement from shorter to longer to still longer and back to shorter once again.

This is a process, let us say, of enlarging and retracting: or of stretching and shrinking. And it seems to me revealingly artful of Whitman (revealing both of the essential nature and achievement of this poem, and of an artfulness he had already acquired) that the line in stanza one that represents the shrinking movement should be just the line accentuated by the word "stretching" as the line "And that object became part of him for a day or a certain part of a day" fades back in quantitative length to the short line that nonetheless bespeaks the greatest spread of time —"Or for many years or stretching cycles of years." The stretching is thus asserted in the moment of shrinking: and the stretching impulse is what finally triumphs and defines the poem.

These considerations lead, easily enough, from the external forms to the substance or better yet to the organic experience those forms are seeking to realize. The external and quantitative enlarging and retracting serve to give us an internal movement of qualitative change. It is a poem *about* stretching and shrinking: a poem about that sistole and diastole of psychic energy that for Whitman was so much at the center of experience and hence of poetry. But in this poem, as in the poems that gave the first edition of *Leaves of Grass* its determining tone and character, the impulse to enlarge, to stretch, to grow is the impulse that is in command, and that articulates itself through all the resources of Whitman's disposal. We can turn, now, from the syntactic re-

source to the verbal resource, drawing attention to the series of
verbal allusions to entities just born and beginning to sprout,
to blossom, to grow; "lilacs . . . lambs . . . litter . . . foal . . . calf
. . . . brood . . . . plants . . . . . sprouts . . . . blossoms . . . .
fruits"; to the increase of the year, from "the Third-Month"
(Whitman's later and somewhat affected emendation of the
simpler "March") to "Fourth-Month" and "Fifth-Month" (April
and May). And all those recently born and growing things—the
new year in its springtime, the animals on the farm, the flowers
and plants and apple-trees: these are not only paralleled by the
main human figure, the child freshly arrived in the world and
setting forth on his own career, his own sprouting and burgeoning and blossoming, they are the very means of the child's outward and forward thrust.

The key word here is, of course, the much repeated word
"became." The child *becomes* the objects he looks upon, and
they become a part of him. This, in short, is a poem about growth
as the process of becoming, not of becoming this or that, but of
becoming in the metaphysical or root sense of coming to be, of
growing into being; in particular, of this child coming or growing into being by virtue of organic and vital and nourishing
relationships with the contents of the world he moves forth into.
And you will notice how rich and complete the process of those
relationships is. After the elements of nature, the animals and
the plants, the child goes on to encounter and become human
entities—his schoolmistress, the boys and girls at school, his
mother and his father, men and women he sees flashing by in
the streets; and finally, as it were, the world at large—the nearby
streets, the village seen from afar, the hurrying waves of the sea,
the clouds in the sky, the horizon's edge. This is a poem that
gives us the process of coming to be, of psychological stretching
and enlargement, not only through a particular sensitivity or
responsiveness to the natural and human and inanimate contents of the world but through a gift for identification with,
absorption of those multicolored things, from the nearest lilac
to the horizon's edge. And I see no reason why, at this stage of
comprehension, students should not be asked how far each of
them feels any genuine and vital relation with the things and
persons and places he or she regularly looks upon; how far each
has ever felt the sense of enlargement through association with

the world outside of him or her; and how far that world remains, for him or her, something separate, unrelated, distinctly *other.*

But it should be emphasized that, in this poem, it is not only the child who comes into being; the outside world undergoes the same process—and it does so by virtue of the third element that *becomes,* namely, the poem itself. These three phenomena—the child, the crowded world, the poem—assume at last their permanent size and shape through the action they share in common and through which they affect each other; that action of stretching, then shrinking a little, then stretching out to the final completed condition. The poetry assembles the world by various devices of linkage: by enclosing a teeming variety within a single grammatical sentence (as in sentence-stanza three, which binds together the field sprouts, the winter grain sprouts and light yellow corn, the esculent roots and the apple trees, an old drunkard, a schoolmistress, friendly boys and quarrelsome boys, fresh-cheek'd girls, a barefoot Negro boy and girl, and the changes of city and country): by the encircling evocation of the phrase "became part of him": and by no means least, through the activity of the meter.

Whitman's metrical experiments deserve a long and close study in themselves, though perhaps such study would be more rewarding with some of the poetry written after 1855. But for our limited purposes, only the following need be said. Whitman was the first American poet to break through the convention of iambic pentameter as the principal and most appropriate and decorous meter for poetry. It was a major act of technical liberation, for which every poet who followed him has cause to be grateful. It was not, however—and as it is sometimes alleged—an act of purely negative liberation. It was emancipation with a purpose: it freed Whitman, first to attempt a closer approximation of metrics and the sense of experience he aimed to express; and second, to recover, eventually, the older conventions of meter in rejuvenated form. Both purposes are admirably reflected in "There Was a Child Went Forth." The seeming looseness, even casualness, of the rhythm is indispensable to the poetic intention. The processes I have been describing—the enlarging and contracting and enlarging—could not be conveyed with anything approaching the same effect by employing a recurring five-stress line, or iambic pentameter, however much play and variety were permitted, nor by a regular alternation, let us say, of five-stress line with four-stress line. What Whitman has done, here and elsewhere, is to depend, not on the alternating metrical current of the iambic but rather on a series of rising and falling rhythms that correspond very well (if not always exactly) with the rising and falling within the experience—that is to say, with the flowing and ebbing, with the stretching and shrinking. And one can scarcely doubt that an achieved technical mastery is at work in the poem's conclusion. Here the movement into being is completed, a world fully and finally created and the child, psychically speaking, full grown—even as the unconventional meter rises to its own consummation and ends in a more conventional line which neither rises *nor* falls any longer, but which rests in a sort of permanent stillness, a subdued iambic of almost perfectly *even* stress composed of a long slow series of monosyllables broken only and properly by the words "became," "always," and "every." "These became part of that child who went forth every day, and who now goes, and will always go forth every day."

"There Was a Child Went Forth" is quintessential 1855 Whitman. Many of the qualities and developments I have been pointing to in it can be discovered in other poems in the first edition of *Leaves of Grass,* and especially, of course, in "Song of Myself," a poem of enlargement and expansion and coming to be on a gigantic scale. I have gone into a greater amount of technical and structural detail than most of you are probably inclined to do in your classes, with the aim, however, of suggesting that the Whitman you discuss deserves respect—and admiration—not only as the chanter of morning and the seedtime of life but also as an engrossingly subtle and resourceful poet. And a correction of the blurry image of Whitman as spontaneous and artless in technique (just as it was necessary, a century or so back, to correct the image of Shakespeare as the artless singer of wild untutored woodnotes free) is indispensable to the correction of the image of Whitman as unfailingly cheery and boisterous in content.

The burgeoning and forthgoing Whitman of 1855 continued to announce itself in the expanding rhythms of the poems added to the next edition, in the following year, 1856; for example, in "This Compost," which salutes (though not without a feeling of awe amounting almost to discomfort) the "calm and patient" earth that "renews with such unwitting looks its prodigal, annual, sumptuous crops:" and in "Spontaneous Me," which in a single grammatical sentence that uncoils over some sixty lines swears a great "oath of procreation" amid a virtual orgy of indiscriminate begetting; and best of all in the splendid poem "Crossing Brooklyn Ferry," which sounds the note of endless outward and onward movement with all the poetic dynamism that Whitman possessed.

But somehow and at some time between 1856 and 1860 a radical change set in, with results that are effectively visible in the poems added to the 1860 edition. The causes are not clearly known. There are biographical rumors of a deeply unhappy love affair in the late 50s; and there are biographical rumors that this alleged affair was of such a nature as to leave Whitman in a state of guilty shock. These rumors, however, have definitely *not* been confirmed, not even by the most strenuous and learned Whitmanian pryers and voyeurs. What we can take account of are the poetic consequences. The most striking is the sense, voiced in a number of poems, that the poet's creative genius had abandoned him or was about to abandon him: a sense of the loss of creative power accompanied, more somberly, by a loss of confidence in everything that power had previously brought into being. I suspect myself that the fear of artistic sterility was the main cause, rather than the effect, of his almost paralyzing melancholy, and that such a fear was due to a familiar climacteric in Whitman's life—what is called *la crise de quarantaine,* the psychological crisis some men pass through when they reach the age of forty. Whitman was forty in 1859. This, I think, is what is implied in the poem "So Long!"—a poem precisely stating the fear that he is, artistically speaking, dead: "It appears to me I am dying . . . . My songs cease, I abandon them": a poem written in 1859 or 1860 and which the aging Whitman, so characteristically, transferred to the very last portion of *Leaves of Grass,* insinuating thereby that it was an old age poem of farewell and concealing the whole nature and extent of the crisis it originally grew out of.

Whatever it was, that crisis was given one of its most remarkable expressions in the second poem, "As I Ebb'd with the Ocean of Life," a poem that seems to me, the more I consider it, one of the genuinely great American lyrics.

This is, of course, a good deal more complex and difficult than "There Was a Child Went Forth," but its complexity is subject to the same kind of careful probing we accord any great and complex lyric, for example, Keats's "Ode on a Grecian Urn," which Whitman's poem in certain oblique ways somewhat resembles. We will not be far wrong if we take it as the opposite, in substance and to some degree in technique, of "There Was a Child Went Forth," or as an inversion of that earlier work; this, at least, has the rhetorical advantage of juxtaposing the two Whitmans, or the two sides of Whitman, that I have been trying to identify. As against the forthgoing Whitman and the floodtide Whitman, this is plainly the Whitman of *ebb,* as against the Whitman of morning and of spring (the early lilacs and the red morning glories); this is the Whitman of the decline of the day and of the year, a poet who is found "musing late in the autumn day." And all the sprouts and blossoms and fruit of "There Was a Child Went Forth" are here replaced, in the poetically stunning second stanza, by

> Chaff, straw, splinters of wood, weeds, and the sea-gluten,
> Scum, scales from shining rocks, leaves of salt-lettuce,
>   left by the tide . . .

to which are added, later, "a few sands and dead leaves," "a trail of drift and debris," and finally

> Froth, snowy white, and bubbles, loose windrows,
>   little corpses,
> (See, from my dear lips the ooze exuding at last. . . .)

Metrically, there is a marked advance in versatility, so marked that it is not possible to give a faithful account of it here. But we can at least underscore the fact that, of Whitman's chief metrical innovations, the rising and falling rhythms, it is the falling rhythm that, properly enough, particularly catches the ear. As against "There Was a Child Went Forth Every Day," we now hear:

> Where the fierce old mother endlessly cries for her
>   castaways . . .

a technical dying fall that conveys the slide toward death the poem is otherwise enacting. And the stanzaic composition shrinks almost to the verge of disappearance in section III, before the poet gathers enough energy to voice the prayer of survival in the concluding part.

A simple grammatical notation is, once again, worth making; to overlook it is to miss the heart of the poem. And that notation is the shift from the past tense of section I: "As I ebb'd . . . As I wended . . . As I walk'd"—to the present tense of section II:

"As I wend . . . As I list . . . As I inhale." The shift corresponds, of course, to the shift from the known to the unknown, from "the shores I know" to "the shores I know not": a shift not so much from past to present as from the temporal to the timeless. This takes us close to the center of the poem; for what the poem confronts and what stimulates in the poet the feeling of disintegration and death is exactly the whole timeless realm of genuine truth and reality, which, as he now feels, his poetry has never known, never touched at all. The reason why he is "baffled, balk'd, bent . . . [and] oppressed" is that he now perceives that "I have not really understood anything, not a single object, and that no man ever can." The essential reality he has quite failed to grasp is rendered as "the real Me": and to get the full forces of that naked confession, we should need to place it next to the whole of "Song of Myself," and especially next to the section of that poem in which Whitman exultingly proclaims the exact opposite, the perfect *union* between the actual Me and the real Me: between, shall we say, the here-and-now everyday Whitman and that higher reality, that timeless being, that (perhaps) creative genius that he addressed as the Me Myself. This, as I have suggested, is the important disunion, this is the love affair that seemed to the Whitman of 1859 to have ended; and disjoined from the real Me, the actual Me feels itself coming apart, collapsing into a trail of drift and debris, with ooze exuding from dead lips.

Still, as the most rewarding commentator on Whitman, Richard Chase (in his fine book, *Walt Whitman Reconsidered*) has insisted, this poem is altogether saved from the slightest suggestion of whimpering self-pity by the powerfully and courageously voiced note of self-mockery, the image of the real Me ridiculing the disintegrating Me:

> . . . before all my arrogant poems the real Me stands
>   yet untouch'd, untold, altogether unreach'd,
> Withdrawn far, mocking me with mock-
>   congratulatory signs and bows,
> With peals of distant ironical laughter at every word
>   I have written,
> Pointing in silence to these songs, and then to the
>   sand beneath.

The effect of those lines is literally immeasurable: an image of total desolation made more not less persuasive by the extraordinary image of the poet's genius offering mock congratulations in a series of silent signs and bows and pointings.

In a poem that deals with the crushing sense of the unfathomable mystery as well as the impalpable tears of things ("the sobbing dirge of nature"), it is to be expected that there will be unsolvable mysteries of content. I should be inclined not to press too hard at the symbolic allusions, to allow the poem to retain that feeling of the ineffable that is part of its subject. But we can notice that the poet seems to address the land or shore as his father and the sea as his fierce old mother; and that the pervasive sense of alienation—of the actual Me from the real Me, of the poet from his genius—is intensified in the felt alienation of the poet, as child, from his symbolic parents. He prays to each of those parents to restore in him the power to create, to renew his poetry-making energy, "the secret of the murmuring I envy." And indeed, "As I Ebb'd" is one of the supreme instances in literature of a profound paradox that we could see illustrated in Keats or much more recently in Hart Crane; that is, the poem of distinction that has as its subject the feeling of poetic *extinc*-tion, triumphantly successful poetry about the abject failure and loss of the poetic power. Here, as in "Ode on a Grecian Urn" and in Hart Crane's "The Broken Tower," the terrible threat of poetic exhaustion is overcome exactly by converting that threat itself into poetry. This is the reason why, at the very nadir of his ebbing, Whitman can say parenthetically in section IV that the ebb will return. And this is why, in the final stanza, the creative impulse, even while dealing with its own loss, can fulfill itself in a poetic thickness and extension so far beyond the precarious brevities of the third section.

There is, needless to say, more to the story of Walt Whitman —to the drama of his psychic career and the development of his poetry—than I have been able to encompass. A fuller account would carry Whitman past 1860 on into the Civil War, and it would record the effects—beneficial effects, for the most part— of that war upon Whitman, both as man and as poet. But the first and most important thing to establish, I venture, is the fact that his psychic career did constitute a drama, and that his poetry is the account and the allegory thereof. Whitman thus restored,

Whitman (or *Leaves of Grass*) put back together again in proper order, Whitman—one might say, punningly—no longer dismembered but re-membered; this is an immensely impressive and fascinating figure, whose acquaintance we ought to make if we desire to understand American literature and, by means of it, to understand the experience it has reflected: ultimately, I suppose, if we desire to understand ourselves.

WALT WHITMAN: SELECTED POEMS

Poems

1855

The Sleepers
Song of Myself
To Think of Time
There Was a Child Went Forth

1856

This Compost
Crossing Brooklyn Ferry
Spontaneous Me
To You

1860

Scented Herbage of My Breast
Whoever You Are Holding Me Now in Hand
I Saw in Louisiana a Liveoak Growing
Hours Continuing, Sore and Heavy-Hearted
A Hand-Mirror
City of Orgies
A Glimpse
As I Ebb'd with the Ocean of Life
So Long!
Out of the Cradle Endlessly Rocking

1867

Cavalry Crossing a Ford
Bivouac on a Mountain Side
The Wound-Dresser
Reconciliation
When Lilacs Last in the Dooryard Bloom'd

1871

Sparkles from the Wheel
A Noiseless Patient Spider
Passage to India

1881

The Dalliance of the Eagles

1891

Good-Bye My Fancy

THERE WAS A CHILD WENT FORTH
Walt Whitman

There was a child went forth every day,
And the first object he look'd upon, that object he became,
And that object became part of him for the day or a certain part
     of the day,
Or for many years or stretching cycles of years.

The early lilacs became part of this child,
And grass and white and red morning-glories, and white and red
     clover, and the song of the phoebe-bird,
And the Third-month lambs and the sow's pink-faint litter, and
     the mare's foal and cow's calf,
And the noisy brood of the barnyard or by the mire of the
     pond-side,
And the fish suspending themselves so curiously below there, and
     the beautiful curious liquid,
And the water-plants with their graceful flat heads, also became
     part of him.

The field-sprouts of Fourth-month and Fifth-month became part
     of him,
Winter-grain sprouts and those of the light-yellow corn, and the
     esculent roots of the garden,
And the apple-trees cover'd with blossoms and the fruit afterward,
     and wood-berries, and the commonest weeds by the road,
And the old drunkard staggering home from the outhouse of the
     tavern whence he had lately risen,
And the schoolmistress that pass'd on her way to the school,
And the friendly boys that pass'd, and the quarrelsome boys,

And the tidy and fresh-cheek'd girls, and the barefoot negro boy
    and girl,
And all the changes of city and country wherever he went.

His own parents, he that had father'd him and she that had
    conceiv'd him in her womb and birth'd him,
They gave this child more of themselves than that,
They gave him afterward everyday, they became part of him.

The mother at home quietly placing the dishes
    on the supper-table,
The mother with mild words, clean her cap and gown,
    a wholesome odor falling off her person and clothes
    as she walks by,
The father, strong, self-sufficient, manly, mean, anger'd, unjust,
The blow, the quick loud word, the tight bargain, the crafty lure,
The family usages, the language, the company, the furniture,
    the yearning and swelling heart,
Affection that will not be gainsay'd, the sense of what is real, the
    thought if after all it should prove unreal,
The doubts of day-time and the doubts of night-time, the curious
    whether and how,
Whether that which appears so is so, or is it all flashes and specks?
Men and women crowding fast in the streets, if they are not
    flashes and specks what are they?
The streets themselves and the facades of houses, and goods
    in the windows,
Vehicles, teams, the heavy-plank'd wharves, the huge crossing
    at the ferries,
The village on the highland seen from afar at sunset, the river
    between,
Shadows, aureola and mist, the light falling on roofs and gables
    of white or brown two miles off,
The schooner nearby sleepily dropping down the tide, the little
    boat slack-tow'd astern,
The hurrying tumbling waves, quick-broken crests, slapping,
The strata of color'd clouds, the long bar of maroon-tint away
    solitary by itself, the spread of purity it lies motionless in,
The horizon's edge, the flying sea-crow, the fragrance of salt
    marsh and shore mud,
These became part of that child who went forth every day,
    and who now goes, and will always go forth every day.

AS I EBB'D WITH THE OCEAN OF LIFE
Walt Whitman

I

As I ebb'd with the ocean of life,
As I wended the shores I know,
As I walk'd where the ripples continually wash you Paumanok,
Where they rustle up hoarse and sibilant,
Where the fierce old mother endlessly cries for her castaways,
I musing late in the autumn day, gazing off southward,
Held by this electric self out of the pride of which I utter poems,
Was seiz'd by the spirit that trails in the lines underfoot,
The rim, the sediment that stands for all the water and all the
    land of the globe.

Fascinated, my eyes reverting from the south, dropt, to follow
    those slender windrows,
Chaff, straw, splinters of wood, weeds, and the sea-gluten,
Scum, scales from shining rocks, leaves of salt-lettuce,
    left by the tide,
Miles walking, the sound of breaking waves the other side of me,
Paumanok there and then as I thought the old thought
    of likenesses,
These you presented to me you fish-shaped island,
As I wended the shores I know,
As I walk'd with that electric self seeking types.

II

As I wend to the shores I know not,
As I list to the dirge, the voices of men and women wreck'd,
As I inhale the impalpable breezes that set in upon me,
As the ocean so mysterious rolls toward me closer and closer,
I too but signify at the utmost a little wash'd-up drift,
A few sands and dead leaves to gather,
Gather, and merge myself as part of the sands and drift.

O baffled, balk'd, bent to the very earth,
Oppress'd with myself that I have dared to open my mouth,
Aware now that amid all that blab whose echoes recoil upon me
    I have not once had the least idea who or what I am,

But that before all my arrogant poems the real Me stands yet
    untouch'd, untold, altogether unreach'd,
Withdrawn far, mocking me with mock-congratulatory signs and
    bows,
With peals of distant ironical laughter at every word I have
    written,
Pointing in silence to these songs, and then to the sand beneath.
I perceive I have not really understood any thing, not a single
    object, and that no man ever can,
Nature here in sight of the sea taking advantage of me to dart
    upon me and sting me,
Because I have dared to open my mouth to sing at all.

III

You oceans both, I close with you,
We murmur alike reproachfully rolling sands and drift, knowing
    not why,
These little shreds indeed standing for you and me and all.

You friable shore with trails of debris,
You fish-shaped island, I take what is underfoot,
What is yours is mine my father.

I too Paumanok,
I too have bubbled up, floated the measureless float, and been
    wash'd on your shores,
I too am but a trail of drift and debris,
I too leave little wrecks upon you, you fish-shaped island.

I throw myself upon your breast my father,
I cling to you so that you cannot unloose me,
I hold you so firm till you answer me something.

Kiss me my father,
Touch me with your lips as I touch those I love,
Breathe to me while I hold you close the secret of the murmuring
    I envy.

IV

Ebb, ocean of life, (the flow will return,)
Cease not your moaning you fierce old mother,
Endlessly cry for your castaways, but fear not, deny not me,

Rustle not up so hoarse and angry against my feet as I touch you
    or gather from you.
I mean tenderly by you and all,
I gather for myself and for this phantom looking down where we
    lead, and following me and mine.

Me and mine, loose windrows, little corpses,
Froth, snowy white, and bubbles,
(See, from my dead lips the ooze exuding at last,
See, the prismatic colors glistening and rolling,)
Tufts of straw, sands, fragments,
Buoy'd hither from many moods, one contradicting another,
From the storm, the long calm, the darkness, the swell,
Musing, pondering, a breath, a briny tear, a dab of liquid or soil,
Up just as much out of fathomless workings fermented
      and thrown,
A limp blossom or two, torn, just as much over waves floating,
    drifted at random,
Just as much for us that sobbing dirge of Nature,
Just as much whence we come that blare of the cloud-trumpets,
We, capricious, brought hither we know not whence, spread out
    before you,
You up there walking or sitting,
    Whoever you are, we too lie in drifts at your feet.

READING
EMILY
DICKINSON[1]

RICHARD B. SEWALL
Yale University

My impression is that as teachers we are hesitant about Emily
Dickinson. She is a puzzle and a problem, of which the difficulty
of handling her tense little lyrics in class is a surface symptom.
Where does she stand in the hierarchy of the poets? What does
she stand for? Anyone with a grain of sensitivity realizes in reading her that he is in the presence of something remarkable. But
just how remarkable? And what are the distinguishing qualities
of her remarkableness? We know where we are with the dozen
other major poets we discuss yearly and confidently in our classes.
Their outlines are set, their measurements taken. But this is not
so with Emily Dickinson. We are uneasy about her and treat her
gingerly. I cannot, of course, settle all these matters in my hour's
conversation with you this morning.[2] All I can offer are some
hints and suggestions as to where and how to begin.

But first let me suggest some reasons for our difficulty. Emily
Dickinson never wrote anything big, like a novel or a play or an
epic, which would establish her dimensions unmistakably. She
wrote some 1775 little things on a bewildering variety of subjects
and representing a bewildering variety of subjects and representing a bewildering variety of points of view. She is, in turn,
and often on successive pages, grave and gay, ecstatic and
despairing, pious and blasphemous, ingenuous and ironic.
Which one is the "real" Emily Dickinson? Furthermore, her
poems are difficult, often very difficult—1775 knotty little prob-

---

1 All quotations from the poetry and letters of Emily Dickinson in this paper
are reprinted by permission of The Belknap Press from Thomas H. Johnson, Ed., and
Thomas H. Johnson and Theodore Ward, Eds., *The Poems of Emily Dickinson* and
The Letters of Emily Dickinson. Copyright 1951, 1955, 1958 by the President and
Fellows of Harvard College.
2 This was a speech given in April 1961.

lems which make the search for the "real" Emily Dickinson tortuous and sometimes exasperating. Add to this the fact that until only six years ago we had no text to work with that gave all her poems under one cover, or gave them in any semblance of chronological order, or in the form in which she originally wrote them. Until then, we had her piecemeal, her poems, often consciously adjusted to suit the taste of a conventional, late-nineteenth-century reading public—with much of the sting and flavor extracted. Until three years ago we had only a sampling of her letters, often expurgated, and presented very unsystematically. Indeed, except for three books, George Whicher's *This Was a Poet* (1939), Henry Wells' *Introduction to Emily Dickinson* (1947), and Richard Chase's *Emily Dickinson* (1951), the last six years (seventy years after her death) have given us the first really scholarly and informed studies of her life and work. And two of the most important (Jay Leyda's *The Years and Hours of Emily Dickinson* and Charles Anderson's *Stairway of Surprise*) appeared only in the last year. (To complete the list of indispensable reading, let me add Mrs. Millicent Todd Bingham's two fine books, *Emily Dickinson's Home* (1955) and *Ancestor's Brocades* (1945), the latter of which will give you some of the reasons why this attention to her life and work was so long delayed.)

What it comes to is this: Emily Dickinson, who died seventy-five years ago one of the great poets in English, is news. For until now the "real" Emily Dickinson has been almost hopelessly obscured for the general reader. Jay Leyda wrote a vigorous article on this subject for the *New Republic* a few years ago, to which he gave the significant title: "Late Thaw of a Frozen Image." And the frozen image he had in mind is another of the reasons why we as a profession have been hesitant about her. Unable to correct it for ourselves by reading an authentic rendering of her poems in print(and in approximately chronological order) or by getting the true flavor of the woman herself in her own matchless correspondence, we have until very recently been victimized by the legends and myths and sentimentalizings that have come down in pious reminiscences, memoirs, fictional renderings, Broadway plays, and Amherst gossip. And quite rightly we have found them repellent. As teachers with a job to do, we think of the football players and the track stars squirming in the back rows of our classrooms—and we head for sturdier stuff.

I may not be able to tell you how to read—or teach—Emily Dickinson, but I can tell you how not to. The first thing to do is throw away all your old Emily Dickinson valentines, the line-a-day calendars, and "thoughts for the week." Disabuse yourself of the legend of The New England Nun, The Shy Recluse, The Moth of Amherst, The Woman in White, The Angry Father, The Blighted Romance, The Forsaken Lover, The Great Renunciation. Be very skeptical of any one with a "key" to Emily Dickinson or a solution to her "riddle." The truth of the matter seems to me at once more simple and more complicated. She is tough stuff, and there is no royal road. We have had difficulty reading and teaching her because we have had difficulty knowing her; and we have had difficulty knowing her because we haven't had the materials. Not only have we been all but helpless before the legend but, it should be added, in the hands of the anthologists, who almost invariably reprint the "easy" poems, those on the romantic, sentimental, orthodox side, or the verse epigrams, the brain twisters, that exhibit little more than her cleverness. And the anthologists perforce follow the old inadequate text. So give over the anthologies along with the valentines and get hold of the three-volume Harvard edition of the poems and the three-volume Harvard edition of the letters—or at the very least the one-volume edition of the poems published by Little, Brown (and following the text, except for variants, of the Harvard edition). Unless you are willing to go this far, there is very little I or any-one else can do for you.

Now that the decks are clear, what next? My advice is to begin at the beginning, reading the letters and poems concur-rently, and reading as if you'd never heard of Emily Dickinson before. You will find the Moth of Amherst and The Shy Recluse vanishing in the presence of a spirited, vigorous, loving, witty woman, intensely aware of life around her and of the vital issues of her day. You will find a daring experimenter in all phases of life, very conscious of her powers and glorying in them. Far from the Amherst Moth, you will find a woman of great strength and almost frightening energy, who went to bed later and got up earlier than anybody in her hard-working New England house-hold; did more than her share of housework and nursing; kept up a steady conversation with the world in hundreds of extraor-dinary letters and with herself in hundreds of extraordinary

poems, most of which (as far as we can determine) she must have
written when the rest of the family were asleep; and (most remarkable of all) made herself one of the great poets in English
under the very eyes of her family and friends—without their
slightest suspicion of it. As early as her late teens, I think, she
recognized her vocation; and she pursued it with a fortitude and
relentlessness that belie all the romantic legends. She knew who
she was, and the most remarkable achievement of her career was
the success with which she kept the secret. Only recently have we
been getting in on it.

But now to the problem of her poetry. A good place to start,
I think, is with the *word*. As Henry Wells wrote, "In the beginning was the word" is most true of Emily Dickinson. As with all
literary artists (see the famous opening pages of Joyce's *Portrait
of the Artist as a Young Man*), from the beginning words had
for her a peculiar existence and power of their own. A casual
remark in a letter written when she was fifteen expressed an attitude toward words from which she never departed, although, of
course, it deepened and subtilized:

> I was very unwell [she wrote her friend, Abiah Root] at the time
> I received your letter & unable to busy myself about anything.
> Consequently I was down-spirited and I give you all the credit of
> restoring me to health. At any rate, you may have your share. It
> really seemed to give me new life to receive your letter, for when
> I am rather low-spirited nothing seems to cheer me so much as a
> letter from a friend. At every word I read I seemed to feel new
> strength & have now regained my usual health and spirits.
>
> [September 26, 1845. *Letters*, Vol. I, p. 21]

"At every word I read . . ." Her early experiments with words,
some of them published for the first time in the Harvard editions
of the letters and poems, show a glorious verbal extravagance.
She squandered words at first, and you should see her at work
in the early letters and the valentines in verse. She deluged her
friends with her rush of words, badgering them for not answering
her letters, pouring out her heart and her gossip with the zest and
enthusiasm of any healthy young virtuoso of words discovering
the joys of expression and composition. "How lovely are the
wiles of words!" she wrote later, and it's exciting to watch her
trying out their wiliness, dazzling her colleagues with her wit
and dexterity. We get a sense in these early pieces of what Mrs.

Bingham calls "the mill-race of her mind," the tumultuous thoughts that surged through her even in these early years. "Seems I could write all night," she wrote to a friend, "and then not say the half nor the half of the half of all I have to tell you."

But as she matured, and by what stages we can only guess, her early joy in the rush of words gave way to a kind of awe or reverence for the Word itself. How and why she developed, from her early loquacity, the tense and terse style we know her by is a fascinating but unanswered question. There have been various suggestions. She was a New Englander and believed in thrift. Waste was a sin—and that included the waste of words. She grew up in a lawyer's family and may have reacted violently against the mouthy and stereotyped phraseology of the law. She became fascinated by the prosody of the hymns she sang in church and decided to make something of it. (That is true, but why did she develop almost no other form?) She detested imitation and refused to slip into the easy, lilting, pseudo-Tennysonian verse of her day. There is truth in all such suggestions, but none suffices. Enough for now that, beginning as early as the letter to Abiah Root ("At every word I read . . ."), she evolved an intuitive poetics with the Word at the center.

She saw that words—the Word—had power not only to heal and create but to hurt and destroy. "I'll heal you," she wrote to her Norcross cousins during their illness: "Tell the doctor I am inexorable, besides I shall heal you quicker than he. You need the balsam word." "Let Emily sing for you," she wrote to them later, after a bereavement, "because she cannot pray." And to another friend, "Wish I might say one liquid word to make your sorrow less." But later on, to an Amherst professor who asked if he could call: "I have no grace to talk and my own words so chill and burn me." And again: "Amazing human heart, a syllable can make to quake like jostled tree." A word could overwhelm, drown, destroy: "A word is inundation, when it comes from the sea." And so she concludes another letter to her cousins, "We must be careful what we say," and appends the poem that begins, "A word dropped careless on a page . . ." It could be said that her aim as an artist was never to leave a careless word on a page; every word must work. "Whenever my words are fluent," she wrote, "I know them to be false." The economy she ultimately achieved was the result of extraordinary discipline and endless practice. We have reason to believe, for instance, that she made practice drafts of even her simplest and shortest letters; and many of the poems that have come down to us are merely practice drafts which she never brought to final form. Apparently, she wasn't content until she had pared away all the nonessentials, all the connectives, transitional phrases, and stylistic signposts that make life easy for the reader. In her best poems, every word bears its ultimate weight until (as in some of Shakespeare's later plays) the lines fairly burst with meaning. She often sacrifices grammar and syntax to pack more meaning in. Her poetry is full of ellipses that only a most attentive and sensitive reading can bridge.

But it's high time we got to some examples. I will start with a relatively simple one to illustrate how important it is to be alert to the full connotative reach of every word—its overtones and undertones, resonances and implications. Take the famous "Because I could not stop for Death" (#712). See what "kindly" does. It announces at once that this poem will be very different from the mawkish, sentimental, or horrific death poems that litter our tradition. Here is no fear, horror, or the "Come sweet death" note of the sentimentalists. The word obviously suggests gentleness and grace but also "gentility," the proper decorum and distance that characterize relations between gentlemen and ladies —or that peculiar kind of personal-impersonal concern of the medical attendant who ushers the patient into the doctor's office. Death comes gently but firmly—and we see in the rest of the poem how the sense of firmness and inevitability and awe grows gradually, as the carriage passes the children at recess *striving* in the ring (not *playing*, note, but striving with that curious concentration and obliviousness to all else with which children work at their play) and as it passes the field of *gazing* grain—that is, staring fixedly, impersonally, unseeingly, even (it has been suggested) with a kind of deathlike gaze. There is no hysteria, no panic, no clutching at life, no tears at parting, no sad farewell. She is saying simply, "This is what the passage from time to eternity must be like." Death is awesome, inevitable, final—yes; but, in a curious way it is "kindly." How unsentimentally she has domesticated a horror! She has found "the balsam word."

This leads me to another rule-of-thumb in reading (and teaching) her poems: the matter of context. As in this poem on death, be mindful always of what she is *not* saying. By saying what she did about death (in this and many other poems) she is indirectly criticizing the usual treatment of it. The poem must be read not only in the context of the conventional death-and-the-maiden lyric but in the context of the endless sermons of her day (of which she was an acute critic): the hellfire sort that scared her (or made her laugh) and the sentimental, consolatory ones that disgusted her. One must see the poem as part of the perennial dialectic on the mystery of death: "It's *this*"; "No, it's *this*," and the reader (and our students) must be somehow brought into the conversation.

Take another poem which calls for the understanding of a quite different context and "conversation." Everyone knows the one on the railroad, "I like to see it lap the Miles . . ." (#585), and almost everyone knows that it refers to the opening of the Amherst to Belchertown railroad in 1853. So far, so good—but not nearly far enough. What only a few others, like Jay Leyda and Charles Anderson, can tell us, is indispensable. The railroad was the result very largely of the vision and the untiring efforts of one man: Mr. Edward Dickinson, the poet's father. The opening of the railroad, with a nineteen-gun salute and a parade led by Mr. Dickinson himself, was one of the proudest moments of his career. It symbolized for him and for the community the dawn of a new era for Amherst and for New England: the expansion of trade, growth of prosperity, and spread of culture. It was a triumph of modern science, engineering, technology, organization. It was a serious matter, to be fittingly commemorated, celebrated, even (I suppose) prayed over. Emily Dickinson saw the whole thing from a distance—literally as well as figuratively. Here is how she records the event in a letter:

> The . . . Day passed off grandly, [she wrote]—so all the people said—it was pretty hot and dusty, but nobody cared for that. Father was as usual, Chief Marshall of the day, and went marching round the town with New London at his heels like some old Roman General, upon a triumph day. Mrs. Howe got a capital dinner, and was very much praised. Carriages flew like sparks, hither, and thither and yon, and they all said 'twas fine. I spose it was—I sat in Prof Tyler's woods and saw the train move off, and then ran home again for fear somebody would see me, or ask how I did.

> [June 15, 1853. *Letters*, Vol. I, p. 254]

The distance was physical—she sat in the woods, viewing the affair from her Olympian perch—but spiritually and imaginatively she was miles away—from her father and from her community. Notice what she *doesn't* say: there's not a word about trade or progress or cultural possibilities; there's no salute to the new era that science and technology are opening up. Her silence on these matters is ironic—indeed, Charles Anderson sums up the poem as "her ironic tribute to modern science and progress." In a way, she *is* poking fun at the whole bombastic business. Her father, who saw things pretty seriously, especially railroads, would not have been amused. But it isn't all ironic; if the vein is comic, it is high comedy, not ridicule. About the same time she wrote to Austin, her beloved and absent brother: "While I write, the whistle [of the train] is playing, and the cars just coming in. It gives us new life, every time it plays. How you will love to hear it, when you come home again!" And this is what she saw in this marvelous new phenomenon: unlimited power, gorgeous energy, —a little "horrid" and appalling; maybe even a little ominous; but spectacular, thrilling, exciting, a tonic to the nerves, a creator of new life—but a new life quite different from the "New Era" envisioned by the public orators of the day.

So be mindful of the "conversation" implied in Emily Dickinson's poems. She spoke of her poems as "My letter to the world"; and her actual letters are extraordinary for—among other things —their marvelously immediate conversational quality. She says often, in so many words, "I take up my pen to chat with you awhile"; or, "I feel like talking to some one tonight." It is as if, in her poems, she suddenly cuts us in on one of these conversations and leaves it to our perception to fill in the context. Unless we know the context, much of the meaning and half the fun are lost.

Take another example, which Anderson explicates brilliantly, the poem "I cannot dance upon my Toes . . ." (#326). On the face of it, she seems to be saying that although she doesn't know much about ballet and opera, she can imagine what they're like and can score great dramatic triumphs in her imagination. Thus on one level it's a poem about "life in the imagination"— as Robert Frost once remarked about her, "To write about falling water a poet doesn't have to go to Niagara." But we know for a fact that this poem was part of a conversation—a literary conversation—she held with a noted contributor to the *Atlantic*

Monthly, Mr. Thomas Wentworth Higginson, to whom she had
sent some of her poems, asking for criticism. He criticized them—
adversely. The rhymes were imperfect [he wrote], the meter irregular, the gait "spasmodic," the meaning unclear. Good man
though he was, he failed her completely; and his obtuseness is
now notorious. The gist of his advice to her was to write more
like other poets, like the conventional versifiers of the day. It is
as if he had just been saying, "You can't be a ballerina unless you
know the ballet steps. These must be learned. Poetry, too, has its
conventions. You can't write just as it pleases you. You must conform if you ever expect an audience." Of course, she had no intention of conforming, even though she sent Higginson many
more of her poems—including this one, which is a polite, indirect
way of saying, "Thank you, Mr. Higginson, *just the same.*" You
remember her famous lines, "Tell all the truth but tell it slant—/
Success in Circuit lies." In the poem, she gives him the whole
truth, told slant—and my guess is that Higginson missed it cold.

    "Tell all the truth but tell it slant." Here I come to my final
suggestion about reading and teaching Emily Dickinson. Remember that she was a born wit. Her niece tells us that "She loved
to fence in words with an able adversary. . . . She loved a metaphor, a paradox, a riddle." Not that she couldn't—or didn't—
speak out directly. "Circumlocution," goes on her niece, "she
despised. Her conclusions hit the mark and suggested an arrow
in directness . . ." And in her poems she could "scalp your naked
soul" with appalling efficiency, when she wanted to. But her
favorite and characteristic way of thinking was metaphoric—
telling the truth slant. This operated on at least two levels: first,
plain enjoyment; she loved getting at things that way, for the
sheer intellectual joy of it—as witness an exuberant valentine
letter she wrote when she was twenty to an Amherst student:

> Our friendship, sir, shall endure till sun and moon wane no more,
> till stars shall set, and victims rise to grace the final sacrifice. We'll
> be instant, in season, out of season, minister, take care of, cherish,
> soothe, watch, wait, doubt, refrain, reform, elevate, instruct. All
> choice spirits however distant are ours, ours theirs; there is a
> thrill of sympathy—a circulation of mutuality—cognationem inter
> nos! I am Judith the heroine of the Apocrypha, and you are the
> orator of Ephesos. That's what they call a metaphor in our
> country. Don't be afraid of it, sir, it won't bite.
>
> [February 1850. *Letters,* Vol. I, p. 92]

She loved to play with metaphor, and many of her metaphors are playful. It is the triumph of the teacher of poetry when he can convince his students that metaphors won't bite—indeed, that they're the cream of the jest. Poetry, wrote Robert Frost, *is* metaphor, "saying one thing in terms of another, the pleasure of ulteriority." Dickinson's poetry is full of this kind of ulteriority —and, I'd say, the *pleasure* of it—of "saying one thing in terms of another." For instance, "Until the Desert knows" (#1291). But, say our reluctant students, riddle me no riddles. Why can't she say it directly—right out? Well, she could. But it would take many lines of prose, and I doubt if any amount of exposition could quite catch all the resonance of "That Caspian fact."

Metaphor became more than play to her, of course. It became her characteristic mode of expression, of distancing life, mastering if, even of surviving it. This last may seem an extravagance; but I am not the first to suggest it, and I think it's true. "I sing," she wrote Higginson (and "to sing" meant in her language "to write poetry"), "because I am afraid." When "a sudden light on Orchards, or a new fashion in the wind troubled my attention," she wrote him again, "I felt a palsy, here—the Verses just relieve." Her capacity for feeling, the sheer intensity of her emotions (if her poems and letters can be taken as even an approximate record of them), can scarcely be equalled in our literature. Compared to her side-piercing thrusts, much of our lyric writing seems like so many literary set-pieces.

> Dare you see a *Soul at the White Heat?*
> Then crouch within the door—
>
> > [*Poems,* No. 365]

The reference is almost surely autobiographical.

> The Martyr Poets—did not tell—
> But wrought their Pang in syllable—
>
> > [*Poems,* No. 544]

But how to tell the truth—and yet not tell it? How to fashion a "syllable" (that is, a poem) out of the suffering—how to make a poem from a "pang"? She grew impatient when people talked about holy things in her company—"They embarrass my dog," she wrote. She was a true New Englander in her reticence. Every now and then it came out straight, as in the breathless: "At least - to pray - is left - is left - " (#502). But more characteristically she would step back a bit, distance her "pang"—it could be of joy or ecstasy as well as grief—and subject it to a searching, clinical, examination as if to see what she could learn from it. Note the cool, even scholarly way she begins this poem: "One Crucifixion is recorded - only - " (#553). "I measure every grief I meet," she wrote in another poem; and in the very process of measurement she would gain detachment and command. Hence her many poems, as Henry Wells points out, that begin like so many academic definitions: "Exhilaration is . . ." "Bliss is . . ." "Crisis is . . ." "Delight is . . ." "Paradise is . . ." "Power is . . ." "Death is . . ." "Denial is . . ." "Love is . . ." In exploring "Being's Centre," the poet, unless he is to be lost in the chaos of his own internality, must proceed with the objectivity of the philosopher and the exquisite care of the surgeon operating on a patient. If his control weakens he is lost.

But Emily Dickinson's material was not quite that of the philosopher or the surgeon. Analysis and probing will never get the actuality of "Being's Centre," no matter how shrewd or cunning. Her characteristic recourse was metaphor, which is only a way of saying, "I can't tell you *exactly* how it is, but it is *like this*." Or, as in one of her finest bits of extended metaphor, "I cannot describe despair precisely. I cannot tell exactly how I felt (when I got the news, or when my friend died, or the blow, whatever it was, fell)—but it was something between numbness, paralysis, a state of trance on the one hand, and yet acute consciousness on the other, as of something happening in my innermost being—steady, dreadful, that could only end in loss of being; an awful loneliness, a nightmarish sense of falling through endless space. It was all this and more—and all at once: "I felt a Funeral, in my Brain" (#280). By making a poem of it—her despair—she distanced it, withdrew from it, mastered it. ("I sing because I am afraid.") There is no doubt that the orthodox religious comforts and consolations of her day were for her largely unavailing. ("Let Emily sing for you because she cannot pray.") She never joined the church, although she attended worship fairly regularly up to her midtwenties. Her life was a sustained, extended search for meaning, for answers to the ultimate questions which she was always posing to herself and with which she continually bombarded anyone who appeared to her at all likely to give her an answer: Higginson, to whom she turned for much more than merely literary advice; the Rev. Charles Wadsworth of Philadelphia and San Francisco; Samuel Bowles of Springfield; Dr. and Mrs. Holland of Springfield and New York, to whom she wrote some of her finest letters; and finally Judge Lord of Salem. But ultimately she had to rely on herself. Like many a poet since the Renaissance, cut loose from the ancient verities she had to grope her way along, make her own unguided pilgrimage, figure it out all over again. "I wonder when we shall cease to wonder," she wrote a cousin who had lost a daughter, "how early we shall *know*." And again: "I suppose we are all thinking of Immortality, at times so stimulatedly that we cannot sleep . . . [But] speculate with all our might, we cannot ascertain." Meanwhile, all she could do was love her friends ("We must love with all our might") and write her poems—that is, create her own world, her own reality. This is why she placed such extraordinary importance on the word, the metaphor, the poem. This was the nearest she got to viable truth—truth incarnate, vital, sustaining. From heaven, or from her minister, came hints and intimations only, which left her baffled. She made her own pilgrimage; and her distinction is that she was honest, as many of her pious contemporaries were not, to every step of the way.

THREE VIEWS
OF THE
HUMAN PERSON
The Scarlet Letter, Walden,
and
The Red Badge of Courage

CHARLES FEIDELSON, JR.
Yale University

Undoubtedly, the naïve, spontaneous way to read a book is to read it solely for itself. But I suppose that the task of the teacher is somehow to push students beyond their pristine innocence—many kinds of innocence, as we know, but in this case the innocence of reading without a context. A teacher, without destroying that naïve joy, must divert it into the study of relations, comparisons, and contrasts. Only when we begin to relate, to pair and then to group writers, either explicitly or by implication, does the study of literature properly begin.

In the field of American literature, as it happens, a critical effort to generalize, to discover patterns of theme or patterns of form common to large groups of writers, has been going on since the 1920s, and notably since Matthiessen's *American Renaissance* of 1941. Some notable instances are D. H. Lawrence's *Studies in Classic American Literature* (1922), V. L. Parrington, *Main Currents in American Thought* (1927), Ivor Winters, *Maule's Curse* (1938), Constance Rourke, *American Humor* (1939), Alfred Kazin, *On Native Grounds* (1942), H. N. Smith, *Virgin Land* (1950), R. W. B. Lewis, *The American Adam* (1955), Harry Levin, *The Power of Blackness* (1958). It occurs to me that a body of literature which is undergoing such extensive definition and redefinition may be especially well adapted to the needs of the teacher. Here if anywhere may be an opportunity to push beyond the individual book into questions of larger import. Indeed, there would seem to be a kind of challenge in the very claim that there is an *American* literature. Is the adjective "American" merely a handy label or does it mean something? I suspect that the demand for generalization presented by that word is what inspired all the critical works I have mentioned. And I suspect that this question has also floated before the American writer, whose need to make "American" mean something must have existed long before the critics began to define what the writers had made it mean. I suspect that beneath the diverse subjects of American books, there is always this common preoccupation with "Americanness"; and in this sense American literature positively demands large-scale study, comparison and contrast of writers, rather than emphasis upon separate authors or works.

However this may strike you as a reason for studying American literature, it is my basic assumption in what I want to say today about Hester Prynne, Henry Thoreau, and Henry Fleming. (We need not be bothered because two of these are invented characters and the other, Thoreau, was an actual man: Thoreau, to all intents and purposes, invented himself.) I assume that these three persons and the books built around them—*The Scarlet Letter, Walden, The Red Badge of Courage*—came into existence as part of a communal inquiry, were addressed to a common question, even though their authors had little or no interest in each other. The question is an obviously important subdivision of the larger issue of "Americanness." It is simply this: *What is a person?* Just as democratic political theory hinges on the nature and function of the public "individual," American moral theory hinges on the nature and function of the private person. I suppose there is no major work in American literature that is not concerned with the problem of the person in some degree. One of the characters in Melville's novels, *The Confidence Man*, asks the question quite explicitly: "What are you? What am I?" And he answers with a sweeping agnosticism that sets one limit to the inquiry: "Nobody knows who anybody is." At the opposite extreme we might place Whitman's equally sweeping assertion that everyone knows himself and thereby knows everybody: "One's-self I sing, a simple separate person,/Yet utter the word Democratic, the word En-masse." The personal identities of Hester Prynne, Henry Thoreau, and Henry Fleming exist somewhere within these theoretical limits. They constitute a kind of spectrum of inquiry into personal existence, each putting the question somewhat differently and answering it with a different emphasis.

Suppose we begin with Henry Fleming, who comes closest to the grim world where "nobody knows who anybody is." *The Red Badge of Courage* is a book about the Civil War, but more fundamentally it is about Fleming's effort to know himself and thereby perhaps to know something about other men. It is impossible for him to proceed the other way—to define himself by means of the world outside him. Neither the tumult of battle nor the quiet life of camp can provide the "courage," the basis for a personal, self-determining existence, that he seeks. Society is here represented by the will of the officers, who are totally indifferent to his will and are themselves mere instruments of forces beyond. Henry and his companions have no information about causes and consequences that would enable them to partake personally in the events of the war; they feed on illusory flying rumors. Physical nature is equally unavailable as a ground for his personal identity. Nature offers only contradictory and mocking images: on the one hand an image of life intent on preserving itself—the lively squirrel who peers down at him from a tree—and on the other hand, immediately after, an image of brute death—the dead man devoured by ants. Nor can immediate human companionship provide him with models for himself. At most, the signs of inner integrity that he notes in others suggest that such a thing may be, but none can tell him how to attain it or what it is. He is thrown back in time and again into the posture he adopts in the first chapter, when he symbolically crawls into his hut to be alone with his thoughts.

As if this predicament were not enough, his very consciousness seems to be irrelevant to his problem. He cannot determine what he will be, but must wait to see what happens in him. When he stands his ground in battle, he does not do so because of conscious self-control; when he runs away, no conscious determination could have prevented it. And which is the real Henry Fleming—the man who involuntarily stands or the one who involuntarily flees? All that his consciousness can do is to project pictures of himself which remain mere abstract possibilities: himself as hero, as coward, as sensible man, as dead man. His conscious self hangs helplessly between his unknown inner being and the unknowable world outside him.

Given all this, it would seem that Fleming cannot hope to attain any sense of personal identity except perhaps by a kind of miracle. Crane seems to be intent on constructing an inhuman and dehumanizing world that will block any effort at human self-realization. The events after Henry gets his second chance merely deepen the ironies of the first half of the story. His wound, his "red badge," is a mere accident suffered while acting on a confused impulse, not a token of resolution and purpose. Having gained his "badge," he lapses back into foolish postures, strutting before others and before himself. Most strikingly of all, when he actually does become a hero in the public eye, hurling himself at the foe, he is moved by unconscious impulses that are no more *himself* than the blind fear that had made him run away. When his intelligence comes back into "the glazed vacancy of his eyes," he observes that a stranger has acted in him while he slept.

Still, the ultimate aim of Stephen Crane in heaping up these ironies is to transcend them—quite literally, to picture a miracle. It is not a miraculous supernatural intervention, but rather the miracle of human existence in the face of all that militates against it. Human existence in the *Red Badge of Courage* is validated by the fact of human intelligence, which is free to swing round upon the blind forces that determine it—to contain them by acknowledging them. This is what Henry Fleming finds that he can do at the end of the story, and this is what gives him dignity and poise in his final meditations. He is no longer trying to discover the ultimate principles either of his own unconscious or of the world outside him. At the same time, however, he is resisting the temptation to abdicate, to become passive before the arbitrary forces of life and death, fear and bravery, that have controlled him. His business is to make what he can from the inner and outer conditions of his life without pretending fully to understand them. The courage of his intelligence lies in facing the double fact of his own blind courage and his own blind terror, as well as the ambiguous creativity and destructiveness of nature, and in realizing that the human state begins rather than ends in these phenomena. This is the basis on which Crane can assert that Fleming "was a man" and that now "the world was a world for him." As he marches off "under a low, wretched sky," he possesses both himself and human reality, precisely because he views both as what he must construct, not what can be given to him.

That is a tough doctrine; but Crane has put the case in extreme terms. At least he does not veer off in the direction of Dreiser, whose greatest failing is a lack of this very sense of specifically human personal identity. But I do not think that Crane could have envisaged the miracle that saved Henry Fleming if he had not had a secret memory of something outside his premises—the older unquestioned faith in persons that preceded his own age of radical questioning. I mention this because the vision of someone like Thoreau may seem relatively facile, too easily asserted; he begins by assuming the truth that Fleming attains only at the cost of great suffering. One of Thoreau's values, however, may be that he fully expressed and made available a standpoint that could still be used by men like Crane, who were more desperately besieged.

Thoreau himself would hardly have welcomed such an apologia, and I don't wish to write him off in that way. Obviously he puts the question quite differently from Crane, and he has his own kind of struggle. Though the "I" of *Walden* is not menaced by the danger of its own loss of identity, this "I" shoulders an enormous burden—nothing less than the salvation of nature and of society. Thoreau's problem is not to demonstrate the existence of a self—he can assume that—but to know himself, as it were, in his deeds; and the only deed large enough to reflect him in the transformation of the world. His personal identity is the beginning and the end, not the substance, of his enterprise. For example, the explicit theme of the final chapter of *Walden* is that all geographical exploration is merely a symbol for the prior exploration of "continents and worlds within." And Thoreau begins the book with a vigorous assertion that "the I, or first person," is the proper subject of all books. But his characteristic stance is not really introspective. His "inner" exploration proceeds, paradoxically, by an outward movement. It is, in fact, a kind of imitation of God's activity—an investment of the world with grace. This grace recalls the world to itself and thereby makes it a fitting mirror for the power that has redeemed it.

The world needs redemption because it is prone to fall into two forms of lifelessness: the inertness of matter and the abstraction of the rational intellect. The first of these lapses is really the fall of nature. Though "nature" has, of course, a highly favorable connotation for Thoreau, he also must see it as a potential menace. He fulminates against the insidious tyranny of lifeless matter, the enslavement of men who are "serfs of the soil." The other fall is the enslavement of the human mind to the limited schemes it has projected, whether these are abstract preconceptions in the moral sphere or the narrow goals of the practical reason. The rational mind is the specifically social devil; its vicious "economy" turns the life of the spirit into the death of theory. Thus nature and society become false to themselves. They can be restored only by a transformation scene, a sort of divine drama, engineered by the heroic self. Thoreau represents his removal from Concord to the shores of Walden Pond as just that; not a flight, not even a disengagement, but the deliberate construction of a sacred precinct where grace will be operative. Within this temple, he endlessly sets up sacramental rites. Consider the incident of "The Bean-Field," one of the most elaborately contrived of these episodes. Here the primal act of settled human society, the cultivation of the earth, is freed of its pragmatic limits, and simultaneously the natural soil is permeated by eternal life. Without ceasing to be a labor for human good, and without ceasing to be a submission to physical nature, the growing of beans becomes a revelation of something potential in both man and nature—a freedom, an openness, a principle of growth —that man and nature always forget when left to themselves.

The world's potentiality becomes actual because of the presence of Thoreau, the man in the bean field. He contains the one freedom and growth and openness that never fails—the fountain deep within the individual man—and he comes to know his own secret powers by awakening the same powers in the objects of nature and in human activities. We may be tempted to say that Thoreau merely projects himself on the world and thereby sees it in a new light. But he would maintain that a far more substantive transformation of things occurred when he went to Walden and recurred within every sacramental moment of his sojourn there. If we grant him this, we may also be tempted to say that he has not really transformed *society*—he has really done away with it.

And I do not think that he has any ready answer to this indictment. The rich flood of the personal being may be able to awaken nature, but it washes away the foundations of the social order. Instead of a purified husbandry, the beginning of a larger philosophy of farming, "The Bean-Field" actually gives us a man uncommitted to any social role and pretending for the moment to be a farmer.

In its own way, then, Thoreau's concept of the self is just as aberrant as the minimal self conceived by Crane. Neither has the moral centrality of Nathaniel Hawthorne, who was perhaps the only major nineteenth-century American writer who could define a person without claiming too much or too little to satisfy our sense of the possibilities of meaning in the word. This is not to say that it came easily to Hawthorne. If the subject of personal identity has been all-important in American literature, the reason has been that the writers did not know exactly what they meant by a "person" but knew that as Americans they must make this term mean something. In his patient, brooding way, Hawthorne managed to invest it with a broad yet balanced meaning. In *The Scarlet Letter* he carefully poses Hester Prynne against two large backgrounds: the social order of the Puritan community and the freedom of the wilderness.

The society of *The Scarlet Letter* is neither unknowable, like Crane's, nor devitalized, like Thoreau's. The Puritan community has massive dignity and a profound vision that commands respect. But it has no place for *persons* at all. Hawthorne consistently treats it as a huge system operating by general laws and incapable of even becoming aware of particular human beings. It is large, but invariable. The ministers who try to deal with Hester's case cannot view her as a particular case: these "sages of rigid aspect" cannot perceive the specific creature, the personal "mesh of good and evil," that stands before them. On the other hand, the wilderness—embodied in the forest and the sea that surround Boston town—is fluid, paradoxical, various: it is dark and light, sad and gay, menacing and comforting. Unlike Crane's "nature," it is relevant to man; unlike Thoreau's, it is bigger than any man who confronts it. And it is impressive in its variety, its primeval organic fecundity. But it is as destructive of the human person as is the Puritan social order, though in a different way. The wilderness is not antihuman, like the Puritan system, but prehuman: a place of whimsical biological powers that are alien to the human mode of individuality. When Hester goes to the forest she finds herself full of creative energies, liberated by an upsurge of instinct; but the price of such freedom is a loss of personal free will; the forest gives power but denies moral choice.

These two realms, the town and the wilderness, provide the language of Hester's inquiry into personal identity. Of course, *The Scarlet Letter* is about sin and repentance, but the problem of sin, as Hawthorne poses it, involves another question: *who* sins, and *who* repents? Hester's answer to that question is forged by keeping herself distinct from the moral mechanism of the town and the amoral freedom of the wilderness, either of which would destroy the specific and human person she wants to be, and thereby would destroy the meaning of sin itself. The significance of sin depends entirely on whether there is anyone present to do the sinning. Hester emphatically wants to be present. But she can think only—indeed, can exist only—in terms derived from the forest and from society. That is the symbolic meaning of the dwelling place she selects—in the indeterminate zone between wilderness and town. A person, as that idea is gradually defined in her character, is at once a lawful social being who possesses the freedom of nature, and a free natural being who possesses the responsibility of society. More precisely, a person is the channel by which natural creativity enters the social world. Sin—as she comes to see it, not as the Puritans define it—is simply the obverse of her proper human function: thus her sin of adultery was the eruption of prehuman natural forces into an antihuman social order. It follows that her salvation from sin and her attainment of personal identity are one and the same. Her function as intermediary between the natural and social realms, her function as a free and responsible person, is the conversion of blind passion and rigid dogma into creative social action. That is what Hester half-consciously means when she first covers her scarlet letter with rich embroidery and that is what in the end she vindicates when her "A" comes to stand not for "adultery" but for "ability."

Although I think that Hawthorne is a greater writer than Thoreau, and Thoreau is a greater writer than Crane, my purpose in moving from one to the other has not been primarily to set up the scale of relative value. Rather, I should like to picture these three writers as experimenters, each approaching the same unknown quantity, but each from a different direction and with different equipment. To Hawthorne was given the larger angle of vision of traditional Western thought. Deeply skeptical and full of doubt as he was, he could state and deal with his question in balanced terms that derived from ages of greater moral security. Thoreau and Crane, each in his own way, were more completely involved in the fragmented nineteenth century, yet strove to make the most of the perspectives open to them. In this sense a comparison of these writers would end not so much in a judgment of their individual achievements as in a sense of their common predicament and their honest dealing with it. And at this point we should recognize that it is our predicament as well. They had to find out what it meant to be American, and bound up with this was the question of what it meant to be a person. The answer is still in the making.

THEME
AND
HISTORY
three poets on a
single theme

G. ARMOUR CRAIG
Amherst College

Every teacher of literature is troubled from time to time by the student who wants to know the value of the poem, play, or novel being discussed in class. "Value," of course, is not the right word: the right word is "rating." For even the serious and conscientious student, no doubt educated by the rating systems of mass entertainment, wants to know whether "On His Blindness" is "considered" a "good" poem, or how Boswell's *Life of Johnson* "is rated" in world literature, or "where" Keats's "Nightingale" is "ranked" in the vast hierarchy known as "Enterprising Productions of the English Poets." And distressing as such questions are, wrongheaded as may be the attitudes that generate them, they seem to be inevitable. If we answer, "Oh, in the top ten," we are not only dogmatists we have also accepted the audience-reaction-research criterion of our students. And if we answer, "Well, it all depends," we infuriate the quetsioner with what to him seems an evasion. The only way out of the dilemma, at least the only way I can see, is to try to change the grammar of the questions. Our students say "is considered," "is ranked," "is rated"; we can try to show them what is involved in transforming these passive verbs into active ones. We try, that is, to forestall their questions about rating and rank by an approach to literature that makes them irrelevant—or at least makes them irrelevant in this exasperatingly simple form.

For there is no doubt that some of our practices encourage this simple-minded attitude toward the values of literature. On the one hand, many of us are experts in rhetorical and aesthetic analysis: we are experts in the elucidation of tone and attitude, we trace metaphors and symbols, we discriminate rhythms and pauses. And such analysis does often get the poem off the page, so to speak, and into the student's awareness of something more than a fancy or fanciful statement; it does often reveal to him that a poem is not a message but a gesture. Again, many of us are experts in background, in biography, in historical considerations such as the character of the Elizabethan stage that often enable the student to see that he is reading not mere antiquarian relics but works that once had audiences even as "Playhouse 90" does today. But because we so rarely do these things simultaneously, because we are so likely to be analysts on Monday, Wednesday, and Friday, but historians on Tuesday, Thursday, and Saturday, our students, like us, on their day off listen and pay heed to works of proven, obvious, demonstrable ratings. There can be no mistake about it: our students, our trustees, our school boards, and even some of our colleagues, have accepted the new dogmatism completely: if such and such has sold three million copies, or if such and such program had a Neilsen rating of five million, then it *must* be good.

I do not, of course, believe that we can put the comic book industry out of business or that we can turn the television net-

works into academies of the higher arts. I only believe that we
can face more directly than we do the issue of how we judge
a work of literature—and not only how but where. I believe, that
is, that if we supply our students with a context in which judgment is both inevitable and complicated, is both called for and
at the same time checked even in the utterance, then we shall do
much to silence the questions about ranks, ratings, and billings.

Consider, if you will, the three following poems:

A CONTEMPLATION UPON FLOWERS

Brave flowers, that I could gallant it like you
And be as little vain!
You come abroad and make a harmless show,
And to your beds of earth again;
You are not proud, you know your birth,
For your embroidered garments are from earth.

You do obey your months and times, but I
Would have it ever spring;
My fate would know no winter, never die
Nor think of such a thing;
Oh, that I could my bed of earth but view
And smile, and look as cheerfully as you.

Oh, teach me to see death and not to fear,
But rather to take truce;
How often have I seen you at a bier,
And there look fresh and spruce;
You fragrant flowers, then teach me that my breath
Like yours may sweeten, and perfume my death.

ON A BED OF GUERNSEY LILIES
WRITTEN IN SEPTEMBER 1763

Ye beauties! O how great the sum
    Of Sweetness that ye bring;
On what a charity ye come
    To bless the latter spring!

How kind a visit that ye pay,
Like strangers on a rainy day,
  When heartiness despaired of guests:
No neighbour's praise your pride alarms,
No rival flow'r surveys your charms,
  Or heightens, or contests!

Lo, thro' her works gay nature grieves
  How brief she is and frail,
As ever o'er the falling leaves
  Autumnal winds prevail.
Yet still the philosophic mind
Consolatory food can find,
  And hope her anchorage maintain:
We never are deserted quite;
'Tis by succession of delight
  That love supports his reign.

THE SMALL CELANDINE

There is a Flower, the lesser Celandine,
That shrinks, like many more, from cold
        and rain;
And, the first moment that the sun may
        shine,
Bright as the sun himself, 't is out again!

When hailstones have been falling, swarm
        on swarm,
Or blasts the green field and the trees
        distrest,
Oft have I seen it muffled up from harm,
In close self-shelter, like a Thing at rest.

But lately, one rough day, this Flower I
        passed
And recognized it, though an altered form,
Now standing forth an offering to the blast,
And buffeted at will by rain and storm.

> I stopped, and said with inly-muttered
>   voice,
> "It doth not love the shower, nor seek the
>   cold:
> This neither is its courage nor its choice,
> But its necessity in being old.
>
> "The sunshine may not cheer it, nor the
>   dew;
> It cannot help itself in its decay;
> Stiff in its members, withered, changed of
>   hue."
> And, in my spleen, I smiled that it was
>   grey.
>
> To be a Prodigal's Favourite—then, worse
>   truth,
> A Miser's pensioner—behold our lot!
> O Man, that from thy fair and shining
>   youth
> Age might but take the things Youth
>   needed not!

Now it is clear enough at first glance that each of these poems is in a general way about man and nature, certainly one of the largest subjects in English poetry from the days when April was the time when longen folk to goon on pilgrymages to those when it has become the cruellest month. Each moreover is a poem in which the speaker finds through his relation to nature an awareness of a power or a destiny that embraces them both. Each poem presents a situation in which the speaker considers himself as he meditates upon some flowers—first, upon flowers so general that we know only that they are bright colored; next, upon flowers that bloom when all others have departed; and finally, upon a flower so particularly described that we see its very shape.

The first poem is commonly but not certainly attributed to Henry King, a seventeenth-century Bishop of Chichester, the contemporary of George Herbert and Robert Herrick, a prominent churchman and poet of the generation just following that of John Donne. Its very title, "A Contemplation Upon Flowers," suggests its meditative character: it sees in the flowers' gallant, handsome acceptance of their cycle of life a comment upon man's proud resistance to his destiny and death:

> You do obey your months and times, but I
> Would have it ever spring;
> My fate would know no winter, never die
> Nor think of such a thing.

And, with the kind of pun that both Herbert and Donne so often used to express their sense of the natural and the spiritual in the same phrase, the speaker, looking at the flowers, exclaims

> O, that I could my bed of earth but view
> And smile, and look as cheerfully as you.

For his bed of earth is his grave, and his pride—indeed, his mortal pride—prevents him from accepting, as inevitably and as cheerfully as the flowers, the certainty of his death. But in the last couplet, in a figure that Herbert used more than once, he discovers an analogy between himself and the flowers through which he can attain the cheerfulness, the serenity, of their gallant acceptance of the seasons:

> You fragrant flowers, then teach me that my breath
> Like yours may sweeten, and perfume my death.

For just as the flowers give off a fragrance that to us sweetens their passing away, so we, in prayer, in example (no doubt, if Bishop King did write this poem, in devout churchmanship), and in all deeds that renounce pride, so we may give off a fragrance to God, and in that fragrance sweeten even our own passing. From the opening address, "Brave flowers," when he speaks to the flowers directly and admiringly, this poet brings us into a situation in which man and nature are intimately related as only a religious view of experience can relate them. There is no self-consciousness in the address: it begins a contemplation in which the speaker moves from considering his difference from the humble flowers to an awareness of how he, in his own way, and yet in a way like that of the flowers, shares with them a life under a larger power, a power as transcendent to both of them as he, in his way, transcends the flowers.

The second poem is by Christopher Smart, though perhaps it seems unlikely from the writer of the *Hymn to David*. Here, the speaker contemplates a bed of lilies. They are an ornament of what we should call Indian summer, for they bloom when all other flowers have passed their prime, and their appearance is compared to the visit of persons from outside our own household when we have been shut in on a rainy day. The appearance of these late-blooming lilies, that is to say, is compared to the unexpected continuance of the round of polite social visits. The flowers are seen in social terms—they are even seen in terms of the polite but determined social rivalries that Jane Austen was to write about forty years later:

> No rival flow'r surveys your charms
> Or heightens, or contests!

The speaker then turns away from these beauties of the meadow and generalizes upon the occasion in larger terms. "Gay nature" may grieve, "Autumnal winds" may prevail, the seasons may move on as certainly as they do for that seventeenth-century poet who "Would have it ever spring." But for man there is finally something different from "fragrance" in the fact:

> Yet still the philosophic mind
> Consolatory food can find,
>   And hope her anchorage maintain;
> We never are deserted quite;
> 'Tis by succession of delight
> That love supports his reign.

Here, the speaker sees himself as participating in a systematic "succession"—unexpected, to be sure, and perhaps even undeserved, and yet as decorous, as open to the "philosophic mind," as the society in which visits are exchanged despite the adversities of weather and season.

The last of the three poems is by Wordsworth, and it is one of three poems he wrote on the celandine in the years 1802–1804. The celandine is the common pile wort, an herb with flowers like the buttercup, and in a note on the first of his poems upon it Wordsworth observed:

It is remarkable that this flower, coming out so early in the spring as it does, and so bright and beautiful, and in such profusion, should not have been noticed earlier in English verse. What adds much to the interest that attends it is its habit of shutting itself up and opening out according to the degree of light and the temperature of the air.

At once we notice what is quite literally a dramatic difference between this poem and the two preceding: the speaker does not at any time address the flower; instead he begins in the tone of the naturalist, telling us in a graceful expository way the habits and the habitat of this small herb. Moving from his general exposition, he draws nearer to the flower by recalling how he saw it "lately, one rough day," and he moves even more deeply into his experience when he tells how, as he saw the celandine "standing forth an offering to the blast,/ And buffeted at will by rain and storm," he spoke to himself with "inly-muttered" voice. The celandine is old:

> It doth not love the shower nor seek the cold:
> This neither is its courage nor its choice,
> But its necessity in being old.

And he concludes his inward mutter with a wry, melancholy smile of recognition. For he has found a kinship between himself and the flower that is far beneath the level of public, consolatory philosophy, and even more concealed than the pious fragrance given off by devout worship. It is a kinship different, perhaps, from that which inspires the deep power of joy with which Wordsworth reaches the spirit that rolls through all things in "Tintern Abbey," but one, I think, not more superficial or indeed less Wordsworthian. But with the discovery of the kinship comes the change of tone from that of the "inly" muttering observer to that of the hard, clear moralist:

> To be a Prodigal's favorite—then, worse truth,
> A Miser's pensioner—behold our lot!

The life of the celandine is an emblem of the life of man, a life that both share through "necessity":

> O Man, that from thy fair and shining youth
> Age might but take the things Youth needed not!

Like the seventeenth-century poet who is troubled that man would have it ever spring, like the delighted (unfortunately only temporarily so, since he would again suffer his terrible mental illness) welcomer of the September lilies, so Wordsworth finds in his kinship to a flower a large, and this time pathetic, meaning that unites them.

Such a juxtaposition as this can of course be paralleled a hundredfold, and from such a juxtaposition many more inferences can be made than I have even begun to suggest. We can see the difference between seventeenth-century wit and eighteenth-century formality in the contrast between "Brave flowers" and "Ye beauties." We can see the difference between a prescientific world of discourse in which "fragrance" binds the fate of man to that of a flower, and a postscientific world in which the idea of "succession" constitutes the binding. We can contrast the open address to the flowers in the seventeenth-century poem—an address that in itself assumes what is a problem to be solved by the later poets—with the fact that Wordsworth can only muse or mutter to himself. But whatever inferences we can make, to the history of literature, to the history of the idea of Nature, to the history even of society, as we think about these three poems, we must admit that the literary distinctions we make are also large historical distinctions. If we think only of tone—of whom the speaker in the poem addresses—we are immediately involved in the most considerable matters that any literary or intellectual historian can face. For we see that the seventeenth-century poet never changes his tone: he is talking to the flowers throughout; he never moves from them to some larger or higher audience. And this is our evidence that he assumes from the beginning a world that embraces both him and the flowers in whose life he so easily and so neatly finds the analogy he seeks. The eighteenth-century poet, however, speaks to two audiences: first to the flowers, and then to all mankind, to whom he appeals in the name of the "philosophic mind." And with Wordsworth we reach yet a third mutation, for he speaks first to us, then moves into his solitary experience, and finally emerges to speak not just to us but again to all philosophic men. In the first poem, the words are all addressed to "you"—to inhabitants of a nature "out there" that is not alien and nonhuman. In the second, half is addressed to "ye," to a formally conceived inhabitant of all that is "out there," while the rest is addressed to anyone who can and will overhear. But the third is never addressed to a "you" or a "ye": here, the flowers are an "it"; and yet the relation that the speaker establishes with them is a more intimate, more startlingly close one than either of the other two achieves.

Whatever inferences you draw from them, the dates of these poems are relevant to their structure. Wordsworth could not write about flowers as did Bishop King; he wrote about the celandine, and he did not speak to it, but about it. And Bishop King did not write about the consolations of a visit from autumn flowers, but about an analogy he believed in between his life and that of any flower at any time. To see the literary differences here is inseparable from seeing historical differences, and historical differences, moreover, that most matter to the student of literature. But if such perceptions were the end of our examination of three such poems, the study of literature would indeed be as pedantic as our students would like it to be. For what matters most here, I am sure, is that even as I have been talking about these poems, each of you has been judging them for himself. You have perhaps listened to detect my bias, my admiration for one of them above the other two. You have perhaps—probably—been disagreeing with my account of one or more of them; you may feel that I do less than justice to Wordsworth, say, or that, like too many college teachers, I am too interested in the neatness and elegance of the seventeenth-century lyric. But whatever your response, I venture to say that it is impossible for anyone to consider such a sequence of poems as this—to consider them however deeply or superficially—without wanting to judge among them. Yet at the same time that each of us finds himself admiring one, say Wordsworth, he simultaneously finds himself qualifying and checking his judgment by his inevitable awareness of history, by his inescapable knowledge that whatever their similarities may be these are three poems in three quite different idioms, and that they could no more be the same, or "say the same thing," than any of us can really live and think and breathe in seventeenth-, eighteenth-, or early nineteenth-century England. It may be that we shall be tempted to persist even so, to say, for example, that the first is the best, the greatest poem. But if we do so, even if we yield, let us say, to a temperamental or craftsmanlike preference for the first poem, we cannot dodge the fact that we are committing ourselves to a preference for a religious view of life that is a good deal larger and more demanding than the idea of simple "preference" would imply. In other words, even if we do persist, even if we do declare ourselves as ranking one of these poems over the other two, we cannot fail to discover something about ourselves, about the values and assumptions that matter most to us. And we also cannot avoid in its turn the knowledge that some of our preferences—our values and assumptions—are decidedly not shared by others, among them some very great poets. We cannot avoid the temptation to judge, to rank, to rate —we would be inattentive to what is before us if we did not. We must, however, see that judging and valuing, placing and ranking, involve the playing of our preferences against our knowledge. We cannot escape the impulse to judge, but we cannot carry it out without modifying it by our knowledge. And this play of the mind between inference and predilection, between preference and knowledge, is the discipline to which our study, our subject, most commits us.

The thematic approach to literature, then, as I have tried to suggest it in something like slow motion here, does enlist our best efforts as both historians and critics because it must reveal to us and our students alike the seriousness of the business and evaluation. The three samples I have proposed here are of course limited, and one could go on from either chronological end. I recall the delight with which a colleague of mine once juxtaposed Dylan Thomas' "The Force that Through the Green Fuse Drives The Flower" with a passage from Thomson's "Spring" and a poem by Henry Vaughan entitled "The Evening Watch": it taught him, he said, among other things, what the Thomas poem was really about. I recently found it highly instructive to myself and to my students to set for them an essay on Robert Browning's "Prospice," Hardy's "The Darkling Thrush," and Yeats's "An Acre of Grass." In each of these poems, as you may recall, the speaker is at the end of life, or at the end of a phase of life that has exhausted him. Browning, you remember, wrote his poem soon after the death of his wife in 1861, and it begins with the question, "Fear death?" It turns in the center to a gesture of defiance: "No! let me taste the whole of it, fare like my peers/ The heroes of old," and moves on to a heroic, though I frankly must say a somewhat muddled, refusal to stop fighting. Hardy, dating his poem December 31, 1900, finds "The Century's corpse outleant"—laid out for burial—and finds the "ancient pulse of germ and birth" is "shrunken hard and dry,/And every spirit upon earth/Seemed fervorless as I." And if there is not defiance for him, there is a tentative hope, hesitant and infirm as the sound of the line with which he marks his turn: "At once a voice arose among/The bleak twigs overhead." It is the song of "An aged thrush, frail, gaunt, and small" who sings a song that by its strange music, though not by its message, almost converts the listener to the hope that came so easily to Browning:

> So little cause for carollings
>   Of such ecstatic sound
> Was written on terrestrial things
>   Afar or nigh around,
> That I could think there trembled through
>   His happy good-night air
> Some blessed Hope, whereof he knew
>   And I was unaware.
>   [Hardy, "The Darkling Thrush"]

And Yeats, in a desperate poem, "Here at life's end," finds in himself something like "Midnight, an old house/Where nothing stirs but a mouse." In a terrifying pun he exclaims, "My temptation is quiet." But for him the turning upon death is accomplished not by an appeal to moral heroics, nor yet by the sense of a tentative and faint possibility of life in nature; he would defy his death with art. In these three confrontations of death there is indeed much history and any choosing among them is difficult.

Other comparisons, the tracings of other themes, suggest themselves readily enough. But whatever works we thematically juxtapose, and whatever the knowledge we bring to bear upon them, only, I think, by some such approach as this can we recognize and do justice to our students' eagerness, indeed their anxiety, to know values, to make judgments, and even, heaven help us, to rate and to rank.